Social Justice
Philosophical Perspectives

Utkal Studies in Philosophy

General Editor
P.K. Mohapatra

Editors
T. Patnaik, S.K. Mohanty
G.P. Das, S.C. Panigrahi

Volume One
ACTION, FREEDOM AND RESPONSIBILITY

Volume Two
GOD, TIME AND EVIL

Volume Three
STUDIES ON THE PURUSARTHAS

Volume Four
REALITY AND MYSTICISM

Volume Five
SOCIAL JUSTICE

Utkal Studies in Philosophy - V

General Editor : P. K. Mohapatra

Social Justice

Philosophical Perspectives

D. K. Printworld (P) Ltd., New Delhi

in association with

Department of Special Assistance in Philosophy

Utkal University, Bhubaneswar

Cataloging in Publication Data — DK

Social justice: philosophical perspectives/
edited by P.K. Mohapatra.
(Utkal studies in philosophy; v. 5).
Includes bibliographical references.

1. Social justice. 2. Philosophy.
I. Mohapatra, P.K. (Prafulla Kumar), 1942 –
II. Series: Utkal studies in philosophy; v. 5.

ISBN 81-246-0119-4

First Published in India in 1999

Published by:
D.K. Printworld (P) Ltd.
Regd. office : *'Sri Kunj'*, F-52, Bali Nagar
New Delhi - 110 015
Phones : (011) 545-3975, 546-6019; *Fax* : (011) 546-5926
E-mail: dkprint@4mis.com

in association with
Department of Special Assistance in Philosophy
Utkal University
Bhubaneswar (Orissa)

Printed by: DP's Impressive Impressions, New Delhi - 110 059

Prefatory Note

SOCIAL Justice is the fifth volume published under the "Utkal Studies in Philosophy" series which is a publication programme undertaken by the Department of Special Assistance in Philosophy of Utkal University. This is yet another work in Analytical Philosophy of Value which is one of our major thrust areas under the Special Assistance Programme. Faculties of this department and eminent philosophers and scholars from other universities have enriched this volume with their critical observations on the diverse aspects of the concept of social justice and its applications to various aspects of our social life.

The editors are deeply indebted to the authors not only for their illuminating contributions but also for their interest in our publication programme. We are sure, this book will be of immense use for students and researchers in this important area of philosophy. We are grateful to the University Grants Commission for granting us the status of D.S.A. which has made this publication possible. We also thank M/s D.K. Printworld, New Delhi for collaborating with this Department in publishing this book.

Oct. 1st, 1998 — ***P.K. Mohapatra***
Utkal University

Contents

1

Editorial Introduction

Justice, Equality and Just-making Considerations

Prafulla K. Mohapatra

IF much of human history has been an incessant quest for justice, the same history has witnessed an almost inseparable link between justice and equality. For the struggles against slavery, racial discrimination, economic exploitation, political subjugation and discrimination of classes and castes have all been centering round one demand — the demand for equality or equal rights for all men. Besides the testimony of history, the close tie between justice and equality is manifest in language and general usage, so much so that even those who meant to break the conceptual link by pleading for unequal apportionment on grounds of differing merits could, nonetheless, stick to the verbal link. This is evident from the fact that "the meritarian view of justice paid reluctant homage to the equalitarian one by using the vocabulary of equality to assert the justice of inequality".[1] Even Popper, holding on to 'general usage', becomes intolerant of Plato's account of justice in terms of unequal allotment. "Why did Plato claim that justice meant inequality if,

1. Gregory Vlastos, "Justice and Equality" in *Social Justice*, ed. by Richard Brandt, Prentice Hall, Englewood Cliffs, N.J., 1962, p. 32.

in general usage, it meant equality?", he asks in his *Open Society and Its Enemies*,[2] and he goes on to say, "To me the only likely reply seems to be that he wanted to make propaganda for his totalitarian state by persuading the people that it was the 'just' state. . . . His attack on equalitarianism was not an honest attack." Thus from common usage to definition of justice and from Plato to Rawls the conceptual closeness of justice to equality is more than manifest. If Plato said that justice is rendering to everyone his due (*Republic*) and Rawls said that everybody has equal right to the basic liberties unless an inequal distribution of any social value is to the advantage of everyone (*A Theory of Justice*), the notion of justice — be it individual or social justice — bears clear stamp of equality on it and the familiar formula of social justice — treating similars similarly and dissimilars differently — stands solidly on the foundation of equality and equitable distribution. The principle of equality can, therefore, be dubbed not only as a part of justice but the distinguishing feature thereof. "The principles of justice are distinguished from other principles of morality by being governed by the ideal of equality."[3]

It follows, therefore, that any plausible theory of justice largely depends on the correct analysis of the concept of equality. In other words, much depends on a proper understanding of what equality means. It is not that we do not understand the meaning of equality in common conversation, that this is a very hard word to be understood easily. But taking the word in its etymological sense — in the sense in which it is the opposite of 'inequality' and is incompatible with 'difference', for example, — might lead one to, as indeed it actually has as we shall see, mistaken theories of justice and unreal opposition between justice theories based on such superficial grammatical

2. K.R. Popper, *The Open Society and its Enemies*, Routledge and Kegan Paul, London, 1949, pp. 79-80. Emphasis added.
3. "The Concept of Social Justice" in Brandt (ed.), *Social Justice*, p. 17.

understanding of the word. It is necessary, therefore, to distinguish between this understanding of 'equality' and knowing the correct analysis of its meaning. What I have in mind is reminiscent of that salutary distinction made by G.E Moore between knowing what a word means and knowing the correct analysis of its meaning.[4] To know the latter, one has to delve deep into what Wittgenstein calls its depth grammar — what the word means in a specific context and the surrounding circumstances. In default of that, a grammatical understanding of the word would create fixed pictures and obscure understanding. Such type of understanding of equality is likely to leave one wondering as to how can a theory of justice based on merit and desert be a theory of *justice* at all or even make sense, since people differ in respect of merit and worth and justice is inseparable from equality. We have seen this sort of perplexity in the case of many a philosophical problems, like how can a person be the same person over a period of time if nothing about him remains unchanged, or, how can an arrow move at all if, at each moment during its motion, it is at one particular point of space! Similarly we are perplexed about the controversy between equalitarianism and meritarianism as theories of justice: if equality is built into the concept of justice then there is no controversy here, since equalitarianism is the only theory that could be there, and yet the other theory seems to make a lot of sense! So there must be something seriously wrong somewhere. Yes, it is our grammatical habit of understanding 'equality' torne out of its use in specific contexts. What is to be considered here is that if justice requires equality — equal treatment to all, — what kind of equal treatment is meant here? Does it rule out all types of unequal treatments, e.g., treating people differently on the basis of their merit, worth and need — as *unjust*? An

---

4. "A Defence of Commonsense" in *Contemporary British Philosophy*, 2nd series, ed. by J.H. Muirhead, George Allen & Unwin, USA, 1925.

appeal to the common usage regarding justice will show that not all types of equality is required to make our actions, individual and social, just. Granting of equal liberty, equal opportunity and equality of the fundamental rights to all is just since each individual has equal human worth; but granting of equal status to a judge and a criminal is certainly not in keeping with the principles and procedures of social justice. Differential treatment and unequal distribution of benefits and burdens in certain circumstances are very much in tune with the principles of justice. What is more to the point, some such differences and inequal treatments are required in the interest of equality in the long run. So, not all forms of equalities and all sorts of differences are just-making conditions; which ones are will depend on their reference to the specific situations. Justice requires that all should be given equal opportunity to promote their good life in the sense of their happy life. But the good life and its conditions differ from person to person because of their needs and the situations in which they are placed. Equal distribution in such cases will necessarily require differential treatment, viz., to give food to the hungry, books to a student, a musical instrument to a musician and a car to a business executive and so on. Even *different* musical instruments *need* to be given to different musicians, even if they form one class by themselves. In all these cases people are treated differently *yet equally*. Indeed, in such type of situations equality *means* and *requires* differential treatment. Thus, though equality is the *prima facie* requirement of justice, a just society must also respect *some* differences as just-making conditions. Considerations of merit, need and potentialities are some of the prominent just-making considerations in justicising differences, just as consideration of human worth and natural rights are some of the just-making considerations in justicising equality. Considerations of the former type give content and sense and justification to the meritarian view of justice. I shall shortly argue that the controversy between meritarianism and egalitarianism is only apparent, since the claims of both boil down to the demand for equality in the long run, as would be revealed by a correct analysis of 'equality'.

Sticking to the just-making considerations for the moment, it should by now be clear that these are related to and contingent upon what I have been indicating as the proper understanding of the meaning of 'equality' *vis-a-vis* 'inequality' or 'difference' and similar *vis-a-vis* differential (or even preferential) treatments. Once again, though the primary condition of justice is to treat similars similarly and dissimilars differently, yet not all similarities and not all differences are just-making. It would not be unjust to treat some similars differently and some dissimilars similarly. For example, debarring Veerappan from holding any public office and nominating Deve Gowda to the Rajya Sabha will not be unjust, though both of them are citizens of India, nor was it unjust on the part of the British Queen to confer knighthood on Bertrand Russell and Alfred Ayer though they differed in respect of race and blood. Sameness of nationality is not just-making in all cases, nor is difference in blood, race and colour. Indeed, it can be said that Droṇa did a great injustice by refusing to teach the art of archery to Ekalavya whereas Duryodhana, notwithstanding his motives, committed an act of justice by conferring the status of a king on Karna. Consideration of birth and caste is by no means just-making in the context of learning while that of valour, heroism and personality most certainly is in the context of kingship.

It should be pretty clear from the above discussion that what is a just-making consideration is not a matter of definition, nor is it something absolute or even amenable to general agreement. All that can be said is that there *must* be some just-making considerations on the basis of which actions and conducts of individuals and societies could be judged as just or unjust. What they are will depend on the context and a proper understanding of the meaning and implications of 'equal' (and 'unequal' and 'different'). We may quote Frankena to substantiate my contention: "Justice", he says, "is treating persons equally except as unequal treatment is required by just-making considerations of *substantial weight in the circumstances*."[5]

In what follows, I shall concentrate on what I think to be a correct analysis of the meaning of equality in the context of justice — what sort of inequalities are compatible with the ideal of equality and what sort of departure from equality are allowable. Our analysis will naturally have reflections on the egalitarian-meritarian controversy as well as on differential or preferential treatment. And I hope to show that both the meritarian view of justice and preferential treatment are required by the ideal of equality and are, hence, subservient to it in the long run.

In this endeavour, I shall have to address myself to two crucial questions: (1) whether there are (or can be) principles of justice, or just-making considerations, which overrule equality? and (2) if there are, can they render the principle of equality otiose? As would be evident from the foregoing, my answer to the first question is in the affirmative while that to the second, negative. To this purpose, let me begin by that crucial remark of Aristotle in his *Nicomachean Ethics*,[6] which is at once simplistic in verbiage but cryptic in implications. Aristotle says, "Justice is equality, as all men believe it to be, quite apart from any argument." It is quite natural to say this for a Greek, since the Greek word for equality, *to ison* or *isotes*, is closer to being the right word for justice than the Greek word *dikaiosyne* which is a usual translation of the word 'justice'. Thus, for a Greek-speaking person it is quite plausible to *say* 'equality' and *mean* 'justice'.[7] But a closer scrutiny of the use of the word *isotes* shows that it means 'geometrical equality', i.e., proportionality, hence

5. William K. Frankena in Brandt (ed.), *Social Justice*, p. 10. Emphasis added.
6. Book V, 1131a 13.
7. I owe this formation to Gregory Vlastos, *op. cit.*, p. 31.

the 'equal' (or just) distribution of the benefits and burdens of the society to persons will have to be proportionate to their merits and capacities. This is what equality or equitable distribution *means*. In a society of different types of people with different needs, for example, giving the same one thing to everybody, an expensive guitar or a motor car each, will not only be a parody of equitable distribution but will neither be just nor equal treatment. For some would need a house, some others clothings and still some others two meals a day. Equal treatment, therefore, will have to be differential and even preferential treatment, proportionate to the needs, merits and capabilities of people. This explains the apparently startling revelation that Aristotle, like Plato, propounded the view that a just distribution is, in effect, an unequal one.[8] What would look to be more startling is that, if 'equal' is one's word for just, as it is for a Greek-speaking person, one would have to say that an *equal* distribution is an *unequal* one !

But far from expressing a self-contradiction, this only brings home the point that some inequalities, though not all, are built into the concept of just and equitable distribution. When merit, or need or capabilities and so on is the just-making consideration, an equal (just or fair) distribution to persons of unequal merit, etc., will have to be inevitably unequal. Unless one chooses to take an extremely literal view of equalitarianism, one can speak in a perfectly matter of fact way of 'equitable inequalities' and 'inequitable equalities'. In fact, Plato was more emphatic on the logic of *just inequalities* justified on grounds of merit and worth. He had not only made his equalitarian rivals — the democrats in particular — intellectually defenceless by his cryptic quip that democracy distributes a very 'odd sort of equality to equals and unequals',[9] but also challenged them to say if they really

8. Plato, *Georgias*, 508a, *Republic*, 558c and *Laws*, 744bc. Also Aristotle, *Nicomachean Ethics*, 1131a 15ff.

9. *Republic*, 558c.

meant to universalise equality, say if there are no just inequalities, no rights in respect of which men are unequal? Understandably, the equalitarians have never come up with a clear answer to this and Plato's question has gone by default. We have come across profound declarations like 'Men are born and remain free and equal in rights'.[10] But in actual practice and application of the concepts, men have remained neither free nor equal in respect of all rights unconditionally and without exceptions. One of the most obvious departures (justified departure, I should say) from the ideal of equal rights can be illustrated as follows. The holder of a unique public office, like the office of the President of India, is not equal in all rights to all other men, for no other man has a right to this office except Mr. K.R. Narayanan, though every Indian has equal right of *eligibility to this office*. To be sure, the equalitarian, the democrat in particular, can draw comfort from the last, but he should not fight shy of conceding that men are (born and remain) equal in *some* rights but not in respect of a great many others. Further, there are justified exceptions to fundamental rights and even to our natural rights as human beings, when equality is denied and freedom is curtailed under compelling circumstances. Contrary to the claims of equalitarianism — literal equalitarianism, as I have indicated above — even natural rights or human rights, in respect of which all men are supposed to be equal, are not absolute and unexceptionable. If I have natural right to a certain benefit, it does not follow that I ought to be granted that benefit in *all* circumstances, no matter how it affects the rights of others and even some others of my rights. John Rawls, quite to the point, has prescribed his two principles of justice[11] with exceptional ingenuity, the first of which (of the second, shortly later) says that every person has

10. Art, I of the *Declaration of Rights of Man and Citizen* (enacted by the Constituent Assembly of the First French Republic in 1971).
11. *A Theory of Justice*, Cambridge, Mass: The Bulkan Press of Harvard University, 1971, esp. Sec. 11.

equal right to the basic freedom compatible with *similar freedom* for all. This clearly envisions the fact that one can enjoy equal natural rights (e.g., right to life, liberty, property, security, etc.) only so long as they — some of them, or any of them — do not adversely affect those of others and, we may add, some others of *one's* own. Even John Locke who, some claim, is known for his advocacy for the view that natural rights are absolute,[12] allows justified exceptions to natural rights in approving imprisonment as punishment for crime and detention of beggars in corrective homes,[13] etc. Natural rights, therefore, can be construed as *prima facie* rights which are *defeasible*, i.e., can be overruled in special circumstances which provide just-making conditions. All we need, perhaps, is to find *reasons for our natural rights which will be the moral reasons for just exceptions*. Reasons can be many in specific circumstances. Rawls provides one in his second principle of justice (what he calls the *difference principle*): all social and economic inequalities are to be so arranged as to be (a) reasonably expected to be to everyone's advantage and (b) attached to positions and offices open to all. Here differences and inequalities are justicised on the same ground on which equality (i.e., equal basic liberty) is also justicised, namely, equity or equitable distribution which is *to everyone's advantage*. This is what I wish to call liberal equalitarianism (as distinct from what I have described as literal equalitarianism) which construes equality as *compatible with* unequal treatment in some respects as seen above. This view which, I think, is perfectly in keeping with our normal intuitions on justice, not only recognises meritarianism as a respectable theory of justice but also shortens the gap between this theory and the equalitarian theory of

---

12. See, for example, E.F. Carritt, *Ethical and Political Thinking* Oxford University Press, 1947, pp. 154ff and R. Brandt, *Ethical Theory*, Prentice Hall, Engleweed Cliffs, N.J., 1959, p. 442.
13. See H.R. Foxbourne, *Life of Locke*, London, 1976, Vol. 2, pp. 379-81.

justice. The unequal treatment in meritarianism seen as a requirement for the principle of equitable distribution, the gap becomes almost non-existent (i.e., there is seen to be virtually no conflict between the two theories), unless one wants to obstinately stick to an extreme form of equalitarianism.[14] Indeed, the differences and inequalities justicised in meritarianism and other non-equalitarian theories of justice are not only compatible with, but are subservient to, the ideal of equality in the long run. In the rest of this lecture, I shall try to supplement this contention by considering differences and preferences (in justified treatment of people) which are either required by (hence built into) the concept of equality or are intended, as we shall see, to restore equality in society which had been disturbed by actions of individuals or the state.

It is a well-known fact about penal procedures that, notwithstanding the equal basic liberties of individuals, a criminal has to be treated differently from his victim and also from other persons, for by committing the crime he has harmed some others and has disturbed equality (i.e., equal right of people not to be harmed and deprived of one's property) and so has to be punished in order that the equality disturbed by his action can be restored; in the process the criminal has justifiably lost his right not to be harmed or deprived of his property. Yet, as a human person, he retains the basic natural right not to be treated unequally before the law. Even though the criminal is a cruel person it will be unjust to treat him equally cruelly, for although he has broken

---

14. The extreme form of equalitarianism issues from taking a literal view of equality. Such a tendency is displayed even by a very discriminating philosopher, William Frankena, perhaps in one of his unguarded moments, when he says: "In opposition to the classical meritarian view of social justice I accepted as part of my own view the principle that all men are to be treated as equals, not because they are equal in any respect but simply because they are human", *op. cit.*, p. 19. (emphasis added).

the law he is still within the purview of the law and deserves equal protection except the punishment as required by his desert and in the interest of equality he has disturbed. The extreme retributive policy of punishment, followed in some fundamentalist Islamic countries, does not care to take this into account and therefore fall far short of a justice-theory. Similarly in the case of taxation policies. The unequal concentration of wealth in the society is usually sought to be rectified by progressive taxation so that an equitable distribution can be effected. Marx's maxim "from each according to his capacity" is an eminent pointer and this, together with "to each according to his need", sought to restore equality in society.

If justice is giving everyone his due, then to deprive someone or some group of men of what is his or their due is denial of justice, i.e., injustice. The struggle for social justice has been to undo this wrong by compensating the victims of such denials and deprivations — the Blacks in America, the Jews in Germany and the so-called lower castes in India, for example. With a view to restoring equality of rights that has been disturbed by denial of justice, a just society has to make provisions for *preferential treatments* to the members of the victim class. This would of course mean that in the process of dispensation of preferential justice some members of the non-preferred class will suffer injustice. For example, taking the reservation policy followed in post-Independence India,[15] a candidate belonging to the P-caste, despite securing 75 per cent marks, may have to lose his chance of admission to a professional course because an R-caste candidate with only 30 per cent marks got the seat, since it was *reserved* for the R-caste candidates. This is inevitable, because the provision of this concession to the R-caste candidates is the only way available to the society for correcting the social or

15. This example and the arguments that follow owe their source largely to the following contribution of Professor Rajendra Prasad, especially secs. 6.2 and 6.3 thereof (pp. 30-38).

moral imbalance and restoring equality of rights and opportunities; the particular student of the P-caste can take his non-admission to the course as *his share* of the cost of social development or restoration of social justice. Preferential treatment, thus, though unequal distribution, is only a means to the ideal of equality (equitable distribution) in the long run and is subservient to this ideal.

Why, then there is so much of controversy and resentment over the reservation policy, if preferential treatment is an essential element of social justice and subservient to the ideal of equality? The reason, I reckon, is a misunderstanding (I hope it is not a willful misunderstanding). The misunderstanding relates to the 'reason' for the resentment of the P-caste candidate for being denied what he deserved on merit. I have said that this candidate has been *wronged* and so his resentment is genuine. But instead of admitting this, the general trend of thinking, thanks to excessive politicisation of the issue, has been to consider his resentment and frustration as unjustified and as an expression of attachment of the privileged class to the powers and privileges it has wrongfully acquired and has been enjoying for centuries. What is unfortunate is that, not only some reservation enthusiasts and its beneficiaries, but the people in power, the politicians, seem to think that the P-student's caste is a good enough *reason* for his non-admission and that there is nothing for him to complain against or to have a feeling of having made a sacrifice ! This is a blatant misunderstanding of the just-making consideration for preferential treatment in this context. The fact that one belongs to a particular caste cannot, by itself, justicise granting to, or withholding from, him anything whatsoever. It is counterintuitive to our moral common sense to make one's caste (for which one is not responsible) the *reason* for giving him something which he does not deserve on merit or for denying something he does deserve. The right reason, as we have seen, is restoration of social balance and the P-caste student has to be made to see that his non-admission to the course is his share of the burden, nonetheless recognising and sympathising for the sacrifice he makes and injustice he suffers. (Compare the case of a child who must, nonetheless, be praised for decent manners despite the fact that his manners are largely due to decent upbringing or constant and careful conditioning by his parents.) And since, I argue, this is an injustice, it should not go on for ever. Considering the fact that we are in the 50th year of our country's Independence, the government and the society must start working for a healthy social order in which such injustices become uncalled for and the occasion for depriving a deserving candidate in order to accommodate a less deserving one does not arise at all. The weaker section too has an onerous role in making this possible. They must realise the important truth that it is 'more dignified and self-respecting' for the young people to earn something on merit than to get it under the protection of a *concession*, and they must work earnestly towards realisation of this truth. Professor Prasad rightly deplores that neither our government nor our educational planners nor even the national media is making any effort in this direction. But social justice will be a far cry unless such conditions are created in which everyone deserves what he earns or what benefit he gets.

2

Social Injustice, Retribution and Revenge

An Examination of the Indian Experiment

Rajendra Prasad

1. Justice as Criterial

SOCIAL Justice is distributive Justice. Even if there is some difference between the two, I am going to use, in this essay, the one to mean the other. The term 'social justice' has the advantage of being emotively more juicy than 'distributive justice'. The latter, on the other hand, appears to be dull and dry. But it has the advantage over the former, like some other non-emotive, or emotively emaciated, terms of being more precise or matter of fact.

The question of social or distributive justice arises when something is to be distributed among a group of people by an agency which has the authority and responsibility to do that. The distributing agency could be an individual, e.g., the king of a monarchical state, a group of people, e.g., the syndicate of a university, or the representative of a group of people, e.g., the prime minister of a democratic state. But the conceptual and substantive problems which the exercise of distributive justice is likely to give rise to and for which it must have some solution, if the exercise is to be successfully done, are likely to remain, by and large, unchanged, whatever be the nature of the distributing agency. Even if all of them are not, at least those with which I shall deal, it seems to me, are.

Justice is a criterial concept. This means that giving *X* to *A* would be just if and only if *A* fulfils the criterion (or criteria) which entitle him to have a justifiable claim on *X*. This would also mean that not giving it to him, or giving it to *B* who does not fulfil the criterion (or criteria), would be unjust. The criterion, thus, exercises a restrictive as well as a facilitative function. It restricts the distributor of *X* from giving it to someone who does not satisfy it, and facilitates his task of deciding whom to give it to. This in no way means that the distribution of justice, where a criterion is available, is an extremely easy affair. It becomes a difficult affair, for example, when it is not clear whether or not a subject fulfils the relevant criterion, or which one, or ones, fulfil it better than some other, or others. All this generally happens when the available criterion is not sufficiently precise or discriminative, or when the situation in which it is to be applied is very greatly complicated, or unusually different from earlier situations. In such cases the applier may not feel sure as to whether it should, or should not, be applied, and if it should be, whether it should be applied as it is, or in a modified form. In the latter case, he may not know in which way it should be modified.

But in spite of such difficulties, dispensation of justice cannot do without some criterion (or criteria). The criterion used in a case must be relevant to it, and, by and large, our normal intuitions about the relevance of a criterion are right, or right enough to enable us to proceed in a just manner. For example, to make the fatness of the neck of an individual, which makes his neck fit into the noose of the hangman's rope, a criterion for putting him to death by hanging, is, our intuitions would say, absolutely wrong. That is why Bhārtendu calls the king who used this criterion senseless (*caupaṭa*) and the city in which it was done lawless (*andherapura*).[1]

This is an exaggerated example of an irrelevant criterion. But it very clearly is a good example of a criterion which our normal intuitions would reject. In moral matters, and so also in matters pertaining to the dispensation of justice, our normal intuitions play the role of a touchstone. That is why when a theory of justice offers a criterion for being a rightful claimant of a benefit or burden, which goes against our normal intuitions, our reaction is that there is something wrong with the theory, or that the theory needs to explain or justify its counter-intuitive stand.

We generally talk of distributive or social justice when what is to be distributed is a benefit, i.e., something preferred, desired, wanted, needed, etc., by those who believe to have a claim on it. But this does not have to be the case. Justice, or injustice, may be done in distributing even a burden, i.e., in distributing something unwanted, avoided, despised by, or even hurlful to, the recipients. The distribution of public land among the landless could be done justly or unjustly, and so can the imposition of collective fine on the residents of a village for their allegedly demolishing a police station. Therefore, when I speak of distributive justice, I would have in mind both, the distribution of benefits and of burdens, though I may not always mention both of them.

Goods to be distributed may not be sufficient in the sense that there may not be enough of them to be given, or given in

1. In a Hindi dramatic satire, *andherpura nagari, caupaṭa rājā; take sera bhājī, take sera khājā*, Bhāratendu Hariśchandra portrays the administration by the king of a city which ordains that if the neck of the criminal to be hanged is so thin that it slips out of the noose of the hangman's rope, anyone else whose neck is fat enough to fit into the noose, be hanged and the thin-necked criminal be let off. The result is that, instead of the real criminal, who is thin-necked, a fat-necked young recluse is hanged.

equal quantity, to each one of the claimants. Strict adherence to the criterion of just distribution then would help the distributor to eliminate those whose claims are not tenable, or are comparatively inferior to the claims of some others, though both the groups, in some way, satisfy the criterion, i.e., possess the property or properties which ordinarily make the distribution of the concerned goods to them just or justified, and the act of distribution an act of justice. I would call such a property a justice-making, or simply, a justifying, property. When, in a distributive act, a justifying property is ignored, or a non-justifying property is invoked, injustice is committed. Droṇa invokes a candidate's possession of the property of being a prince (*rājaputra*) as the justifying property of his being admitted in his school. Since Ekalavya did not have it, he was not admitted. But the property invoked is not a justifying property. Therefore, Droṇa's non-acceptance of Ekalavya is an act of (social) injustice.

Reference to a justifying property is equally important even when the goods to be distributed are available, or can be made available, in abundance. Suppose the chief minister of a state decides to give a job to every unemployed engineering graduate, and has the resources to create as many jobs as are needed. Suppose, further, that he assigns the job of supervising the generation of electricity to a chemical engineer and that of supervising the construction of a highway to an aeronautical engineer. He has given a job to each one of the claimants. But he has ignored the relevant justifying properties the possession of which by the job-claiming engineers has to be taken into account in deciding which specific job has to be given to which engineer, keeping in view his area of specialization. He has done, therefore, an injustice to both, the chemical and the aeronautical engineers, the injustice of giving each one of them the jobs which should not have been given to him, or, to put it a little differently, of not giving to him the job which should have been given to him. It would be another matter if both of them, since they were unemployed, are extremely happy, and, instead of calling the chief minister's act an act of injustice, extoll him as an apostle of social justice. But it is obvious that such acts would be acts of societal injustice, i.e., injustice to society because they would ultimately lead to the impoverishment of the society's, or the country's, resources.

Maybe, the chief minister had no criterion, or, justifying property, in mind in distributing the jobs. Still, the way he did it was unjust. A distributive exercise which uses no criterion, as well as one which uses a wrong one, e.g., the size of an individual's neck in deciding whether he should be put to the gallows or let off, would, in all likelihood, result in injustice, and if it sometimes does not, that would be only by a fluke or accident. Therefore, in the dispensation of justice the desirability of being clear about the justifying property or properties for making the distributive process just can never be brushed aside, or taken in a casual manner. The justifying property must really justify the distribution, and in deciding whether or not it does, our normal intuitions about justice are extremely helpful. They may not be so important in the dispensation of legal justice because in it the legal system provides in a codified manner the set of justifying properties. But even here when the codification is not adequately clear, and sometimes it is not, the judiciary has to take the help of relevant normal intuitions about justice.

2. Social Justice and Retribution

The concept of social justice definitely, and perhaps that of justice *per se*, involves a sense of retribution from which follows a sense of pride or self-dignity in the recipient of the benefit justly given to him.

What I deserve to get, what I have a right to, or claim on, I ought to get, or, must get, simply because, in a timeless, or moral, sense, it is *mine* though it may not at the moment be in my possession. The agency which is involved in making it available to me, therefore, ought to, or must, make it available to me. If it does, it would be doing only justice, or social justice, to me, and not an act of favour, or charity; it would only be giving to me what is mine, and not a gift or an alm. Therefore, in receiving or accepting it, I do not have to compromise my self-respect. Rather, I should have a sense of pride, self-dignity, or elevated satisfaction, for having got what I ought to have. This means I would not be doing anything wrong, rather I would be doing something commendable, courageous, or heroic, if I fight to get it in case it is withheld from, or denied to, me. One who withholds it from, or denies it to, me, does an act of gross injustice.

Such feelings can become very strong. Sometimes they do in a natural way because of some gross injustices having been really perpetrated for a very long period of time on an individual, or a group, by another individual or group. Sometimes they do because of having been pumped up by some interested persons, say, politicians holding an ideology of a certain type, or hoping to get, in the coming general election, the votes of the allegedly wronged people by posing to be the protectors of their rights.

Such feelings, in an individual, or group, become generally strong when the concerned individual, or group, *believes* that a gross injustice, or a set of gross injustices, has been perpetrated on it by another individual, or group, for a very long period of time. For the feelings to rise high it does not matter whether the belief is or is not true; only the belief must be there. In the case of a false belief, however, sometimes rational persuasion by a Gandhi or a Jai Prakash, may succeed in convincing the alleged victim that no injustice has really been done to him and thereby in calming him down. But this is a very difficult job and becomes more difficult when a large group, say, a caste-group, or a religious group, of people hold the (false) belief. But this also is true that rational persuasion by a neutral person, or a group of persons, is the only peaceful way of assuaging the strong feelings by showing the untenability of the belief or beliefs concerned.

The belief that a gross injustice has been done retributively causes, in the believing individual or group, the urge to get the injustice undone. This urge makes the believers agitational, sometimes in a natural way and sometimes because of having been whipped up by some interested individual or group. Such an agitation is very likely, given certain conditions, to become violent because the agitators think they have a retributive justification to use violence to get back what has been denied to them. Their thinking proceeds in some such way: We deserve to have *X*, but it has been denied to us. The existing social machinery is not sincerely trying to restore it to us. Therefore, even if we use violence to get it back, we would be doing nothing wrong.

3. Retribution and Revenge

A natural ally of the feeling of retribution is the feeling of revenge: *A* has taken *X* from me; therefore I must take it back, and even if I hurt him in the process, nothing wrong would be done by me. He would deserve the hurt because of what he has already done to me. Retribution and revenge do not have to go together; they are only likely to go together. The retributive agent sometimes, and generally when he becomes revengeful, forgets that the feeling of revenge very often overshoots its target and then it takes away a part, small or large, of the *moral* merit of retribution. Draupadī's insulting Karṇa by not allowing him to compete in her *svayaṁvara* on account of his (allegedly) low parentage, gives to Karṇa the retributive right to make Draupadī give him the respect he deserves and repent for her misbehaviour. But his feeling of revenge overshoots the retributive target when, in the game of dice, he calls her a whore, for which he himself later repents. A large part of the moral merit of his retributive right to get undone the injustice she has done to him is destroyed by his own act of injustice, or immorality, committed through his revengeful act of calling her a whore.

The conceptual line which separates retribution from revenge is very thin, and very often it is either not noticed, or unwrittingly crossed over, without letting one realize that thereby he has entered a different kind of territory, that from the moral he has passed into an amoral or immoral territory: "That *A* has deprived me of what, in a timeless, moral, sense, is mine — my land, social status, opportunity for advancement, etc. — retributively implies that I have a moral right to recover, or get restored, what he has taken away, or damaged." This is what retributive morality, retribution within the bounds of morality, means. That *A* has deprived me of *X* does not imply that I have a moral right to take away from *A* what in a timeless, moral, sense belongs to him, i.e., to do him an injustice in return. That Draupadī does an injustice to Karṇa does not (retributively) imply that he has a moral right to do an injustice to her. It is a moral truth that nothing can give one, or imply that he has, a moral right to do an immorality which an act of injustice obviously is.

The revengeful person does not clearly see what retribution really implies and what it does not. Partly because of his conceptual dim-sightedness and partly because of his disturbed emotional state he thinks that retribution implies, or justifies, revenge, or is indistinguishable from it. But the fact of the matter, as mentioned above, is that retribution only justifies the restoration of the moral balance disturbed by an immorality, or a set of immoralities. It does not justify the commission of a counter-immorality for the simple reason that nothing can. To think that it does is a gross error, conceptual as well as moral. But so many people, philosophers and non-philosophers alike, very often commit it. It is committed by all those who define the doctrine of retribution as sanctioning taking an eye for an eye, a tooth for a tooth.

4. Revenge as Contingently Moral

The motivation behind a retributive action is moral; it is an urge to get a moral wrong, an injustice, undone in a morally right or permissible manner. When a landless labourer, with the help of the village *pañcāyata*, legal machinery, social persuasion, or even use of violence when no other means is available, or other means fail, gets back his plot of land which had been wrongfully grabbed by someone else, he gets an injustice undone. If he is a retributivist, and does all this with the motivation of getting the injustice undone, after getting back the lost plot of land, he would become satisfied. He would not like to hurt the land-grabber further. A retributive act, or system, aims at restoring the disturbed moral order. The injustice of his plot's having been grabbed had disturbed the moral order which has now been restored with the return of the plot to him. It could also have been restored, had anything else, equivalent to it, would have been returned to him by the grabber himself, or as a result of a governmental decision. There is a form of theism according to which God is the greatest retributivist who administers the world in such a manner that everyone gets in return of what he does what he is entitled to, and so does the law of *karma* according to the classical Indian world-view.

On the other hand, the motivation behind a revengful act is merely the satisfaction of a grudge, no matter whether the grudge is justified or not. Since the grudge does not have to be a moral grudge, a revengeful action has no moral boundaries. It is contingently, and not necessarily, moral in the sense that it does not have to operate within the bounds of morality. It may be moral, immoral, or non-moral. The revengeful landless labourer may collect a group of other landless labourers and kill all members of the family some ancestor or ancestors of which had grabbed the land. As enacted in the Hindi movie *Umraon Jan*, a revengeful criminal, after being released from the prison, kidnaps the small daughter of the person who had given true evidence against him in the court on the basis of which he was convicted. He then sells her to a prostitute, who forces her, when she attains her youth, to lead the life of a prostitute, and the circumstances so contrive that the young lady ends her life by drowning herself in the Gaṅgā. Here the kidnapper does not get anything back. He only gets the satisfaction of having hurt the man who had given evidence against him which involved no immorality.

But very often the distinction between retribution and revenge is forgotten, or not clearly recognized, and a revengeful act is taken to be retributive and therefore justified. For example, the labourers may think that they have acted retributively and therefore justifiably in killing innocent members of the family because some ancestor or ancestors of it had, according to their belief, taken possession of the land by means of fraudulent legal devices. But they would be mistaken because retributive morality justifies only such an action which is at least morally permissible, and not any immorality like the one they have done. The aim of retribution is to restore moral order, to set moral imbalance right. Killing innocent persons would upset, and not restore, moral balance. It would be an act of revenge and not of retribution. Perhaps only a feeling of revenge can push a person, or a group, to commit such gruesome acts.

It is also possible that a retributive measure may be mistaken for being a revengeful one. Suppose members of the caste *B* are not allowed to enter a Hindu temple, and they are agitating against it. The management of the temple realises that by so far not allowing entry to them, it has done great social injustice. To compensate for this moral lapse it makes the rule that the members of *B* will henceforth not only be allowed but given preference over others in entering the temple. This would be a retributive, compensatory, moral step. But the members of *B* may mistakenly think that they have avenged their injustice on the so far favoured castes and even the latter may do the error of thinking that they have been. But the fact of the matter is that no caste has avenged or been avenged. Rather, a moral lapse, or injustice, an immoral social practice, has been rectified by a counter-moral, or retributive step, perhaps in an over-enthusiastic manner.

To avenge on someone for something he has done is, in some

sense, to hurt or humiliate him, to make him feel small. The avenger himself, on the other hand, when he successfully avenges, feels, in some sense, great, or more powerful than the person avenged on. All this happens no matter what is the moral quality of the revengeful action and of the action of the person avenged on for which he is avenged on. Therefore, it is very likely that the person avenged on, if he can, or when he can, would take counter-revenge on the avenger. In this way, the process of revenge and counter-revenge is likely to continue and to keep the social or moral order more or less disturbed. On the other hand, if the wronged person takes retributive action against the wrong-doer, keeping himself well within the bounds of morality, the situation is likely to be much better. For example, if the landless labourer gets his lost land recovered through his own, or through society's, morally permissible efforts, the person from whom it is taken back may feel a sense of loss. But then there is a reason available to the person whose land it really is, and to any neutral observer, which can be used to convince him that he has not really lost anything. We can tell him that what has been taken away from him is not really his; it really belongs to the person to whom it has gone. Therefore, in taking it away from him, nothing *his* has been taken away; or in loosing it, he has not lost anything which is *his*. If all this is done in a proper setting and if the social surrounding is amicable, it is very likely that he would get convinced and would not feel any animosity with the recepient of the land, or with one who has helped him in regaining it. He may, rather, feel a sense of relief or satisfaction, indistinguishable from a sense of purification, a sense that a wrong has been righted. If such things happen, they would certainly strengthen the moral order, the moral fabric of the social order.

5. From Revenge to Retribution: The Philosopher's Way

Both the retributive and the revengeful propensities are natural to man. But social-moral planning has to aim at strengthening the former and weakening the latter. How this can be done is a very important question in practical or applied ethics, the area to which the administration of social justice belongs. There cannot be a simple answer to it. I would only say that a number of things are necessary to achieve even the modicum of success in this matter. Some of them are the following: good education, formal and informal, morally motivated and politically unbiased methods of publicity about the wrongs done to some sections of the society and the right methods of compensating for them and of stopping their reoccurrence, meaningful encouragement for retributive correction and discouragement for revengeful attemps, exemplary behaviour from the makers and implementers of social policies, not-political approach to diagnozing and correcting social injustices, etc., etc. Explaining even a single one of them would require me to explain the others, and that cannot be done in this work. I would content myself only with saying a few things about the philosopher's role in this matter.

We may not approve of Hegel's attempt at building a grand philosophical system, but we can never ignore or minimize the importance of his saying that philosophy is a thinking consideration of things. It can influence human beings only, or primarily, by working on their thinking. There is no doubt that it works on human thinking. The conceptual distinction between retributive and revengeful action, and the likely after-effects of each one of them, as I have explained in some of the foregoing pages, when properly understood and acknowledged, can go a long way to strengthen the propensity for one and weaken the propensity for the other.

One who acknowledges the distinction between the two, i.e., acknowledges that retribution has to work within the bounds of morality and revenge does not have to, would have in the acknowledgement itself a very good reason for not letting the retributive effort superseded by a revengeful one. And, if he is a rationally mature person, then, because he would have a reason against becoming revengeful, it is very likely that he would not become revengeful. Secondly, a society's acknowledgement of and respect for the distinction, would facilitate its task of keeping the propensity of revenge in some of its members under appropriate control without subduing, or curbing, their retributive propensity of not tolerating injustices done to them, i.e., without dampening their moral heroism.

The Gandhian struggle for India's Independence is a very good example of a retributive, as against a revengeful, one: a struggle to take back what the British Government had taken away but not to avenge the injustice by trying to take away anything from the latter which belonged to them. This is very clear from the fact that he never agreed to side with Hitler in his war against the British. A revengeful Gandhi would have readily done the latter. Even Nehru exhibited the non-revengeful spirit of India by agreeing, after India's becoming independent, to be a member of the British Commonwealth instead of joining a block hostile to the British.

The philosopher, therefore, can contribute to the individual's and societal efforts for the promotion of social justice, or the removal of social injustice, by doing well his own job, his *svadharma*, the job he is equipped to do. That is, by diagnozing accurately the conceptual distinction between revenge and retribution, stating it clearly, cogently and comprehensively, and making it available to thinking people in an easily intelligible vernacular. He can improve the chances of his conceptualization becoming action-guiding and persuasive by highlighting the differences between the likely consequences of revengeful and retributive actions and policies. Examples of such actions and policies he can easily find in the history of mankind, and if he does not, or does not want to spend time in digging into history, he can hypothesize cases and draw an impressive picture of the consequences each one is likely to yield and their likely effects on the social or moral order, on the targetted personal or social welfare for which such actions and policies are allegedly adopted.

All this is neither unimportant nor easy. It is not unimportant because people who confuse revenge with retribution and therefore consider revenge justified are available galore. Because of the unclarity of the distinction between the two politicians find it easier to call cruelties inflicted on innocent people, done out of revenge, retributive actions justified because of past injustices done by the victims' forefathers. To be convinced that it is not easy to catch the distinction correctly one has only to try his hand.

Duryodhana thought that he was acting retributively in humiliating Draupadī when he tried to get her de-robed and to make her sit on his thighs, because she had humiliated him by saying that being a son of a blind man he also behaved like a blind man. So did Kṛṣṇa when he advised Bhīma to strike his *gadā* at Duryodhana's thigh-joints, the areas prohibited by the rules of *gadā* warfare. He thought, and also made Bhīma to think, that doing so was retributively justified because of Duryodhana's having earlier humiliated Draupadī. One has to do some conceptual analysis to conclude whether what Duryodhana, Kṛṣṇa or Bhīma, did, was really retributive or revengeful.

6. The Indian Experiment

I. *Imbalance of Social Well-being.*

The present-day Indian society is in a state of moral imbalance. By this I do not mean the oft-repeated saying that there is a collapse of values in all, or almost all, spheres of Indian life. The general collapse of values is not irrelevant to the specific kind of imbalance I have in mind. But I would almost exclusively concentrate on the latter.

The imbalance I have in mind is, to put it in a way not too precise, an imbalance of well-being. A large section of the society has been, for a pretty long time, denied opportunities of growth and advancement leading to the general ill-being of its members.

They have become economically poor, academically backward or uneducated, socially disrespected or neglected, etc., etc. Some of them were, until recently, considered untouchable.

To cause the ill-being of any section of the society is to do an immorality. Such things as poverty, ignorance, low mental development, etc., caused by social practices or policies, and not by the lapses of the individuals or groups suffering from them, are moral, and therefore social, evils. It is important to emphasize, or even overemphasize, this truth because the implications of calling them moral evils are much more far-reaching than those of calling them just evils. Take ignorance, for example. If the ignorance of any section of the society is a moral evil, then it becomes the moral duty of the government and the capable people of the country to get it removed. Ignorance *can* be removed by proper education and therefore proper education ought to be provided. The concerned agencies, if they do not make honest efforts in this direction, would, then, be not only negligent or incompetent but morally condemnable. Moral condemnation is the vilest that can be slung on any individual, group, or even political party.

To characterize this sort of moral evil more precisely, to deprive a section of the society of adequate opportunities for developing their abilities, or ameliorating their living conditions, is an act of social injustice. Independent India has made an experiment to stop fresh occurrences of such injustices, and compensate for the past ones. I shall try to examine this experiment in the light of the theoretical framework presented in the earlier sections.

The Hindu society is basically a caste-constituted society. By this I mean that the broadest or proximate groups or sections into which it can be divided are castes or caste-groups. Every Hindu by birth belongs to some caste. To say that in classical India an individual's caste was determined by his capabilities is only to point at a red herring. That might have been the case at some stage of Indian history, but quite early, even in classical India, castes became birth-determined. Moreover, today castes are birth-determined, and it is the social injustices suffered by, and facing modern, birth-determined, caste-Indians, I am talking about here.

II. *Caste, Concession and Conversion*

The non-Hindu sections of the Indian society are not, in the sense in which the Hindus are, caste-constituted. Among the non-Hindus, Muslims, Christians, and Buddhists, in principle, are casteless groups because neither Islam, not Christianity, nor Buddhism, admits of caste distinctions or divisions. In this respect they are more rational or equalitarian than Hinduism. This means that anyone who is a Muslim, a Christian, or a Buddhist, by birth or conversion, cannot claim to be of this or that caste. Consequently a Hindu, after becoming converted to anyone of these religions cannot retain his pre-conversion caste. He must lose it, or give it up, otherwise he would not be a genuine convert. No one can have two religions. A man of one religion may have sympathy for, or even appreciation of, some aspects of another, but he cannot be a member of two religious groups, an adherent of two religious faiths. This means that a Hindu of caste *B*, after his conversion to, say, Christianity, ceases to be a member of caste *B*. Suppose, sometime after his conversion, the government passes a legislation to give some concessions to those members of caste *B* whose annual income is less than a certain amount, say *M*. Suppose further that the annual income of the convert, before and after his conversion, is less than *M*. But since he is not longer a *B*, he cannot claim the concessions. Concesions are, *ex hypothesi*, available only to him who is both a *B and* an earner of annual income less than *M*. The convert's annual income is less than *M* no doubt but he is not a *B*, and therefore is not covered by the legislation. He would have been covered had it also been applicable to Christians with annual income less than *M*, or to all Indians with annual income less than *M*, irrespective of their castes, or religions.

Therefore, when a converted non-Hindu claims to have a concession, available to a person of a certain caste, on the ground that in his pre-conversion period he belonged to that caste, it means that his conversion is not complete or genuine, or that the caste-system, through this move of his, has entered, or is entering, into the religion he has been converted to, or that he is unscrupulous, with no regard for his new religion, disposed to do anything for his selfish gain.

Let us limit the discussion to the Hindu sector of the society. If individuals or groups, who have suffered social injustices, were classified in some non-caste manner, then the entire gamut of the Indian society could have been uniformly covered by concessional or ameliorative measures. But the policy-makers found it easier to classify them in caste-terms. It was true that members of some castes were denied social justice *because* they belonged to those castes. Even if anyone of them improved his living condition and obtained some respectable job, he was not given the social status a person of equivalent rank but belonging to a so-called upper, or privileged, caste enjoyed. The caste of a person, thus, did become, in a large number of cases, the cause of his ill-being. Therefore, in a good number of cases the caste of a person was taken to be the indicator of the fact that social injustices had been done to him. It was not, thus, completely unreasonable to classify socially injusticed people into some caste-groups. The possibility of reaping a rich electoral harvest, by exploiting caste-feelings of the voting public, was also very clearly seen by the policy-makers and they were keen to tap it to the fullest extent. All this happened because behind such moves political motivation was always very strong. Some would even say that it was stronger than the alleged ethical motivation of preventing the privileged castes from doing further injustices, and of compensating for those already done, to the exploited, unprivileged, or underprivileged, castes.

III. *The Experiment in Operation: Revenge and Retribution*

For making the discussion handy, I shall take up a particular area of social life, simplify it as much as possible, without, of course, making it look unrealistic, and then examine the Indian experiment to restore social justice relevant to that area. My objective would be to highlight some of the problems it is likely to give rise to and to suggest some ways of destroying, or curtailing, their power to disturb social harmony. Perhaps they cannot be completely eliminated, but it would mean a lot if their fire-power is reasonably reduced. Some such problems, it seems to me, have already arisen. That they have begun to disturb the social and moral order, or are not letting us have the kind of social-moral order the restoration of social justice is expected to usher in, is apparent to any neutral observer of the Indian social scene.

The area I want to limit myself to is that of education. Take a caste, which I would call *U*, most of whose members are uneducated, or very poorly educated. Generations of them have been socially neglected, disrespected, and denied facilities of good education. They have neither the economic resources to meet the cost of good education, nor the proper atmosphere in their families to motivate and help their children to do well in their schools which now have been made available to them. Therefore, their children very seldom secure good grades in their examinations. Since very high grades are required of a student to be admitted in a professional college, say, a medical one, none of these children is likely to receive medical education. And, all this is so, they feel and many others as well, because generations of their caste members have been subjected to social injustices. The Indian experiment, to ameliorate this situation, is to provide to some of these children admission in a medical college in a concessional manner, by lowering the admission requirements in such a manner that at least a few of them would meet them. As the number of seats are limited, it so happens that some children of the caste *P*, an advanced one, with much better grades, are denied admission even if their economic and family background are not better than those of the concessionally admitted *U*-caste students. This is possible because some members of *P* may not be economically or familially better than some members of *U*, even though, as a caste, *P* is much more advanced or privileged than *U*.

Let us now imagine some of the possible ways in which the *U*-student and the *P*-student may react in the situation outlined above. The former may think in some such way:

(i) 'Generations of *P* have done social injustices to generations of my people. In giving me a seat in the medical college the government has not really given any concession to my caste. Rather, because of the power democracy has given to it, it has, in effect, snatched some seats from *P*, and thereby has avenged at least some of the injustices.' The latter may also think that a revenge has been taken on his caste by *U* and the members of his caste have not been able to resist because of their weaker position in the country's politics. He may even blame some leaders of his caste to have betrayed it for fulfilling some of their political ambitions.

This kind of thinking may then lead to what generally happens when some people think to have avenged on, or to have been avenged on by, some others. The avengers may feel victorious, or become arrogant, and the avenged-on may start preparing for a direct or indirect counter-revenge. For example, it may happen that when he completes his education, the *U*-student becomes the boss of the *P*-student. The latter may then try to satisfy his propensity of revenge by not giving him the respect and courtsey he deserves in virtue of his official status. Sometimes the reactions of either party could be very strong and even violent. But whether they are mild or strong, concealed or open, the revenge-interpretation of the Indian experiment, of restoring social justice by the method of granting concessions to the undeveloped or under-developed sections of the society, would always be inimical to the protection or establishment of social harmony. Therefore, by means of proper dissemination of information about the relevant facts of social history and value-based education, attempts must be made to reduce, as much as circumstances permit, the possibility and appeal of the revenge-interpretation. One step in this direction would be to get it replaced or countered by what I call the retributive interpretation.

(ii) Suppose the *U*-student takes the Indian experiment as a retributive one: He thinks he has got the concession as a moral recompense for past injustices, the provision of concession as a moral mechanism for correcting social imbalance in the society. To think in this way is to have a retributive, a moral, attitude towards the mechanism of concession, i.e., towards its provision and its consequences for him as well as for others like him, i.e., for the people of his caste and of some other castes. To adopt a moral attitude is to have a care or concern for the welfare of others. Therefore, he would have some care or concern for others if he adopts the moral attitude. This means he would have a concern for the welfare of even those who would be deprived of admission in a medical college though they are, in merit, equal to, or better than, him. It is very likely, therefore, that instead of jubilating over the consequential deprivation of admission to the latter, as he would have done had his attitude been one of revenge, he would feel sorry for them. His reaction to his admission would be something like this: I have got what I ought to have got and thereby an injustice done to me and my caste has been compensated for. But this has caused an injustice to someone else; it has adversely affected his welfare. This means that though my admission, being a case of giving me a moral compensation, is a moral good, it has involved an immorality by adversely affecting someone else's welfare. This is inevitable because the provision of the concession is the only way available to the society for correcting the social or moral imbalance. This sort of immorality is, therefore, permissible, or condonable, *but nothing more than that*. Since it is an immorality, it should not continue for ever. The society must work for ushering in a social order in which resorting to such immoralities becomes uncalled for. This would mean, in this particular case, ushering in a social order in which (a) every, or almost every, candidate deserving admission in a medical college gets admitted and (b) the question of depriving any deserving one of admission in order to accommodate some undeserving, or not equally deserving one, on some non-academic ground, does not arise.

(a) may look like an utopia, but there is nothing wrong in having an utopia as a social ideal. If we aim at an uptopia, we may achieve a social order in which the majority of deserving candidates get admitted and even the remaining ones get something which may not be exactly what they wanted, but something very near to it, say, admitted in a management school which is their second choice.

(b) also has some far-reaching implications. The need for accommodating a weaker candidate, because of some non-academic reason, for example, because of social injustice done to the members of his caste by the members of some privileged castes for a pretty long time, would not arise only if the number of such candidates is nil, or very negligible. This means that either the society does not have what we call its weaker section, or if there is one, it is very small. In the latter case, it would be easier to raise the status of the weaker section and also to accommodate weaker candidates belonging to it without depriving many deserving ones from the better sections. We can hope to realize such a state of affairs only if successive governments work for ushering in a social order of this type and not remain satisfied with making more and more provisions for concessional admissions. To make the latter state of affairs real, one of the things which they must do is to provide to the existing weaker section the necessary resources and opportunities for raising the level of competence, academic abilities, etc., of the students belonging to it so that they become more equipped and able to compete with those from the better, or privileged, sections. Greater the number of such students from the weaker section, lesser will be the need of concessional provisions, and in due course they would become uncalled for.

But the society, or governments, alone cannot achieve this goal. The weaker section as well must cooperate with them. By properly utilising the available resources and opportunities for developing their talents, the weaker section students must exert hard to make themselves better equipped so that they may claim to have on their own merit what they are now given because of a concessional provision. Education, formal as well as informal or non-formal, must get it instilled into their minds the great truth that it is more dignified and self-respecting for a young man to get something on account of his merit than to get it on account of a concessional provision. Even the media has to emphasise this truth. It is a pity that neither our educational programmes nor the media are making any effort in this direction. About the politicians, less said the better.

Concessional provisions for helping a weaker student have built into them a pernicious possibility. If he can get admission in a medical college by securing 20 per cent marks in the admission test, while a *P*-student can do so only by securing 70 per cent, then the former may think, there is no need to work hard to improve his merit. This thinking would make him lethargic and he may stagnate at the academic point where he presently is. This kind of thinking is likely to be popular and if it really becomes popular, it would make the weaker section remain perpetually weak. The weaker section must realise that an earned dry bread is sweeter than an unearned buttered one.

Suppose we succeed in shaping the outlook of an *U*-student in the above way. That is, he takes the concession given to him as a moral compensation for the social injustices done to his section of the society, and admits that it involves some immorality in the consequential denial to a *P*-student what he deserves on the ground of his merit. He also admits that such a measure cannot be made permanent and also that he must make himself better equipped because getting something on the basis of one's merit is more self-respecting than getting it on account of a concessional provision. His attitude towards the *P*-student, who has been denied a seat, would, then, in all likelihood, be one of sympathy and not of arrogance, or of having avenged on an exploiter or oppresser. If the *P*-student also takes the matter in the retributive, and not the revengeful, way, his reaction to his loss and the *U*-student's gain would, again, in all likelihood, be very different from what, in most cases, it is found to be. We may describe it in some such way as this:

I have lost what I ought to have got, and so have many others. But this is inevitable to compensate for the injustices done to the *U*-students. Not giving me the admission and preferring one with a poorer merit is morally wrong. But the end to achieve which it has been done is morally commendable; it is a wrong, or not a very desirable, means to achieve a right or desirable end. It pinches me, but the pinch is unavoidable because of the critical state the Indian society is passing through.

When the *P*-student reaches this point, his and the *U*-student's understandings of the situation and attitudes towards it converge to the same point, or almost to the same point. This convergence is likely to reduce, to a large extent, the social tension caused by the provision of concessions.

IV. *Concession-caused Resentment: A Fake Argument Refuted*

To say all this is not to deny the unhappiness of the *P*-student. His feeling unhappy is natural because it arises out of his thinking that he has not got what he deserves simply because he belongs to a certain caste. But if he has taken the denial as a retributive, moral, consequence of the policy to raise the social status of the *U*-student by using the mechanism of concessions to give him medical education, he would be able to have a rational, tolerant, attitude towards his own unhappiness. This attitude would give him the fortitude to take it in an impersonal way and therefore to reduce or soften his resentment against what he has been denied.

That the provision of concessions and its implementation have made the *P*-student unhappy has been recognised even by the strongest supporters of the policy of concessions. In fact, it is difficult to unsee or unhear it without closing one's eyes or ears because it has been expressed several times in very strong, even violent or self-violent, ways. But the general trend of thinking about it is to consider it unjustified, politically instigated, or as an expression of the attachment of the privileged class with the powers and privileges it has wrongfully acquired and has been enjoying for centuries, and to treat the *P*-student's anger and frustration as the outcomes of his realisation that the power and glory of his caste are going to be very much reduced by the implementation of the policy of concessions. That there is a point, an element of reasonableness or righteousness, in his unhappiness or resentment, is generally missed. Those few who see it find it unsafe, or unfashionable, to emphasise it.

The result is that neither the leaders of society, nor the intellectuals, have tried to properly understand what the *P*-student's unhappiness and resentment really connote. Consequently, they have not been able to suggest any ethically sound way to contain them without hurting any interest of his or of the *U*-student. It is no wonder, therefore, that none of them has emphasised the desirability of creating a climate of mutual understanding which would motivate the *P*-student to be a little detached or impersonal, so that he may take his unhappiness not as the result of some injustice done to him, but as an inevitable sacrifice he has to make, or rather should smilingly make, to help those, who happen to be in the last rung of the social ladder, to come up to a higher one in order that they may have a meaningful and dignified social existence. This mode of thinking, if cultivated by the *P*-student, may inspire him to feel great instead of feeling agrieved. He may then take his suffering, or deprivation, as an inevitable consequence of the society's efforts to promote a larger social good, to evolve a better social order. If such is the perspective from which he looks at his social scene, his feeling of unhappiness, caused by the implementation of the policy of concessions, would surely become much less bitter than what it presently is.

Anyone with a sound ethical perspective would admit that there is a very good reason for him to be unhappy because he has been denied what he thinks he ought to have got, and his thinking that he ought to have got it is right when he really has the merit which entitled him to what has been denied to him. The alleged reason for denying it to him is his caste for which he is in no way responsible. Nor is it possible for him to get rid of it even if he wants to. The pointfulness, or righteousness, of his unhappiness and resentment, thus, lies in (a) his having a good moral reason, i.e., academic merit, to have got (i.e., the medical admission as per my example) what he has been denied, and (b) the alleged reason for which he has been denied, i.e., his caste, really being no reason at all for denying it to him.

The fact that one belongs to a certain caste cannot by itself justify, or be a reason for, granting to, or withholding from, him anything whatsoever. It is counter-intuitive to moral common sense to make it a reason for giving someone somethig he does not deserve on his own merit, or for denying him something he meritwise deserves. We cannot, therefore, say to the *P*-student that you deserve your non-admission because you belong to a certain caste. We can only say that you should take your non-admission as your share of the cost of social development, or, of the restoration of social justice to the weaker section. To me this seem to be the best attitude to take towards the policy of concessions and its fallouts; the best attitude for those on whose shoulders it puts some extra burdens as well as for those who are its beneficiaries.

But some enthusiasts of the policy of concession as well as some of its beneficiaries seem to think that the *P*-student's caste is a good enough reason for his non-admission and for making his unhappiness resulting therefrom well-deserved. Therefore, there is nothing for him to complain against, or to feel great for having made any sacrifice.

The upholders of this view give an argument in support of it. I have not come across any written version of the argument. I have only heard some people using it to justify things of which the *P*-student's non-admission is an example. Generally it is used in an emotional manner, or in an emotionally tense situation. But keeping aside the emotional overtones, it can be presented in a cut and dry manner. Only then we can clearly see whether or not it really achieves what it is claimed to. The argument can be put as follows, assuming that it is directly addressed to a complaining *P*-student:

It may be true that you yourself have not done any injustice to any member of an *U*-caste. But this also is true that your ancestors have done many. You inherit their assets, the wealth accumulated by them. You must also then inherit their liabilities, the demerits or blameworthinesses attached to the injustices done by them. Therefore, you ought not to mind suffering, if per chance you have to, the consequences of the measures adopted to rectify, or compensate for, their injustices. Denying you the admission, you say you deserve to get on your own merit, is one of these consequences. It should not make you unhappy and if it does we cannot help it. We can only say that no wrong is being done to you. Since your ancestor's injustices have made you deserve the non-admission, they have also made you deserve the unhappiness the latter may be causing to you.

This argument has the appearance of a moral argument, i.e., of an argument meant to justify, in the moral sense of the term 'justify', the non-admission of the *P*-student and his unhappiness resulting therefrom. But this it does not really do. Morality or immorality, i.e., moral merit or demerit, of actions are categorially different from material goods. Unlike a material good owned by a person, the immorality (or morality) of an action done by him cannot be transferred, lent, gifted, or bequeathed, etc., to any other person, howsoever close the latter may be to him. Similarly, one can inherit a material good owned by an ancestor of his if he is the latter's legal heir and the good has not already been willed to someone else. Along with his material assets, he can also inherit the ancestor's material liabilities, for example the debts he incurred, the taxes he owed to the government, etc. But he cannot inherit his moral assets or liabilities, i.e., moral merits or demerits, praiseworthiness or blameworthiness, of any moral or immoral action done by him, even if he were a parent of his. It makes no sense to speak of transferring, gifting, lending, bequeathing, etc., the moral merits or demerits of one's actions to anyone else, not to speak of one's inheriting them from anyone else. We cannot praise, or blame, anybody for someone else's moral, or immoral, action, or actions. Material goods are inherited because there are laws of inheritance. But there is no law for inheriting the culpability of a person for having done something wrong, say, an injustice to someone else, for the simple reason that there cannot be such a law. One is punishable or rewardable, in the moral sense, only for what he himself does, i.e., only for that for which he is accountable or responsible. One cannot be sent to the gallows even if it has been proven that his absconding father has committed a number of murders. If it is established that he has concealed him somewhere, he may be punished. But then he would be punished for his own crime of concealing a criminal and not for any crime committed by his father, the criminal.

We cannot, therefore, morally justify the denial of admission to the *P*-student, who himself has done no injustice to any member of the *U*-caste, on the ground that some ancestor or ancestors of his have. The argument concerned, therefore, fails to establish the moral propriety of the *P*-student's non-admission and of his having been made unhappy on that account. As a moral argument it does not, thus, achieve what it is intended to.

The argument smacks of an attitude of revenge, conveying to the *P*-student something like the following:

You might not have done any injustice to any member of the *U*-caste. But your ancestors have done so many. In causing you some unhappiness by denying you the admission and giving it to an *U*-student, nothing more has been done than avenging on you for the misdeeds of your ancestors.

As I have already shown, the concept of revenge is *amoral*. Revenge for what one man has done can be taken on someone else, immediately or remotely, related to the former. And, even if the action, to avenge which it is done, was morally wrong, the revengeful action itself may also be morally wrong. The motive behind a revengeful action is to return hurt for hurt without caring whether or not it is morally right to do that. Therefore, to take the Indian experiment of providing some concessions to the weaker section of the society as a revengeful move would amount to very greatly devaluing or lowering its dignity and objective. The experiment is worth making only if it is a moral experiment, i.e., an experiment to compensate for injustices done, with a view to establishing, in a moral manner, social balance which is a necessary condition for social welfare. Moreover, taking revenge is very prone to cause reactive revenge, i.e., to make the avenged-on retaliate, sooner or later, and therefore to disrupt social harmony. That is why I have argued for making all possible efforts to effectively discourage all those who give to a particular concession, or to the general policy of giving concessions, a revenge-interpretation.

The *P*-student's feeling of unhappiness or frustration can be made, as I have shown, much milder, if good education and enlightened social climate have got inculcated in him a proper understanding of the societal matrix, which has made the provision of concessions inevitable for ameliorating the existing condition of the weaker section of the society. All this involves developing a balanced attitude of moral retribution. Then, he may even develop an ennobled attitude of thinking that by ungrudgingly receiving, without any malice, the consequences of the provision of concessions, which include some unhappiness, he is contributing to the societal programme of helping the members of the weaker section to better their living conditions.

The acquisition of such attitudes is not an easy matter. But it is not impossible either. There are certain concrete things which, if properly done, can go a great way to help the *P*-student look at things in a balanced and dispassionate manner, and get his dissatisfaction watered down, may be in a slow, but stable, manner. For example, his unhappiness can be very greatly assuaged by the society's giving him the assurance of fair play and fulfilling it in admissions in those institutions in which no concessional provision is operative. But if in such an institution his claim is superseded by that of the less meritorious son of a minister, his frustration and anger are bound to reach a very high pitch. They are also likely to increase if concessional provisions are made, or are suspected to be made, permanent. It is not unnatural to have the suspicion because of the implicit, and sometimes even explicit, unwillingness of Indian politicians, who really are in command of the country's present and future, to make political practice conform with the demands of morality. This point needs elaboration.

V. *The Mechanism of Concession: Paying to the Politician But Likely to Block the Beneficiary's Growth*

The politician who argues in defence of concessional provisions for the weaker section claims to be the latter's benefactor and thereby hopes to get their votes. There is nothing wrong in doing so provided his motives are morally pure. But it is extremely difficult to be sure of the moral purity of his motives. The existence of the weaker section is to his advantage because he can exploit it, in elections, to vote for him or his party. He can do that by making its members believe that he was instrumental in making available to them the existing concessions, would do his best, if elected, to see that they are not taken away, and some new ones are enacted, etc., etc. Concessions would be needed by the weaker section only as long as it is weak. Therefore, the politician, who is guided only or primarily by the political motive to capture political power, may wish and in some indirect ways try to ensure that the weaker section remains weak. This he can do, for example, by encouraging its members, in a surreptitious manner, to think that the provision of concessions is the only, or the most effective, means to improve their lot. It seems some of them have been taken in and therefore ask for more and more concessions, and react very strongly against any proposal to drop any of the existing ones. In defending the cause of concessions the politician claims to defend the cause of social justice to the downtrodden. But the truth seems to be the contrary: In making the weaker section prize concessional advantages much more than their voluntary efforts to improve their capabilities, he does a great social injustice to them.

A concession is like a crutch given to a man with a fractured leg. Its use can only make him walk in a limping manner. He can somehow survive; the crutch cannot enable him to run, or to compete with those whose legs are uninjured. That is why it is to be used only until the broken bones join together, and then to be dispensed with. The real ability to walk and run is acquired only when the legs are used without the help of any crutch. The politician, who lulls the members of the weaker section to believe that concessions are indispensable, that they should never be withdrawn, and if the existing ones have not improved their lot, some new ones should be added to them, would make them, if his designs succeed, permanently handicapped, able to walk only with the help of their crutches. Such people would be useful to the politician: He can make use of them to remain in power because they have to depend on him for their crutches, for retaining the existing ones, for replacing the damaged ones, or weaker ones, with better ones, etc., etc. To do, or intend to do such things to a class of people is to do a great social injustice to them. By no stretch of imagination it can be given the name of social justice.

In the present state of Indian society concessions for its weaker section are needed, but they are needed only up to a certain point. They can only make its members survive, and not help them to grow and develop in a dignified manner. That they would do only if they make sincere efforts to develop their talents and capabilities in a self-respecting manner in whichever area they have to work. Suppose the *U*-student gets admitted in a medical college because a concessional provision is there, though he got very low percentage of marks in the admission test. Suppose, further, that he also graduates with equally low percentage of marks. He did not work hard because he was sure of a job, and he really gets one immediately after the graduation because, again, of a concessional provision. He gets a promotion in the same way in a short period of time, and in course of time becomes the head of a medical institute even though he did not try to improve his professional expertise. He has, in a sense, grown and risen to a high status, but he remains a poor, sub-average, or at the most, a mediocre, medical scientist. He could have been a good one only if he had tried to develop his capabilities. Therefore, to make the members of the weaker section occupy a respectable status in the mainstream of Indian society, it has to be instilled into their minds that concessions would only help them to be on the road of development. And, that too they would do only if they are used by them carefully, cautiously, and conscientiously, unvitiated by the temptation to become self-complacent, which really means to become lethargic. They will really grow and develop in a creative manner only if they take pains to develop their personhood, their individuality, their talents, and objective ways of looking at themselves and their surroundings. They must aim at reaching a stage, and the society must help them in reaching it, when they would have the natural urge to say to the politician, trying to woo them by promising to procure some concessions for them, "Don't insult us by such promises, we don't need a crutch, our legs are sturdy enough to take us wherever we want to go."

The stage mentioned above is not easy to reach, and it may even look utopean. But it is extremely desirable to be utopean these days because, in the name of what is called grassroot realism, Indian politicians have almost completely eroded all values from an average Indian's picture of the good life. Not only the members of the weaker section, but every Indian, should aim at reaching this stage, though its description might vary a little in the case of others. Gandhi has made a remark somewhere that one should never wish to get something for nothing. But unfortunately the reverse seems to have captured the mind of Indians. One can very easily find a person, to whichever sphere of life he turns his eyes, gloating over having got something for nothing. It is this idea ensconced in Gandhi's remark which I have tried to emphasise by means of the stage I have talked about.

It is true that concessions are given to a person not simply because he belongs to a certain caste. Economic considerations are also taken into account and those belonging to the creamy layer are not entitled to them. But it is also true (a) that the majority of the members of certain castes, being below the poverty line, or very poor, are entitled to them, (b) that there is some unclarity about *how* thick the creamy layer should be to make one belonging to it disentitled and therefore there exists the possibility of its different quantitative characterizations, and (c) that politicians make frequent references to castes in talking about concessions. The facts (a), (b) and (c) make it highly plausible for the beneficiary of a concession to believe that he has got the benefit because ofhis caste and for the consequential sufferer who has been denied it to believe that he has suffered the loss because of his caste. It is very likely, then, that both of them attach undue importance to their castes and develop casteist biases. If this unfortunate thing happens on a large scale, it is very likely to cause social imbalance and disharmony, just the opposite of what the provision of concessions in intended to achieve. Minimizing, to the utmost possible extent, reference to castes in such matters alone can retrieve the situation. This does not seem to be possible in the near future because of the way Indian politics has been shaping itself in the last few decades. But it has to be done if the Indian society is to survive in a viable manner.

The purpose of granting a concession to a member of the *U*-class, say, a *U*-student by admitting him in a medical college and giving him, again in a concessional way, a job, promotion, etc., should be to make his status socially respectable in a comprehensive manner, and not merely to improve his economic status. Comprehensive elevation of his status can be achieved not merely by giving him a job but by giving him suitable opportunities to shape himself as an elegant, mature, and professionally competent individual. One of the things required, and a very important one, in this connection is to make him go through a specially designed system of education. At present we lower the standards, or, requirements, to accommodate the *U*-student. For example, we admit him in a medical college with low permanent percentage of marks when a *P*-student, with much higher percentage of marks, is rejected. In one sense the *U*-student is a gainer, but in another sense he is a loser. If he is sensitive, he would feel that he is not as good as the *P*-student sitting on his right side. This feeling of inferiority may assume many forms. Even after his becoming a professor of medicine it may keep nagging him, and those who have to deal with him may also retain the feeling that he is a professor not because he has professorial abilities but because he belongs to a concession-entitled caste. Such things are not merely hypothetical probabilities but hard social realities. It cannot be brushed aside as a mere gossip spread by a *P*-class individual that a minister coming from an *U*-caste refused to be treated by a physician coming from his own caste and preferred to be treated by one coming from a *P*-caste. Concessions have done some good no doubt to the *U*-class of Indians, but not as much as it was expected of them. A good, objective, empirical research, conducted on qualitative, and not merely quantitative, lines is needed to assess how far the availability of concessions has improved the overall status of the beneficiaries.

VI. *Well-designed Education as a Prophylactic to the Mechanism of Concession*

It seems to me that the existing situation can be improved a lot if care is taken to adapt the quality and format of education given to *U*-students to their needs and capabilities. A full-fledged programme of the relevant kind of education cannot be outlined here. I would rest satisfied with simply making some general suggestions.

It is said that because of centuries of exploitation, social neglect and injustices meted out to them, the will of an *U*-student to learn and rise in life has been terribly weakened. He has lost his self-confidence, his faith in his own individuality. Therefore, even if he is now given chance to educate himself, he cannot do as well as a *P*-student can; the former's score would very seldom be comparable to that of the latter, etc., etc. Therefore, if he intends to join a medical college, the requirements of admission have to be very much relaxed to accommodate him. I am not questioning all this. I want to reiterate, as I have already made the point, that his concessional admission, even his concessional appointment as a doctor and promotion, etc., may not restore in him his self-confidence, his faith in his own capabilities, in his own individuality. Even if in some cases they do, they would not do as effectively as improving his merit would. Therefore, I suggest an adaptation of the existing system of education in such a manner that when he is drilled through it, the chances of getting his merit improved become much brighter. More specifically, I suggest that syllabii taught to him be staggered in such a manner that he has to carry a lighter load than that of an average *P*-student, and consequently the number of years of schooling required for him has to be greater than that required of the latter. After a *U*-child is given some general schooling, a diagnostic test may be held to judge his aptitudes and abilities. If the average index of his performance is found to be much lower than that of a *P*-student of his age, in the coming classes lighter load may be given to him so that he can perform better. In this way, he would take a little longer, say, twelve years, instead of ten years, to complete his secondary education. But his loss of two years would be very well compensated for by the resulting enrichment of his capabilities. It will boost up his self-image if he becomes able to get, because of his merit, what he is given nowadays because of some concession granted to him.

Some such thing can be done even in the present system, of course, in a limited way. Suppose an *U*-student is given a concessional admission in a medical college, even though his score in the qualifying examination is very low. Instead of letting him run the race in a duckling manner, along with others whose average speed is much greater than his, it would be much better if he is given reduced load and let to complete the courses of studies by taking a few years or semesters more than the minimum number of years or semesters required of a normal student to graduate. If by loosing a few years or semesters at this stage, he becomes as able a doctor as a normal student is expected to be, he would be able to face, in his professional career, the world on the strength of his own merit and abilities, without needing concessional provisions for getting a job, or for getting a higher promotion. He himself, as well as others would then consider him as respectable a professional as any other. He would thus get rehabilitated as a dignified individual in virtue of his being what he himself is, and not because of any favour or concession granted to him by the society or the state.

7. Conclusion

Social justice consists in giving to an individual, or letting him have, what he deserves to have in virtue of his being what he is. Social injustice is the denial of social justice. The victim of social injustice has to be compensated for the injustice done to him. The mode of compensation would depend on the nature of the commodity he deserved to have and which has been denied to him. Making the compensation may cause some suffering to someone else who may be the agent himself who has done the injustice, or to another person related directly or indirectly, immediately or remotely, to the latter. But it is also possible that no link is establishable between the agent, an individual, or a group, who has done some injustice or injustices, to some member or memebrs of the *U*-caste and the individual, or group, belonging to the *P*-caste, who are to suffer, or deprived of something, as the result of some concession granted to the victims of the injustice or injustices. This may happen because of the complexity of the case, or of the situation in which the alleged injustice was done. An unusually long gap of time between the injustice done and the compensation made may also be responsible for it.

The beneficiary of the compensation may have towards the compensation or its consequential sufferer an attitude of revenge or one of retribution. The same is the case with the attitudes the consequential sufferer may have towards the suffering caused to him, towards the beneficiary, or towards the agencies who have made the compensation available to the beneficiary. The attitude of revenge is very likely to cause immediately, or a little later, social, or societal, imbalance, whereas that of retributivity is not. Since the latter is a moral attitude, one who has it would have some care for the welfare of others. Therefore, it can generate some sympathy for the sufferer of the compensation in the mind of the beneficiary of the compensation. In a similar way, it can generate some understanding, even sympathy, in the mind of the sufferer for the beneficiary.

The Indian experiment of providing compensations to some members of some castes to whom social injustices have been done is, in principle, morally right if the motivation behind it is to restore social balance which has been disturbed by social injustices done to the latter. But the way it has been talked about, propagated, or championed, gives rise to the impression that it has been done to avenge on the wrong-doers, or, to put it realistically, on their distant descendents because the majority of the former are dead and gone. It is, therefore, very likely that the beneficiary thinks that his wrong-doers are now avenged on for their misdeeds, and he who suffers in consequence thinks that he is being avenged on for something some of his ancestors have allegedly done. An attitude of revenge, or a revenge-interpretation of a situation, is extremely prone to generate a reactive attitude of revenge in the other side, which may take revenge on the beneficiary in a direct or indirect manner, sooner or later, when he is in a position to. All this will obviously disturb social balance and harmony. To ward off this eventuality it is necessary that a social or moral climate is created in which both the beneficiary of a compensation and its consequential sufferer have towards the provision of concessions or compensations the attitude of moral retribution. This would mean that both the beneficiary of a concession and the consequential sufferer think that the former's benefiting from a concession is a moral compensation for some past immorality done to him or his predecessors, and the consequential suffering or deprivation caused to the latter is due to the peculiar nature of the Indian societal situation, due specifically, for example, to the paucity of resources, extreme poverty of the members of certain castes, etc. If such a climate of understanding is created, each one of them would have some sympathy for the other and both would admit that social affairs should be managed in such a manner that, as early as possible, the Indian society becomes so harmonious or cohesive that the benefit of one member of it does not become a burden on some other member.

A concession granted to an unprivileged, or underprivileged, person, in the present set-up, means, giving something to him by lowering, and more often than not, lowering very greatly, the qualifications which are normally required of a person from the privileged class to be eligible for making a claim to it. This practice is likely to generate in the recipient of the concession a feeling of inferiority which may come in the way of his developing into an elegant, self-respecting, individual. On the other hand, if it generates in him a feeling of pride, or of being a favoured person, allowed to have something with a merit much lower than that of some others to whom it has been denied, it would hamper his growth as a cohesive and cooperative individual. It has been suggested that, to ward off such possibilities, the concession-needing individuals should be given a kind of education specially designed for them, say, by extending the time-span and making provision for a reduced load of work required, so that when they come out of it they become able to stand on equal, or almost equal, footing with claimants from privileged classes. A suitable scheme for developing their skill and abilities can be made and implemented even for the present beneficiaries of concessions who are already holding some responsible ranks in some public or private concerns, or in some professional areas.

The ultimate objective of restoring social justice in the social order, by compensating for past injustices by means of granting to the victims a set of concessions, should be not merely to remove their economic hardships by giving them jobs or opportunities by lowering the criteria of entitlement. It should rather be to help them develop into individuals who are self-respecting, socially cohesive, and promotive of the constructive goals of the nation. One may say, in an objecting tone: But this should be the aim for all individuals. Everyone should develop into such beings. This is true, and I am emphasizing it because it is true. Ultimately, or in principle, all Indian citizens should form a single stream. The two streams, one of citizens entitled to concessions and the other of the remaining ones not entitled to them, must not run separately for ever, or for a long time. Sooner they merge into one, sooner the number of concession-needing individuals become nil or negligible, better for the country even if not so for the politician.

As I have argued, it is an ethical, or a meta-ethical, truth that a social injustice has to be compensated for, since the concept of being compensated for is retributively contained in that of social injustice. And, depending upon the nature of certain empirical factors pertaining to the case concerned, the compensation may sometimes be done by doing something more than the corresponding act of social justice. For example, the Board of Trustees of a temple may not only allow, hitherto disallowed member of the scheduled castes to enter the temple, but also appoint one of its members its chief priest when the existing practice required that the chief priest be a brāhmaṇa. The primary purpose of all such moves is to raise the social, or rather, overall, status of the members of the *U*-castes, and thereby to improve their style of life.

But there are some effects of social injustices, done for a pretty long period of time, which must be separately attended to if their victims' style of life is to be made really better, because they may not be adequately taken care of by compensatory moves alone. Prolonged perpetration of social injustices on a person not only weakens or destroys his respect for himself, his will to develop his talents, but generates in him certain undesirable traits, or habits, of living and thinking. For example, he may develop the habit of keeping his body, children, animals, surroundings, etc., unclean even when keeping them clean requires only his labour.

Similarly, he may develop the mental habit of thinking, or, believing, that there is nothing wrong in his using certain indecent or foul words or phrases in normal communicative transactions with others, even with the members of his own family, in the latter's using them in their's with him, in his charging abnormally high wages for his services when sought by people in some emergencies, in spending on the week-end his day's wage on alcohol and thereby depriving his sick son of his medicine, in looking amorally at his sexual immoralities, in indulging in stealing or pick-pocketing as an occasional hobby, etc., etc. He may as well think that his miserable living condition, his poverty, justifies such things. His style of life would not, then, even from the point of view of his own self-interest, be a desirable one; it cannot be unless such habits are replaced by better ones. It may be that his unhappiness motivates or causes him to acquire such habits, but it cannot justify anyone of them, simply because nothing can. The poverty of a rickshaw-puller would not justify his charging ten times of the normal fare to take an old lady, injured in an accident on the road, from the place of the accident to a hospital, exploiting her helplessness because no other means of transportation is available at the time and she is unable to walk to the hospital. Such an immoral, exploitative, action, would remain unjustified, howsoever poor the agent, and howsoever rich the injured lady, may be.

It is wrong to think that only a rich person can exploit a poor person. Even a poor one can, and sometimes does, exploit a rich one. Exploitation of anyone's helplessness by anyone else is morally wrong. The morally wrong action is wrong, no matter when, where, by whom and to whom, it is done. A *jhuggī*-dweller's asking, or letting, his children dirty every morning the public road in front of his residence is as wrong as a rich housewife's throwing garbage on the road in front of hers. Both of them can ask for spaces for such things, and if the municipal administration does not provide, they have to exert their best to minimise these practices as much as possible. It would be unfair to think that the *jhuggī*-dweller's poverty *justifies* what he has been doing, and the rich housewife's affluence makes *unjustified* what she has been doing.

I am not oblivious of the difficulties of the members of the U-class. I have said what I have above because there is a strong belief in the minds of many that concessional provisions are all that we need to implement in order to better their style of life. This is not true. We have to change their value-structure, by making them go through a process of culturisation in formal as well as informal ways, to undo the effects of malculturisation or aculturisation their adverse physical and social surroundings are likely to have caused in their style of life. Professional or technical education alone cannot do that. The pernicious belief that poverty, or adverse living conditions caused by social injustices, *justify* uncultured behaviours, immoralities, or incivilities, has to be driven out from wherever it exists, because it gives a false sense of propriety to things which ought not to be done and to ideas which ought not to be entertained.

Equipping the members of the *U*-class with a sound value-structure is as bonafide a part of the programme of restoring social justice to them as is the provision of certain types of concessions in education, health-care, housing, jobs, etc. Their behavioural and thinking patterns have to be suitably changed along with making available to them, in a dignified manner, certain facilities which had been until recently denied to them and are not yet being fully utilised by them. Doing the former is necessary because without it they would not be able to properly and judiciously use the resources made available to them. Only then exploitative politicians would not be able to use them as means to their political ends. They do that, for example, by collecting them in rallies to cover up their misdeeds, or by manipulating their votes in elections. I do not mean to suggest here that there is nothing wrong in the non-*U*-class Indians' value-structure. In fact, we have the *U*-class largely because of the latter anaemic value-structure.

3

Democracy and Justice
Assumptions and Questions

Debi Prasad Chattopadhyaya

NEITHER *democracy* nor *justice* is a place-time-invariant concept. The same two words have been and are being used to mean different social and political structures or state of affairs. Democracy in the Hellenic context stood for citizens' rule and not based on the principle of heredity. It may be a form of government or a structure of society or both claimed to be reflecting the will of people. But there is no unanimity among the people themselves who have tried to answer the basic question "how best to reflect popular will in the different forms of government and structures of society?" The text-book parameters of the White Hall and White House models of democracy, — multi-party system, independent judiciary, free press, free trade unionism and periodic election, are quite different from what Aristotle had in mind when he used the term. City-states and tribal societies had their own ways of democratic living. When one recalls the diverse connotations of such expressions as *Social Democracy*, *People's Democracy* and *New Democracy* used in the recent past added complexity crops up. The threat of 'relativism' becomes obvious.

The ancient India had its own forms of democracy or *gaṇatantra* (*gaṇa*=people and *tantra*=rule). It could be of different forms — republican, hereditary or a curious blend of the two. Vedic deities like Marut and Bṛhaspati are described as *gaṇapati* (*gaṇa*=people and *pati*=head). Initially it was an elective office. From literary, numismatic and epigraphic sources and also from Pāṇini's *Aṣṭādhyāyī* and Kauṭilya's *Arthaśāstra* it is gathered that there were many democratic republics, viz., Yaudheya, Vasati and Aprita (Aparyati of Herodotus). The popular two bodies mentioned in the *Ṛgveda*, *sabhā* and *samiti*, the former more select, less popular and political than the latter, wielded considerable authority and formed essential features of the government in the Vedic time. These assemblies were intended to ensure deliberative rationality, rational allocation of responsibility, duty and authority between different individuals and groups.[1]

The above historical references are of little philosophical consequence unless these proclaimed forms of democracy can be rationally justified to be truly democratic. Without some or other accepted paradigm or criterion of democracy the objection of the political and moral relativist can hardly be met.

The same problem we face in deciding what is *justice* and under what conditions are we justified in describing a society or a form of government as just. It is predicated of action, — individual, corporate and state, cause of action, attitude, disposition, administration, procedure, order, legislation, priority, reward, punishment, etc. Instead of characterising an action or administration as *just*, we often characterise it as *right* or *equitable* or *fair*. Meaning of each one of these terms, though extremely important both in ethics and jurisprudence, has been

---

1. A.K. Majumdar, *Concise History of Ancient India, Vol. II, Poltical Theory, Administration and Economic Life*, Munshiram Manoharlal, Delhi, 1980, pp. 131-44. See also, U.N. Ghoshal, *A History of Indian Political Ideas*, Bombay, 1959; and Ram Saran Sharma, *Aspects of Political Ideas and Institutions in Ancient India*, Delhi, 1959.

explicated in various ways and is more or less subject to context of use.

An action is said to be *nyāya* or just when it is found to be performed in accordance with some or other original type, standard, method, rule — general or universal. Fitness or propriety is taken to be the defining property of what justice can be predicted of. *Nyāya-rājya* or just regime is required to be ruled by law and the ruler himself is expected to have certain qualities and to perform his duties (*rājadharma*) to protect and promote the virtues of the law-abiding people (*prajādharma*). King or *rājan* (who may or may not be a hereditary king), though credited to have divine right to rule, must rule according to and as expressive of the collective will. His own life should be disciplined (*vinaya*) and virtuous and he must be advised by efficient, learned and honest officers drawn from the different strata of society. The classical works like *Manusmṛti*,[2] *Arthaśāstra*[3] and *Āin-I-Akbarī*[4] go into details of *rājadharma* and *prajādharma*. Each one of these books (even when its authorship is historically traceable) is to be taken more as description of an obtained tradition than that of a regime at a specific time and place.

Admittedly democracy or justice cannot be established and promoted merely by cultivating individual or collective moral qualities; the rationality and efficiency of institutions are also equally necessary for the purpose. But overemphasis of the institutional and constitutional aspects leading to the relative neglect of the concerned human beings or what I call the

2. P.V. Kane, *History of Dharmaśāstra*, Vol. I, Part I, Bhandarkar Oriental Research Institue, Poona, 1968.
3. R.P. Kangle, *The Kauṭilīya Arthaśāstra*, Parts I, II and III, Motilal Banarsidass, Delhi, 1988.
4. Abul Fazl (1591), *Āin-I-Akbarī*, ed. by H. Blochmann, 2 Vols., *Bib. Ind.*, Calcutta, 1867-77, rev. by J. Sarkar, Calcutta, 1927-39, Vol. I, 1949, Vol.II, 1948, Vol. III.

anthropological basis of ideal polity is bound to obscure our understanding of the functioning of democracy and administration of justice. The point has been well brought out by Confucius when on government he observes that if we rely only on *statute*, people turn out to be evasive but if we govern using the *virtue of morality*, they obey the government willingly. In a somewhat similar vein while enumerating the essentials of government he speaks of the supervenience of *people's confidence* over *weapons* and *food*. What a polity needs *most* for attaining and retaining its ideal character is popular support, not military strength or material inputs.

The hidden assumption of this or that, e.g., pre-liberal or liberal form of democracy is anthropological. If it is assumed that human beings *by nature* are self-centric and inclined to strife for self-promotion, the state needs to be vested with enormous power and authority to check this self-centricity or individualism and also on the understanding that it would effectively maintain peace and order, given which, legitimate extent of individual liberties and properties would be protected. Added accent on individual liberty accounts for the rise of constitutional government and power diffusion and decline of monarchy and power concentration. Its economic fallout is the rise of market as the best possible equilibrating principle of demand and supply of goods and services and the global expansion of the market economy. Evidently the anthropological presuppositions of pre-liberal democracy and liberal democracy are different.[5] But their basic points of similarity — inequality of human beings and of their contribution to social good — explain their common loyalty to market and competition. The anthropological assumption that man by his nature is consumer of utilities and possessive in character underlies capitalism.

---

5. C.B. Macpherson, *Democratic Theory: Essays in Retrieval*, Clarendon Press, Oxford, London, 1973.

The anthropological assumption paving the way for egalitarianism, equal liberties with equal worth attached to them, is that all humans are naturally free and united in will as well as in the pursuit of common weals and avoidance of common woes. This egalitarian ideology is obviously at variance with pre-liberal democracy, liberal democracy and free market economy leading to colonialism, consumerism and exploitation of the poor by the rich.

The radical market economist and the extra-liberal democrat are united in debunking egalitarianism, defending the concepts of minimal state, free competition marked by unequal opportunity and power, and demise of ideology. Many of them think that egalitarianism is somehow affiliated to or influenced by Marxism. Even welfarism, including its moderate forms, is an anathema to them. Market is commended as the supreme dispenser of social justice and defender of liberty. Presumably because of the recent breakdown of the Soviet system the anti-Nazi and pro-democratic role of Russia during the World War II is easily forgotten. Almost with equal ease attempts are made to erase from history the positive effects of Marxism on the freedom-struggle of the erstwhile colonies in Asia and Africa. The Marxian roots of welfarism can hardly be missed by the discerning political and economic thinkers. To recall the positive side of Marxism is not to condone the despotic activities associated with its practice but only to set the history right, pointing out in the process its positive contribution to the evolution of the ideals of democracy and justice in the twentieth century. Without situating the ideals of democracy and justice into their proper practical context it is difficult to evaluate them rationally. Abstract criticism or praise of this or that political ideal lands us in unwelcome negativism or utopianism. To avoid adhocism what is needed is a comprehensive and normative concept of rationality marked by a set of idealised epistemic conditions.

The point may be clarified by referring to and spelling out

the details of the widely felt desire of the world community to reorganise the power-structure of the UN system, especially Security Council, making it more democratic, equitable and just. It is both historically rational and morally imperative. The world-body must express the mankind's needs of today, converging aspirations of tomorrow without being unfair to our sharable civilisational legacy of many millennia.

Man-making, nation-building and unifying the mankind on the basis of shared values are a continuously unfolding and ascending process. It may be viewed both diachronically or anthropologically and synchronically or historically. What unifies the smaller human aggregates is not essentially different from the principle underlying the unity of the larger human aggregates. The basis of unity is the urge for and power of freedom and without which neither growing democracy nor spread of justice is intelligible.

It is true that the concept of democracy as we understand it today has evolved with the time. But this truth is only historical. The content of democracy consists in a form of living which is freedom-seeking. For example, in the Greek city-states most of which are claimed to be democratic, both citizens and slaves used to live together. This means that the co-existence of free citizens and unfree slaves was not only a state of affairs but it appeared to be just to the people and even the wise philosophers of the time. In those days and in the Hellenic world freedom of *some* people was quite consistent with the slavery of the rest. A charitable interpretation of the matter would be like this. But for the hired labour of the slaves citizens could not be free and their freedom preserved.

This restrictive content of the concept of freedom has been defended, for example, by no less an authority than Plato in his *Republic*. To him, like many others after him, there is nothing unjust in a hierarchical society or polity. In this ideal State Plato recognises three classes, the rulers (the men of gold), the fighters (the men of silver), and the farmers (the men of iron and brass) — all professional in their own ways. His main concern is with the upper two classes, the most rationally gifted people and the best of the brave people endowed with the fighting spirit. But the masses lacking in professional education, weak in enterprise and expected to serve all the upper classes in different ways are obviously not recognised and rewarded equally in terms of office and power. Democracy, based on political selfishness, desire and false equality, is as good or bad as, if not inferior to, oligarchy. Without the binding ideal of justice, democracy turns out to be empty, i.e., devoid of content. As per this view, apparently inequality goes well with democracy. The main two ways of justifying this view are (a) one must first *deserve* freedom before it is granted to one individually or to one's group collectively and (b) freedom must be allowed, to start with, only to few so that they can work for the freedom of the rest either by developing the ideals underlying democracy or enabling others to work according to those ideals.[6]

Aristotle is also critical, though less severely than Plato, of democracy because it rests on what he calls the false notions of equality and liberty. Democratic rule amounts to the rule of the poor for the poor and marked by sectional selfishness. Though Aristotle allows the masses to take part in election, he is critical of their lack of respect for law and which, he believes, leads democracy to a political chaos.

If the above broad, admittedly not precise, formulation of a hierarchical society based on the principle of unequal freedom and tilted justice, is accepted, it may help us to understand not only the ancient societies of the Graeco-Roman world but also many non-European societies down the ages.

For example, the Indian society from the ancient to the

---

6. Ernest Barker, *The Political Thought of Plato and Aristotle*, Dover, New York, 1959.

modern time may be understood in terms of hierarchical classes, professional guilds or castes. The brāhmaṇas, because of their learning and advisory competence, are put at the apex of the caste system. Because of their fighting and ruling capacity the kṣatriyas are accorded the second highest stratum. For their business acumen the vaiśyas are ranked third from the top and second from the bottom. The śūdras, servants, are condemned to the lowest position.

This unjust and hierarchical society is sought to be justified by arguing that it cannot be held to be contrary to the God's scheme of things in which all human beings are *either* equal and free actually *or* destined to be so in principle. *Karma*, causation and retribution are believed to be linked concepts. The form of society which stands in the way of realising the higher human potentiality into practice is bound to be considered irrational. It is mainly reason, *ṛta*, which facilitates the process of development of the inner human potentiality to be free and equal. In a sense the dynamic law of nature is the law of reason as well, the former being the outer condition of the latter and being affine to it. By virtue of its rationality, rational reflection, the human *nature* is related, not antithetically but positively, to human *freedom*.

But the truth of this philosophical proposition has to be taken in a qualified manner in the context of our caste system or *varṇa-vyavasthā*. *Varṇa* literally means colour. The Āryans who are believed to have arrived here from the northern and the north-western countries had been of fair complexion. The complexion of the local people was generally dark. Obviously because of thier mixture or marriage (of different recognised types) over the millennia one finds in India today many brāhmaṇas of dark or brown complexion and many *dāsa*s or scheduled caste people of not so dark complexion. Four broad recognized castes are brāhmaṇas (priest and the master of the Vedas), kṣatriyas (rulers and fighters), vaiśyas (the business community) and śūdra (serfs or *sevaka*s) of the other so-called upper castes.

Different writers on the caste system have expressed widely divergent views on it. Some attribute this highly hierarchical system to "the learned and wicked social engineering" of the brāhmaṇas. Henry Maine sees it as "the most disastrous and blighting of all human institutions". There are several others who find it 'marvellous' or 'stability-imparting'. I find no special reason to praise it. In the name of imparting stability to the multi-ethnic and multi-religious society of India, basically it hindered and harmed the orderly emergence of a pluralist and flexible culture here. The determinants of caste — heredity, restrictive rules of marriage, occupation and gradation — praised and raised few, lowered many and separated humans from humans on the basis of the fiction of *varṇa*. The divisive forces which we see today and which have considerably retarded the social progress of India are in no small measure due to this caste system. Equally pernicious in its effects is religious fundamentalism. To swear blindly by caste, religion or nation is a symptom of the split soul. It is anti-libertarian, anti-rational, unethical and inconsistent with the philosophical propositions that we are all God's children and that all human beings are 'essentially' indentical and, given opportunity, may be equal, enjoy equal liberties and primary goods.

To say 'man has liberty' or 'man is free' is to say one and the same thing differently. Liberty is a property which can be owned, enlarged justly or encroached upon unjustly. By owning property, and expression of fundamental right rooted in liberty, man either individually or collectively realises and enlarges his potentiality. If the equality of all human beings is recognised as right, then we need a social state of affairs in which that right can be realised. And that state of affairs has to be defined in terms of qualities, relations and actions of the concerned human beings.

Justice may be advisedly viewd under three heads, *aggregative*, *productive* and *distributive*. An aggregative principle of justice tells us about the total amount of goods and services available for enjoyment by a group of human beings. The productive principle is concerned with the modes of production of material resources such as happiness, satisfaction or fulfilment. The distributive principle, on the other hand, refers to the share of goods and services that different members of the group or different groups of mankind can enjoy. It is often a matter of dispute whether the egalitarian principle of justice is unconditionally imperative or it is so under the condition that human beings must produce first enough to be distributed equitably. For it has also been argued that whatever may be the amount of goods and services it should be distributed in a principled and just manner so that people feel induced to produce maximally.

All these questions relating to liberty, rights and justice prove highly controversial in a hierarchical society. If liberty is not available equally, at least in principle, to all members of a group, then obligation of the less privileged towards the more privileged remains unjustified or only partially justified. If the proprietory rights as expression of liberty remains highly uneven, the conflict between the affluent, the less affluent and the poor is bound to prove itself perpetual.

The main responses to this conflict-situation are two-fold. One: this is purely notional and as a matter of fact this inequality is recognised as hard reality. Two: this conflict-generating inequality is a motive-force of producing more goods and services and therefore provides an incentive to development. These purported justifications of inequality are aimed at perpetuating, if not widening, social conflict on the basis of the dubious claim that it promotes production, justice and social development.

Different types of justice, if not the very conception of it, seem to be under threat in a hierarchical society. It is in this way. If justice is deemed to be right-based and if rights are not equally available to all members of a group or class, how the group or class can be just? If justice in a society is taken to be desert-based and if some less privileged or poor people are denied the very conditions of deserving such values as happiness, satisfaction, education, etc., how the concerned society can be described as just? In a hierarchical society, where needs of different classes or strata of society are defined unevenly *ab initio*, the need-based interpretation of justice is bound to prove unsatisfactory for the poor.

One may point out that the tribal society has in it at least a partial answer to this trilemma between the three interpretations of justice, right-based, desert-based and need-based. Because in it there is a more or less even standard of deciding what is needed by the members of the tribe irrespective of their age and productive capacity. Illness or infirmity does not debar a person from enjoying his or her rights. Rights are also simply, rather unambiguously, defined and well known. Further, the notion of deserving, though diverse, can be arranged in a single scale. For example, while some relatively able-bodied members of a group deserve their food by plucking fruits, hunting animals, catching fish or similar other ways, the children and the old people have their own but different *ways of deserving* either just by waiting patiently for the return of the fish-catchers on sea beach or by helping in building the sea-going boat or in some other way. Thus the very notions of unequal production, rights, needs and desert may be interpreted quite differently.[7] The recognized social criteria of evaluation themselves are different.

One way of containing criterial scepticism is to identify the common qualities (*sādhāraṇa dharma*) available in and expected of *all* human beings. Truthfulness, freedom from anger and enmity, love or compassion (*ahiṁsā/dayā/karunā*) and gift (*dāna*) are often said to be common to all types, classes or *varṇa*s. The

7. Paul Radin, *Primitive Man As Philosopher*, Dover, New York, 1957.

virtues which the famous king Aśoka of the third century BC inscribed on stone in all parts of his vast empire are remarkable in their breadth and depth, viz., compassion, liberality, truth, purity, gentleness, peace, joyousness and saintliness. Both Buddhism and Hinduism defend these virtues and which anticipate a list of virtues enumerated later on by St. Paul in Edicts II and VII. Perhaps most of these *dharma*s or qualities are recognized in the teachings of all the religious leaders and social reformers of lasting significance.

It is true that from culture to culture the *emphasis* on the specific virtues or duties differs. And, what is more, even within the same culture, religion or class one can discern history-specific shift of emphasis on this or that particualr virtue or set of virtues. But it need not necessarily put one into a hopeless form of cultural relativism. Whenever we speak of values we are obliged to speak from within a preferred cultural framework. Even then the content of our discourse has a culture-transcending meaning. Without ceasing to be what we are we know others and we can appreciate others' values even if we do not share them. Whether we call it 'ortho-aestheticity' or self-transcendence, it is very much there. Otherwise we would have been condemned to a sort of cultural solipsism or egology and which would have blocked our way to *objective* sociology of knowledge and value. In the *literal* sense of course we cannot jump out of our skin but that does not mean we cannot *metaphorically*, i.e., supported by some *literal* basis, go out of our habitual or preferred conceptual scheme.

Sharability of views, values and arguments may rightly be claimed to be the main basis of democracy. In spite of its not so encouraging past, positive recent history and ambiguous current meaning, one cannot think of a better form of governance or way of living. Its main strength lies in its tested character. As a form of governance it has emerged out of many trials and errors, trials with other various forms of governance and errors of many insurrections and bloody revolutions. Even the failures of morally planned but cruelly executed revolutions have indirectly contributed to the gradual acceptance of the ideas and ideals of democracy. Another very welcome feather of democracy is that it is open ended and informed of and enriched by the futuristic aspirations of the concerned people. Perhaps the most fundamental strength of democracy lies in its affinity with the consciously *preferred* way of corporate living of the most people. Democracy is not a mere matter of *habit*, social form of habitual living. There is a sound, though inarticulate, element of choice in it. The democratic form of governance or even way of living can hardly be extracted from the passive tradition. It is much more than the moss around the idle stone.

Irrespective of its form, direct or representative, democracy works on the principled communicability and actual sharability of views and values. If, on the one hand, the virtues of communication are not backed up by some or other *principle*, broadly defining the scope and limits of communication, these may be easily mutilated by demagogues of affluent parties or moneyed advertisers through the high-tech telecommunications and media. If, on the other hand, some views, especially these of unconventional or radical character, are not allowed to be *actually* propagated or made public because of the state intervention, obstruction of the ruling or other parties, and restriction imposed by administration or election commission, the electorate is denied in effect the benefit of deliberative rationality. From these seemingly contrary considerations it becomes clear, on reflection, that democracy is a complex web of intricate human relations. It is delicately poised. Herein lies its strength and weakness, resilience and fragility. Democracy may be changed before it becomes intolerably despotic or when it proves to be idle and non-performing.

Another thing that silently sustains democracy is that any body, friend or foe, can argue for or against it. Its openness is not partisan. It is *systematically* rational. Even to his critic the door of the democrat is open. The only limit, if it is a limit at all, which the defender of democracy upholds against its critic is that the actual form of criticism, violent or peaceful, must not be allowed to *destroy* the very system which makes criticism, friendly and hostile, possible. The borderline between *damaging* criticism and *destructive* criticism is not easy to draw. It is drawn and redrawn in the light of received wisdom in the light of constitutional laws, administrative exigency and public opinion. Even then one may find the roles of contingency and irony in the enterprises purported to save democracy.

Going through the endless contingencies and ironies of history it is not easy to answer the question 'What is Democracy?' and in the absence of which one's reflective analysis of the elements is bound to appear off the mark. As already pointed out earlier, the ancient forms of the Indian and the Graeco-Roman democracy, marked by the *hierarchical* society and *direct* participation of the citizens, relatively small in number, are quite different from what we, people living in the non-tribal society and outside the single-party system, understand by the concept. Only by excluding the tribal society and the single-party political system the delimitation of the concept of democracy that we achieve is not enough to arrive at a satisfactory definition. While the *legally* recognised slave system debars the weakest, unless 'liberated', from its access to the crucial decision-making bodies, the rigid caste system, marked by the inhuman institution of *bonded labour*, a sort of serfdom, makes it impossible for the poorest of the poor to exercise his *nationally available* democratic rights. Not only poverty, particularly its highly uneven distribution, is the only enemy of democracy but also the monopolised or cartelised state power by a single partly or/and its various arms stifle democracy. What is worse, often in the name of the poorer efficiency or both this sort of gross distortion is ideologised and sought to be justified.

Used to various sorts of distortion of democracy over a long period of time many of us develop some blind spot and fail (or perhaps refuse) to see some patent weaknesses of democracy not linked, certainly not directly, to poverty. One of the clearest examples of it is provided by the *gender inequality*. One can easily gather it from the ancient sources of Hindu Law, Roman Law and the laws of the women's suffrage in the modern European countries. Apparently concerned with the preservation of "the delicacy, the purity, the refinement, the elevation of [woman's] own nature . . . the present sources of its power", Gladstone was unwilling even in 1892 to grant voting right to women lest it pushed them into the dirty arena of power politics, the exclusive preserve of men. This right was not there for them until 1929. French women did not have this right until 1945. The story of women's suffrage in Switzerland is even more shameful and instructive.

Careful study of the ancient Indian literature on the position of women in general and wives in particular make one thing very clear: the honour and dignity, though limited, that was available to them in the Vedic age was gradually curtailed later on. The discerning scholar can hardly be misled by the high eulogy of women. It is sad to read of their utter dependence on father, husband and son at different stages of life. In such matters as their access to the learning of the Vedas, the rights of inheritance and succession the inferiority of their entitlements, *vis-a-vis* men's, is unmistakable. P.V. Kane, who otherwise tries to take a balanced view regarding the position of women in the ancient Indian society, is obliged to concede that "in the *Mahābhārata*, in the *Manusmṛti*, in other *Smṛti*s and the *Purāṇa*s women are charged with serious moral lapses". They are said to be 'falsehood incarnate', their mind 'uncontrollable' and nature 'poison, snake and fire in one'. Among 'the natural faults' of their character are mentioned lack of *dharma*, fickleness, cruelty, thoughtlessness in action, greed, impurity, trickery and folly. Obviously undeserved, this censure of women may be lightly dismissed, as it has been rightly, by Kane as expression of almost universal male cynicism. His reference to the favourable view of Varāhamihira to the effect that women possess more virtues than men and to Manu himself who observed that men owe their very birth to women is more in the nature of exception than rule. Even the ardent justificationist of Hindu Society cannot deny "an undercurrent among common people of poor opinion about women".[8] Given this attitude, how a society can be democratic? Any attempt to justify this highly discriminatory and anti-democratic attitude in terms of the spirit of the ancient or the medieval age is to concede indirectly that the Indian society of the time was unworthy of democracy in the received sense of to-day. Further, the questions remain: is not history, as distinguished from archaeology, contemporaneous? and why should we suspend our basic moral *judgements* on the ground of self-refuting historical relativism?

Even today our claims to be democrat mainly depend on our success or failure to make the whole people irrespective of their class, caste or sex participate in all decision-making bodies and functions, big and small. Outside the limited context of tribal society and its way of life by *democracy* what is understood is *representative* form of government of this or that sovereign state. Representation without active participation tends to take away the substance of democracy. The obligation underlying participation must also be there. Otherwise mere passive acquiescence may be confused with and accepted as conscious and active consent. If the 'big' affairs of the state are left to the political parties and their leaders and if the government is left to the care of bureaucracy, legislature, judiciary, media, business community, trade unions and farmers' lobby, and we, the common people, take our decision only on the basis of public opinion poll and do not do anything actively to influence that opinion, perhaps we hardly deserve the merits of democracy. State,

8. P.V. Kane, *op. cit.*, Vol. II, Part I, Bhandarkar Oriental Research Institute, Poona, 1974, p. 581.

government, society, community and ways of actual living — in that order — must be seen and acted upon to reap the harvest of democracy.

Arguments against class discrimination, caste system, sex difference and the like, though pro-egalitarian in their inspiration, need to be taken with circumspection. Otherwise the ideal of equality loses its necessary protection against possible undemocratic encroachments. Equality has to be democratic. For example, when the Part III of the Constitution of India in the course of spelling out the concept of Fundamental Rights refers to *Rights to Equality* (Article 14), equality before the law or the equal protection of the laws, and *Rights to Freedom* (Article 19) of speech, freedom to assemble, to form associations or unions, to move freely, to reside or settle in any part of the country, and to practice any profession, simultaneously mention is made of *reasonable* restrictions on the said Rights. The principle of equality of protection is not universal in its scope of application, does not take away from the State the power of reasonably *classifying* persons for legitimate purposes, and (it is conceded that) every classification is in some degree likely to produce some inequality. But that as such does not attract the charge of denial of equal protection. The nature of the rights guaranteed by Article 19 is confined to *civil* rights, as distinguished from *political* rights. Again, it is to be noted, having guranteed freedom by Article 19 (1) *reasonable* restrictions, both substantive and procedural, in terms of clauses 19 (2) to (6) are imposed on its enjoyment in public interest. An attempt to 'abolish' 'untouchability' due to caste system is made under the Article 17 which makes its practice a punishable offence. I say 'an attempt' because any one familiar with the ground-level social reality in India knows very well that 'untouchability' still survives in various forms. The gap between the constitutional provisions and actual practices is wide and distressing. The point becomes very clear when one notices that such extremely important issues as "justice, social, economic and political (Article 38(1)) and equality of all citizens, men and women, in the matter of right to an adequate means of livelihood figure under *non-enforceable* Directive Principles of State Policy (Part IV) and *not* under enforceable Fundamental Rights (Part III) of Constitution".[9]

The reliability of constitutional laws as indicator of democracy in a country, especially in the context of poor countries like India, is very disappointing. Many crucial rights and liberties are not practically available to the majority of people who are poor, ill-informed and do not have the means to reach the appropriate courts, i.e., cannot afford to pay the administered price of *enforceable* justice. It is precisely these people who badly need and rightly deserve justice. To them the price of justice proves frightfully expensive and the process of justice unbearably delayed. What is even more tragic is this. Often in the cases of corruption in high places, political and economic, exploitation of the poor and pollution of environment courts' judgements remain unimplemented for ages by the concerned administration. The powerful and the rich somehow manage to remain outside the reach of the punishing hands of justice.

This again reinforces my view, expressed earlier, that the litmus test of democracy in all societies, in general, and in the poor ones, in particular, is whether it is *lived* or can actually become a way of life. Democratic *form* of polity without a democratic society to support it is an abstract entity. It is here that one has to seek the reason of one's preference for the *tribal model* of democracy. However I am quite aware that in the complex and conflict-ridden structure of our modern society, industrial or even agricultural, this model is *not* politically practicable without a lot of difficulties. But at the social level it has its relevance at least as a model. In the matters of distribution of justice this model is least vitiated by *discrimination* and most

9. Durga Das Basu, *Constitutional Law of India*, Sixth Edn., Prentice-Hall of India, New Delhi, 1991.

informed of *equality* consistently with the *liberty* of the individual as a member of the group.

The attraction of 'natural' or tribe-like society and the 'general will' of its people that charmed thinkers like Rousseau have been critically tested by the course of political events of last two hundred years or so both in Europe and elsewhere and carefully studied by political analysts and working anthropologists. The main two points that emerge out of the history of France under Napoleon and Germany under Bismarck are how (i) in the name of discipline democracy or republicanism and (ii) in the name of national unity all sorts of diversity and dissent may be easily crushed by a charismatic or ruthless and efficient leader. In the absence of internal checks and balances, the critic may point out, the theory of *general will* ideally embodied in a tribal society encourages undemocratic tribalism in a modern society, a miniature form of ultranationalism, which is patently impervious even to the legitimate forces of individualism. *Per contra*, the heavy presence of too many institutional checks and balances makes the administration of justice and the practice of democracy very difficult indeed. One way out of this paradox of democracy, taking cues from Kant's thought, may be found in the *form*, not matter or content, of *universal* good will, i.e., rationally free will. Actions may be said to be just if these are performed according to *free* union of wills irrespective of what is willed by the persons who or the unions which enter into the union. Firmly committed to anti-consequentialism, this view of justice obviously refuses to recognise many pressing complexities of the modern state and its ways of actual governance. For example, Kant excludes women from active citizenship, opposes the reciprocity of relation between husband and wife and argues against revolution even it is found to be necessary to achieve the ideal of republican constitution. All these points highlight the fact that even the idealists like Kant fail to recognise and grapple with the problem of conflict of duties. For they maintain that by their very nature duties know no conflict between them. But it is just not phenomenologically true.

To defend the cause of human unity and, by implication, to discount the role of conflict and difference between humans, various approaches have gained currency. While the metaphysically disposed moral philosophers speak of the *essential unity* of mankind based on reason or God, the anthropologists claim to have discovered universal categories in such diverse areas of different cultures as language, art, social laws, morals and religions. But one feels that most of these approaches suffer from one common handicap. Either these are not empirically checkable at all or these are so only in a very superficial way. Essentialist theories, because of their high metaphysical presuppositions, do not lend themselves to any sort of check; they 'survive' by *definition*. The case of comparative anthropologists is somewhat different. When the so-called anthropological categories appear to be universal, either they embody facile generalisations based on comparative study of innocent data or they beg the very issue to be established. Merely by cataloguing biological universals, environment-related similarities in dresses, food-habits, folk medicines, navigational and building skills are not of much help in identifying the universal human nature, if any.[10] The so-called cultural constants seem to be rooted in the commonness of the problems, material, technological and theoretical, encountered by humans in different cultures and that of the possible solutions of the same. After all the endless variety of problems can be solved or efficiently tackled only in terms of a finite number of ways. The point that is to be kept most in our view in the context of democracy and justice is not the similarity

10. A.L. Kroeber, *Anthropology Today*, ed. by Sol. Tax, University of Chicago Press, Chicago & London, 1962; see, Clyde Kluckhohn, "Universal Categories of Culture". See also, Claude Levi-Strauss, *The Savage Mind*, Weidenfeld and Nicolson, London, 1972; D.P. Chattopadhyaya, *Anthropology and Historiography of Science*, Ohio University Press, Athens, USA, 1990.

between but distinctiveness of different *creative* aspects of cultures, viz., moral values embodied in the recognised facts of widely separated cultures.

Theories and practice of democracy and justice are directly related to conflict of interests and duties mainly due to uneven social, political and economic conditions and the related value-systems, in general, and the laws pertaining to distribution, redistribution and retribution, reward and punishment, in particular. The critic of the idyllic 'tribal' model of thinkers like Thoreau and Tolstoy point out that the social arrangements which by their nature rule out the very possibility of emergence, survival or development of class-conflict, clash of group interests or some such thing can easily skirt, i.e., need not face and therefore solve the problems of administering justice. The task of the tribal chief is easier than the minimal statists of quite different types like Gandhi and Nozick; the former is for the poor and the latter for the informed and the privileged.

If the strong note of the criticism is discounted what remains is this. In a more or less *homogeneous* society, assumed by the tribal model, very simple laws of measuring need, utility, desert, well-being and destitution are available and these are rarely disputed. When disputes arise — given liberties, disputes are bound to arise — the ways of settling the same are equally simple. Therefore it is not at all surprising that uncodified tribal legal systems, compared to ours, are easy to grasp, interpret and administer. What we have to learn from the tribal model is how best to try to minimise the difference between the obtained levels — obtained in our highly heterogeneous societies — of liberties and inequalities.

It is easy to speak of the moral desirability of a simple and pro-tribal model of democratic society but under the present-day conditions of a developed country like USA and a developing country like India it is extremely difficult, if not impossible, to have it established or even to undertake a credible agenda for it.

After the disintegration of the former USSR the pro-market bias of economy is becoming clearly evident all over the world. Deontological primacy of justice is outrightly denied or pushed to a back bench. The ideal of piece-meal social engineering, debunking planning, is highly popular. The principle of minimisation of pain, *not* maximisation of pleasure, is proving attracting presumably because of its damper on the role of the state in the economic affairs.

The concept of democracy is getting perilously close to that of economic efficiency. Most people, from businessmen and policy-makers to academics, talk of development, desert and retribution. Only few recognise the grave and global problems of food, destitution and equitable distribution of global resources. Tariff, patent, agricultural pricing and similar other policies of the rich countries are geared to their narrow national interests. International issues are being left to the market forces to be decided by the latter. The assumptions, though hidden, are not difficult to understand. Economic development is the single most potent factor to make the people happy in the long run. Market is the best mechanism to measure one's desert and to make one pay for one's failure of inability. It is a plain truth that in a competitive situation many individuals or even groups of individuals suffer from poverty or ill-health *not* because of their own failure, idleness or unwillingness to work hard. They find their 'choices' do not work and preferences go unresponded by social circumstances and over which they have little or no control.

What is being said here is not as such a stricture against utilitarianism. In a sense all interests, needs, ideals, wants, and aspirations of humans may be taken as their preferences. This is not to suggest that all these preferences stand on equal footing from a justificatory point of view. For example, one may be interested in promoting one's business profit primarily by displacing the existing labour force by installing the latest capital-intensive technology and another by increasing the current level of R&D investment. A journalist may need some books to be informed of the latest facts and figures so that his columns in the newspapers and journals cater to the taste of his readers and another may need the same mainly to please his boss, the owners of the newspaper and journals with which he is associated. It is *interest as such* but *interest in what*, the content of interest, which truly discloses, at least in part, the moral worth of the concerned interest. Similarly, it is *not* need as such but *need for* which helps us to ascertain its moral worth. The comparable sort of graded, at times very important, distinction may be shown in the contents of ideals and aspirations as preferences and in their possible justifications.

Secondly, preferences or utilities have to be rational or prudential. Otherwise it is difficult for the theoretician or the policy-maker to make use of them in *social* practice. How, for example, can they stand by anti-social, anti-poor or even anti-rich and envious 'moral' attitudes? Somehow the preferences of the members of a social group must be described by some degree of rationality. Otherwise the very basis of sociality is undermined.

Finally, the moral defensibility of utilitarianism depends much upon how *utility* is defined as a pleasure-augmanting or as a pain-removing principle. It may be construed as a *choice* in a stable or in an uncertain situation. Here again the conception of content seems to come up. Some may choose well-being of the poor in a poverty-stricken Third World country, while others may choose to impose more and more fiscal discipline on the economy of an aid-seeking poor country on the plea that this will *ultimately* lead to its well-being. All critics of utilitarianism are not its enemy. What is in dispute is the claim that it is the most rational, unified and comprehensive theory of morality.[11]

---

11. John Rawls, *A Theory of Justice*, Oxford University Press, Oxford, 1972; see also, Robert Nozick, *Anarchy, State and Utopia*, Basil Blackwell, Oxford, 1974.

Utilitarianism may be defined in different ways, viz., the rightness of actions should be decided in terms of the goodness of the consequent state of affairs (consequentialism), and the goodness of state of affairs should be judged in terms of the goodness of individual utilities within the concerned state of affairs (welfarism). Rawls proposes to offer us a pro-Kantian view of morality taking into account the conditions of the most deprived group of persons, deprived of such pirmary good as rights, liberties and opportunities, income and wealth, and the social basis of self-respect. If the *social basis* of self-respect is discounted, self-respect as such loses much of its substance. Though all rational humans have rights in principle to primary goods, but, due to the operation of the difference principle, the relatively poor person's rights in terms of welfare cannot take away in practice the relatively rich person's extensive rights in the forms of opportunities, income and wealth. The taxation policy of the state is not supposed to eliminate the difference between the better off and the worse off classes for the purpose of redistribution of the total income and utilities of the concerned people. The Rawlsian maxim "liberties can be curtailed only for the sake of liberties" preserves so much of unequal liberties in favour of the better off people that it is likely to be resented to and opposed by the worse off ones. Moreover, his formulation of the different principle is unresponsive to the special needs of the sick, the disabled and the poor. The Kantian liberal inspiration of the Rawlsian utilitarianism of the welfarist variety is not satisfactorily preserved in its worked-out details.

Attempts have been made to work out an alternative to *total* or aggregative utilitarianism, on the one hand, and welfarism or *differential* utilitarianism of Rawls defined in terms of primary *goods*, on the other hand.[12] This alternative takes note of such

---

12. Amartya Sen, *Resources, Values and Development*, Oxford University Press Delhi, 1984, *On Ethics and Economics*, Oxford University Press, Bombay, Calcutta, Madras, 1987; see also P. Dasgupta, *The Control of Resources*, Blackwell, Oxford, 1982.

factors as workload and its nature. place, physical fitness and climatic conditions; and it emphasises what may be called basic abilities of primary powers, viz., the power to satisfy one's nutritional requirements, the requirements of clothing and shelter, of keeping oneself fit for working and earning at least that level of income which the better off people earn working much less. The very basis of democracy comes *effectively* under attack or much of its substance is taken away when people's income turn out to be highly unequal, saving from it and expenditure of it are allowed to be primarily governed by self-interest or group-interest, intra-nationally and internationally, and all these are sought to be deontologically justified in terms of intrinsic rights.

In Nozick's model of right-based democracy in defence and promotion of one's rights constraints are put on others' freedom to realise their capabilities. It is well-known that constraints are not equally complied with by all alike. The rich people have both money and information advantages to their credit to disregard in effect much of the constraints they are supposed to be under. Policy-makers and policies are more or less manipulable by their influence, official and unofficial. If the *social* choice of the *individual* is defined within the narrow but nationally constraint-free features of exercised (or exercisable choices) by others, there is not left much for the disadvantaged to choose. Busy in the exercise of his own rights, the informed and advantaged seems to be under no obligation to help the uninformed or less informed and disadvantaged.

What the minimal statists like Nozick fail to appreciate is that unless rights are practically found to be fulfillable or realisable their mere notional availability make little or no sense. The poor's right to live is meaningless in a country where there is neither job nor social service benefits available for him. Availability and visibility of food in the market make one's hunger all the more unbearable when one does not have the necessary income or money necessary to buy, cook and eat it. His arguments in defence of right-based entitlements, in view of Nozick's strong anti-consequentialism, are sought to be legally, but not ethically, delinked from deprivation. Unrestricted legal rights of some to possess, hold and transfer their assets, regardless of others' poverty and starvation, have very little ethical basis. The point has been persuasively argued, among others, by Sen. If democracy rests on the type of right-based justice defended by Nozick, the ideal of good relations between the poor and the rich countries is bound to be affected. The poor does not necessarily deserve poverty and suffering.

4

The Basis of Justice*

Chhatrapati Singh

I

THERE are three aspects to any theory of justice. The first explains why I, the judge or a society ought to be just. The second works out the basic and derivative principles of justice which need to be followed; this is an answer to 'what is justice?'. The third explains the ways and means by which an individual or a society can be just; this is an answer to 'how can I (or we) be just?', given that we have so many shortcomings — psychological, social, political, and economic.

Philosophers of law do not usually propound their theories in a systematic way, dealing with each of these questions separately. They are mostly preoccupied with one of them, relegating the other two to the background. The three questions and their answers, however, are interrelated. The answer to the 'why' question is presupposed by the answer to the 'what' question. The task of spelling out the principles of justice makes sense only because it is assumed that it is necessary to follow them; some answer explaining this necessitation goes along with the 'what' question. Similarly, since necessitation implies

---

* Reprinted, by permission, from *Essays in Social and Political Philosophy*, Allied Publishers, 1989.

possibility (that is, ought entails can), a theory of justice that sets out to answer 'what is justice?' must also tacitly or explicitly imply (or explain) how justice can be attained. Any theory which claims to be a 'theory of justice' must actually address and satisfactorily answer all three questions.

Most, however, do not. To illustrate, Rawls in his 'theory of justice' is in fact seeking to answer mainly the 'what' question; the 'why' and the 'how', therefore, turn out to be very unsatisfactory. Del Vecchio's 'theory of justice', on the other hand, is seeking an answer to the 'why' question. His theory, therefore, lacks a satisfactory exposition of the 'what' question — that is, of principles of justice. We shall look into the details of these theories subsequently; the point here is not to criticise them but to emphasise the fact that there are different related aspects to any theory of justice, and often theories which are presented as competing are in fact complementary or about different aspects.

Not all three aspects of the theory of justice have received the same attention from philosophers. If one were to rank them, it seems far more attention has been paid to the 'how' question than to the 'what', and the least to the 'why' question. The reason for this seems to be as follows: justice and morality are closely related; in fact, the ultimate principles of morality and justice are overlapping, if not the same. The answer to the question 'how can I be moral?', therefore, throws a great deal of light on 'how can I be just?'. The issues concerning acting morally despite our shortcomings have, consequently, received significant attention in moral philosophy and religious discourse. The 'what' question has been the domain of legal and political philosophy. The reason why philosophers have vigorously pursued the question 'what is justice?' can be traced to the development of political philosophy, along with different developing nation-states, on the one hand, and to the progress of epistemology, on the other. Theories of knowledge which seek justification for what we know also provide the motivation for spelling out the basic cognitive elements or structures of what we can claim to know. It would, therefore, be just as important to work out the basic structure of laws as to show the basic structure of languages. From the point of view of politics it becomes important to identify the basic principles of justice, because these have to be embodied in constitutions or in constitutional law in one way or another.

Any theory of justice, however, will be incomplete unless we are able to explain satisfactorily why an individual, a judge, or a society must be just. The reason this question seems to have received much less attention is simply that it is perhaps a far more difficult question to answer. Asking why one must be just is like asking why one must be moral or religious. The answer to these questions leads directly to inquiry about the nature of the self, of society, of the meaning and purpose of one's life in society, and of the purpose of society itself. In other words, it leads directly into metaphysics and teleology. Modern logical and legal positivism has been averse to metaphysics, and the modern natural and social science to teleology. This is another reason why philosophers neglect the 'why' of justice. But, as we have noted, an authentic theory of justice cannot escape this question. The human mind wants to know the why of everything.

Besides this cognitive motivation there is another basic reason why this question has become extremely significant in our age. If human beings are to follow any principle which they are not ordinarily inclined to, they must have a good reason for doing so. The earlier transcendent reason that god wants us to do so, or that there will be reward after death in doing so, does not appeal to most of us any more. The modern political reasons, such as that the sovereign wants us to do so, or that it is the people's will, are also not very convincing. The sovereign often turns out to be unrepresentative, the election process is unable to create a government with which the people can identify, and the conception of the 'people' has become difficult, with so many classes, vested interests, regional, national and international lobbies — all moving in different directions. We shall see the details of these theories in what follows.

In this paper I wish to look at the answers provided to this basic question: why must anyone be just? For unless we have a convincing answer to this, merely enunciating the principles of justice — however clearly and perfectly we may do it — will not suffice. People have to be convinced why they must follow the principles. I think that although some insights relevant to this question are found in the Western tradition, i.e., the Judaeo-Christian, Greek, Continental and American traditions, it is inherently incapable of providing the appropriate answer, partly because of the metaphysics of the self and the world it has adopted from time to time, and partly because of its lack of clarity about the teleology of the self and the cosmos. In my opinion one will have to turn eventually to the Indian traditions to seek appropriate answers. In this paper, however, I do not proceed to the Indian alternatives. The primary task here will be to show the inadequacies of Western thought, since it has become dominant in jurisprudence and philosophy of law. I shall, therefore, limit myself to presenting and analysing various Western theories about the basis of justice, so that having seen their shortcomings we may be in a position to seek other, Indian, alternatives.

It must be emphasised, however, that the task of analysing the Western theories is not merely to prepare the ground for the alternatives; it is a useful task in itself, for it may generate the possibility of internal critiques and improvements within Western thought itself. Not all answers given to the question, within the Western theories, can be correct, especially if they are conflicting. Moreover, the advancement of legal knowledge often requires recapitulating the wisdon of the past. There is little that modern legal theories seem to have learnt from the Greek or the Roman experiences, leave alone the experience of the East. They are expounded as if all our learning about law began with Blackstone or Austin. But, as this discussion will attempt to show, the past within the western theories is just as relevant as the modern.

II

Let us begin by making sure what the question means. As we noted, the 'why' question is different from the 'what' question: 'what is justice?'. There are many principles of justice, some people know more about them, some less; similarly some constitutions or legal systems employ more of them, some less. The question is not about the knowledge of such principles, although enumerating and justifying them is an important task in itself. The 'why' question presupposes that we already know what some of these principles are: principles such as 'give every person his due', 'be impartial in evaluating', 'promises once made must be kept unless there are good reasons to break them', 'all parties concerned must be heard before deciding a case', and so on. There is no reason to believe that our knowledge of what constitutes justice is final; as legal systems advance, both at the national and international levels, our understanding of justice is likely to grow. Given that there are these and other principles of justice, the 'why' question in fact wants to know why these principles must be followed. It should be evident, therefore, that the answer to the question does not depend upon the extent of our knowledge of the principles of justice. Even if there is only one principle of justice and we can identify that principle, the question remains: is there any good reason for me or society or the judge to follow it? The first point, therefore, is that in asking this question moral or legal scepticism is denied. The second point, which too needs to be made obvious, concerns necessitation. In asking this question we are exhibiting (and presupposing) the intuitive understanding that in some sense we are obliged to follow the principles. In terms of the presupposition, therefore, the question 'why must I be just?' takes the form: is it necessary that I should be just, am I obliged to be just, must I compel myself, and what is the reason for this necessity? If there is indeed a good reason which I must hold to be true, then is it necessary that I should be just? Justice is a universal idea which applies to and is available to all men; but sometimes the question can arise within a limited context, most appropriately within the context of the legal system: is the judge obliged to be just, or is he obliged to interpret mechanically the statutes even though they are unjust, or when there are no laws relating to the matter? This becomes pertinent in 'hard cases', or, as it has become obvious, in 'judicial activism' in India and the United States. If we wish to assert that the judge is obliged to be just, the question at once arises: why is he so obliged, why must he be just? But in our day-to-day life we are all judges in one way or another in matters big and small; the question, therefore, applies to us as much as it does to the judge.

The two-assumptions in asking this question, thus, are, first, the denial of moral or legal scepticism or agnosticism, and second, the intuitive understanding that there is some sort of compulsion or necessitation for us to be just. The reason for this compulsion, i.e., the intuition, then needs to be made explicit and explained. The discussion that follows proceeds on these assumptions. I do not propose to prove that there are principles of justice or that there is a common sense understanding that we need to be acting justly.

But before proceeding further it will be important to analyse the question a little more closely so as to explain its relationship with other related questions, such as 'why must I be moral?', and 'why am I obliged obliged to obey just laws?'.

The morality of a society is distinct from its legality. However, insofar as principles of justice are akin to principles of morality, justice becomes the meeting point between morality and legality. The administration of justice in that case becomes the administration of a morality accepted by that society. The administration of justice, within this context, need not evidently be identified with the administration of law, for law may or may not be in conformity with justice. However, for those who believe, as I do, that principles of justice are nothing but principles generated by human reason in its application to praxis and that these principles are the same as the universal principles of morality that a society can legislate for itself, the issues of justice and morality (strictly speaking, external or social morality) become one and the same.[1] The question why I ought to be moral is the same as why I ought to be just. In other words, the answer to the question what necessitates moral obligation (morality here being understood as not what an individual can or will legislate for himself alone, but what he is willing to legislate universally for all). It was Kant who first clearly formulated and attempted to answer the question 'why ought I to be moral?'.[2] Although he identified the juridical realm with that of external morality, he did not apply his moral theory to justice.[3] Otherwise he would have noticed the close relationship between 'why ought I to be moral?' and 'why ought I to be externally moral (that is, just)?'. This is not the occasion to discuss the details of Kant's views; the point to note is the close relationship between justice and morality. For those who do not identify justice with external morality that a society ought to adopt can work out for themselves separate answers to 'why ought I to be just?' and 'why ought I to be moral?'; the answer provided to the first question would none the less be relevant to them.

Let us now turn to see the connection between legality and justice. A just law is supposed to be based on the principles of justice. In fact, a just law is nothing but substantive interpretation and application of these principles. Administration of the principles of justice by the legitimate authority and institutions in a society, and the administration of just laws by the legitimate

1. Chhatrapati Singh, *Law from Anarchy to Utopia*, Oxford University Press, Delhi, 1985, pp. 167-78.
2. Immanuel Kant, *Groundwork of Metaphysics of Morals*, tr. by H.J. Paton, Harper and Row, New York, 1964.
3. For a detailed analysis, see G.F. Murphy, *Kant: The Philosophy of Right,* Macmillan, 1970; and Chhatrapati Singh, *Anarchy to Utopia*, pp. 150-6.

authority and institutions are one and the same thing. The questions why it is necessary for me to follow the principles of justice and why it is necessary for me to follow just laws are then one and the same. What this entails is that if one has explained the basis of our obligation to be just, then one has *ipso facto* explained the basis of our obligation to follow just laws.

Has one then also explained the basis of our legal obligation? I would say yes. It depends on how one defines law. If by laws one means only just laws, as I do, then the basis of juridical obligation is the same as the basis of legal obligation.[4] If one restricts the use of the term 'law' to only just laws, then one has to find other terms for a variety of other elements and rules that are to be found in any existing legal system. For, clearly, the existing legal systems do not consist of only just laws. There is a series of other terms that one may use to describe the elements of a legal system — commands, decrees, political fiats and so on. The distinction would then have to be maintained between law and a legal system. Ideally, a legal system ought to consist of only laws and other conventions, actions, or institutions compatible with these laws; our present legal systems, however, contain many other elements besides laws, many of which are inconsistent with these laws, i.e., just laws. There are both advantages and disadvantages in defining law in this way and characterising the legal system in this manner. The issue here is not of defining law, but of understanding the relationship between juridical and legal obligations. Those who do not wish to define laws as just laws can work out the basis of legal obligation separately. But insofar as they agree that following just laws is the same as following the principles of justice, the answer to the question why I must follow the principles of justice also provides to them the answer to the question why I must follow just laws. And for those who define laws in terms of just laws, explanation of the basis of juridical obligation is also the explanation of the basis of legal obligation. Having set the stage, let us now proceed

4. Chhatrapati Singh, *Anarchy to Utopia*, pp. 252-62.

to analyse what in fact can be the basis of our juridical or legal obligation to follow external morality.

III

Since law is external morality, the classification of moral theories also applies to legal theories. All theories of justice may be classified into heteronomous theories and autonomous theories. Heteronomous theories base the grounds of juridical obligation on factors other than the individual's capacity to determine his actions. Autonomous theories, on the contrary, find the basis of obligation in the individual's capacity to determine his actions.

Since they base the grounds of obligation on factors other than the individual's will to determine his actions, heteronomous theories reduce the obligation into a fear of coercion by the other or by some factor in nature. Such reductive theories can be distinguished in terms of conceptual schemes based on principles of force and based on principles of nature.

Into the first type of conceptual schemes fall the theories of Hart, Kelsen and other legal positivists. Since their theories base the grounds of obligation to follow just laws on factors other than the individual's own will, they reduce the obligation to external compulsion. Obligation in such theories means nothing other than political compulsion, since the external compulsion that they legitimise is the one enforced by the political system. Hence although such heteronomous theories talk about obligation, they fail to characterise this notion. They are in the final analysis talking only about political coercion and not the obligation to follow just laws.

A theory that mistakes political coercion for legal obligation may either permit one to coerce others, or some to coerce others, or all to coerce each other. The first type of theory comes from Austin, who allows the one sovereign to coerce; the second type from Hart who allows some officials to coerce everyone; and the third type from Marx who allows all to coerce all in the dictatorship of the proletariat.

There can also be heteronomous theories of justice which attempt to base the grounds of obligation in some sort of utility. Although there have been various heteronomous utilitarian moral theories, a serious and consistent attempt to come up with a heteronomous utilitarian theory of justice does not seem to have been made. D.H. Hodgson, for example, explores the consequences of utilitarianism for a legal theory. He argues against the act-utilitarian ethics and shows that rule-utilitarianism is also unsatisfactory for the purposes of a legal theory.[5] He maintains none the less that a different type of utilitarianism is tenable. Even if one grants his thesis, his analysis does not bring out what kind of utilitarianism, if any, can justify the grounds of obligation to follow the just law. To say that one must follow the law, or that one has the obligation to follow the law, merely because it is useful, is to assert something which can be seen to be empirically false. To follow what such a theory takes to be law can be of serious 'disutility', for example, in following the commands of a dictator, or in more ordinary cases such as paying fines or accepting punishment. In any case, even if one convincingly argued that following the just law is useful, it would only prove that it is prudential to act according to justice; it would not show why we have an obligation or a duty to follow the law. All heteronomous theories, whether they are based on coercion or utility, are erroneous, because they reduce legal assertions to commands or rules of prudence. The notion of juridical obligation then turns into either the notion of fear or that of external compulsion.

Heteronomous theories of justice which attempt to base the grounds of obligation on some factor in nature also fail to define the sense of obligation. For we do not have the choice of either following

5. D.H. Hodgson, *Consequences of Utilitarianism*, Oxford, 1967.

or not following the laws of nature. If principles of justice were necessary principles of nature, the necessity would be one of causality; the question of obligation or 'ought to' would not then arise. The Stoics and some natural law theorists have attempted to base the obligation on some factors in nature, but since legal obligation cannot be based on any such factor, these attempts can lead to arbitrary rules, such as those supporting racism or casteism.

A second type of heteronomous theory which attempts to ground the basis of obligation in nature is that which eventually grounds it in the will of God. Obligation in such a case really becomes the obligation to follow what God wants us to do, not what the individual's will determines for itself. Such a theory obliterates the grounds for the distinction between religious obligation and juridical obligation, and in fact reduces the latter to the former. The notion of 'god' is understood differently by different religions. God's command can be a good, but not legal reason for action.

The basis of juridical obligation can thus be grounded neither in the will of the sovereign nor in the will of God. It can be grounded only in what the individual himself wills in accordance with his reason. Such an obligation can be explained only by an autonomous theory.

Autonomous theories are based on a conceptual scheme applicable to the created social order. However, such autonomous theories cannot take arbitrary forms which conflict with the possibility of reasoning. Autonomous theories are usually of two types: (i) a conceptual scheme based on individual or communal mystical experiences; (ii) a conceptual scheme based on rational principles applicable to the created social order.

Mystical autonomous legal theories appeal to the individual's or the community's experiences in order to justify legal obligation. Mystical autonomous theories seem to show up only infrequently in the Western tradition. For example, Milner S. Ball has recently attempted to justify legal obligation in terms of a Christian notion of 'the Beginning'.[6] Such theories are untenable, because they appeal to experiences available only to some individuals. The legal system, being a mode of cooperative reasoning, requires that it be based on experiences which are available to all. Law is based on universal principles which all can cognise and on reason.

In the Indian tradition mystical autonomous theories have been more frequent. In Buddhism, for example, the idea of *dharma* is grounded in a cosmology which is ultimately intelligible only through some mystical experience. The difficulty with such a theory is the same as that with Ball's theory. It grounds itself in experiences which are not publicly available at all times. Only the *siddha* or the *buddha* can have such experiences.

The reason why mystical autonomous theories are more common in the Indian tradition while heteronomous coercive theories are more common in the Western is not difficult to understand. In the Indian tradition, the idea of law is often confused with some aspects of religious systems which have various mystical elements, whereas in the West it is often confused with some aspects of political systems which have various coercive elements.

Kant's *Rechtslehre* has many aspects necessary to an autonomous rationalistic theory of justice, but in the end it confuses the grounds of legal obligation. Kant comes up with an autonomous ethical, but a heteronomous legal theory. Such a position makes his philosophy inconsistent.

IV

To assert that the juridical system is an autonomous system does not yet amount to an explanation of the basis of the obligation to be just. It does, however, delimit certain types of explanations — those which make the necessitation external, and provide grounds for analysis in one direction — those which

6. S. Milner Ball, *The Promise of American Law,* Athens, 1981.

make the constraint to act justly internal to the human will and reason. Both what is to be rejected and what is to be accepted need to be explored in detail now.

It will be best to begin with some clarification and recaptitulation of some key notions which may still cause confusion. The idea of law and the idea of justice are not the same. The task here is not to define what is law nor what is justice, but to find the basis for acting justly. The notions of justice and law are, however, also related: therefore assertions about the basis of justice also have direct implications for the basis of law. The relationship is as follows: the demand for justice is in a significant sense the demand for administering just laws; it is the demand for a just legal system. Since the two demands are equivalent, an explanation of the basis of justice simultaneously becomes an explanation of the basis of administering just laws. It is in this sense that juridical and legal obligations are related.

To argue that the juridical system is autonomous is to say that the nature of necessitation involved in acting justly is such that the determination to so act does not involve anyone other than oneself. Necessitation in this sense is self-imposed obligation.

So far it has been argued that if the necessity to act justly was not conceived as imposed by a person's own will and reason, there would be no way of distinguishing between an externally imposed compulsion and an internally imposed obligation. Yet both at the individual and at the social level we can ordinarily distinguish between an action which a person or society does of its own free choice and that which it does under compulsion. We can distinguish between a dictatorship, a colony, and a democracy; similarly at the individual level we can distinguish between a self-determined action and an action under external influence such as of drugs, or under orders from another person, such as when a policeman executes his duties. In fact, we judge a person's or a society's action to be just or unjust only on the assumption that it was determined by the agent concerned. Supposing it were true that all actions are done under compulsion, of one sort or another, not a single legal system would be in existence. The very working of law demands the assumption that there are self-determined actions whose merits or demerits can be evaluated in courts of law. Any theory of justice or law must pay heed to the ordinary day-to-day life situation. If ordinarily we can distinguish between action under command or threat and self-determined action and a theory is unable to provide us with the distinction, clearly it is the theory which is at fault. This is precisely the problem with legal positivism, such as of Hart, Kelsen and others. Having described acting in accordance with just laws as acting under external compulsion by the sovereign or the officials, there is no way their theory can provide a distinction between a just democratic society and a dictatorship, or a just action and an action under pressure from others.

Rationalists such as Kant or Rawls and metaphysicians such as Radbruch, Del Vecchio, or Hegel do not commit this error — of either seeking the basis of justice in the will of other human beings, as the positivists do, or of seeking it in some transcendent will, such as of god, as some natural law theorists do. But are the accounts of such rationalists and metaphysicians satisfactory? Let us scrutinize these alternatives to positivism.

The first major alternative to positivism, and a popular one, is the thesis that I (or we) have to act justly now because I (or we) made a promise sometime in the distant past to act justly. The promise has to be kept. This is the social contract theory. It asserts, in one way or another, that we have made a pact or a treaty which must be honoured. Hobbes and Rousseau would have us believe that this is some sort of social fact.[7] This thesis has

---

7. J.J. Rousseau, *The Social Contract*, ed. by Lester G. Cocker, New York, 1967; T. Hobbes, *Leviathan*, ed. by M. Oakeshott, Macmillan, 1962.

a popular appeal, because it helps to shift the burden of the question; instead of asking why we must act justly now, we ask: did or did we not in fact make the promise?

Numerous authors have shown that this type of *a priori* sociology will not do, for we cannot base our present decisions on a dubious, hypothetical fact. I have myself argued elsewhere that the issue is not one of empirical verification, whether or not such a contract was actually or hypothetically made.[8] There is a logical fallacy in such an argument; the notion of just action is presupposed by the notion of contract or treaty. Both these notions are juridical or legal, which derive their meaning and sanctity from the notion of justice. The reason for a just action, therefore, cannot be derived from the notion of a contract; it is the other way round. In empirical terms this means that a genuine contract or treaty is possible only when people are first willing to act justly. Acting justly, therefore, exists prior to contract. Merely shifting the burden of the argument will not do, because one can still ask: why must I keep my promise (act justly) whether it has been made just now or sometime in the distant past; what obliges me to abide by the past contract, especially one which has no legal existence (legitimisation within the present context), and hence against which no legal sanctions exist?

Such contractarian theories are, in fact, again heteronomous theories. Although they do not base the reason for acting justly on coercion by others, they invoke the will of others, in the distant past, which now constraints our will. All heteronomous theories, as argued, are thus spurious.

Although Kant and Rawls appeal to the notion of social contract, their arguments do not actually depend upon any contractarian theory.[9] Kant mentions the notion of contract as

---

8. Chhatrapati Singh, *Anarchy to Utopia*, pp. 179-98.
9. J. Rawls, *A Theory of Justice*, Harvard University Press, Cambridge, Mass., 1971, pp. 181-3, 513-76.

a postulate; he believes it is a useful notion with sufficient persuasive power. The argument actually employed both by Kant and by Rawls is a Weberian ideal-model-type thesis. For Kant the model is the 'Kingdom of Ends'; for Rawls it is the ideal community of rational beings.[10] The persuasiveness and greatness of both Kant's and Rawls' theories lie in the fact that tacitly (in the final analysis) they appeal to an idea which is very deeply embedded in the human psyche and which in a sense has a cosmic significance. It is the idea of heaven or utopia. The net result of their argument is as follows: here is the picture of heaven (the ideal community), here is how people there actually behave (totally rationally), and here are the principles they follow (Categorical Imperative or Rawls' two principles);[11] and if you want to create heaven on earth behave like them and follow these rules.

Hobbes and Locke had earlier tried the opposite strategy. They had described for us the picture of hell, the state of nature.[12] The net result of their argument was as follows: here is the original state of nature; see how selfish and ill-behaved the people are, see the gross injustice prevalent in it — people cannot protect their property, they cannot punish the wrong-doer; if you want to move out of this state of affairs and create a better society, give the power to the sovereign to protect your property and punish the wrong-doer.[13] Unlike Hobbes, Locke retained some power with the people, in terms of innate rights. His strategy, however, was similar to Hobbes'.

Between Kant and Hobbes, there is a third strategy, that of Karl Marx. Marx finds the present to be the hell, the heaven (the

---

10. Kant, *Groundwork*, pp. 421-37.
11. *Ibid.*, p. 421; Rawls, *Justice*, p. 60.
12. John Locke, *Two Treatises of Government*, ed. by Peter Laslett, Cambridge, 1960, sections 87, 124-7.
13. *Leviathan*, pp. 229-36.

communist society) being a possible future which is to be realised on earth. His strategy is not of giving us the picture of the communist society or the principles of justice that apply therein, but one of fighting the injustices of the present for the sake of realising the heaven of the future.

The point of discussion here is not one of analysing the merits or demerits of any of these theories concerning the metaphysics of the community and its teleology, but of understanding what implications these teleological theories have for a theory of justice. The Kantian and the Rawlsian type of theory yields the principle: act justly now so that the ideal state (heaven) may be realised on earth. Kant tells us: act *as if* you are a member of the Kingdom of Ends, even though such a kingdom has not been realised as yet. Hobbes' and Locke's type of theory yields the principle: act justly so that you may remove hell. Marx's theory implies: act justly (against the exploiters) so that you can bring about heavenly conditions some day.

These maxims are very persuasive; in fact, it is precisely this type of argument which religious discourses employed earlier. But are they conclusive? It must be noted that these are not heteronomous arguments. Kant and Rawls are in fact telling us: if you were a member of the ideal state your rationality would automatically direct your will to act justly. Acting justly would then be self-imposed. Thus, there is no heteronomy of the will involved here.

Impressive as the arguments may be, they still fail to be conclusive, almost for the same reasons as those advanced by religions.

One such reason is that the grounds given for acting justly are contingent. They persuade but do not necessitate just action. The argument does not prove that you have necessarily to choose to be a member of the Kingdom of Ends; if you choose that there should be heaven on earth, then act like this. But supposing I do not, supposing I prefer to live in hell so that I, in my moral uprightness, can bask in my superiority and gratify my ego, or supposing I am a sadist or a masochist, of what use is the ideal state to me? Or supposing I am a priest, how will I practise my altruism in utopia? I would rather stay here.

Besides these existential or teleological problems, there are more serious metaphysical difficulties in this type of autonomous theories. These pertain to ontology. The metaphysics of possible worlds, sustained here tacitly, can be challenged in the Leibnizian way. Leibniz believed that god, being perfect, must create a perfect world, the best of all possible worlds. This is part of his perfection.[14] One does not have to adduce a theological argument to assert that this is the best of all possible worlds. Even a materialist argument will do: this is the best way matter could have construed itself, together with the good and the evil, the beautiful and the ugly; this is the only way it could have construed itself — a stronger argument. How does one disprove this?

The point is not one of showing the Leibnizian argument to be false, but of realising that doing justice cannot be made conditional on the existence (actual or possible) of another states of society or the world. Justice, as we intuitively understand, has to be done *now* even if there be no ideal state, Kingdom of Ends, communist society, or heaven. Justice must be done for its own sake, as Kant realised; a moral duty must be done for its own sake (he did not, of course, apply his moral theory to justice).

The metaphysics of possible-worlds argument becomes more problematic when we consider what Hegel and Marx had to say about the way movement or transformation takes place in the world or in society. Transformation or change takes place, according to dialectical materialism or idealism, in terms of

---

14. G.W. Leibniz, *Theodicy*, ed. by Allen, tr. by Huggard, Dent University paperback, 1966, section 8.

contradictions. Both in Hegel and in Marx one can separate their metaphysics from the conclusions they draw from their own metaphysics. One does not have to accept communism or the ideal German state to understand or accept dialectical materialism or idealism, nor does one have to believe that with communism or Hegel the world comes to an end. In fact, dialectics has a much older history, predating Marx or Hegel. The point of dialectical ontology is that all progression in the world takes place in terms of resolutions of contradictions, which in turn give rise to further contradictions, which then need to be resolved again. Our cognition of such contradictions (the epistemology) must evolve with our ontology. The logical consequence of this thesis is that one cannot hope for a final state, such as the Kingdom of Ends or a communist society; the generation of such states will also produce (or lead to) their contradictions. Similarly, total rationality must also lead to total irrationality, if rationality and irrationality are opposites.

The point here, again, is not of exploring the consequences of dialectics or of the Marxist or Hegelian theories, but of realising what implications dialectical materialism and idealism — insofar as they are viable views — have for any theory of justice. First, they clearly show that progression of the type visualised by Kant or Rawls is impossible, hence any utopian theory of this type will not suffice to answer why anyone must be just. Second, they reaffirm the fact that the act of justice cannot be made conditional on any social or physical fact. Conditionality does not generate necessitation of the type desired. It pictures a contingent situation outside ourselves in which nothing ultimately makes justice an absolute value that a legal system or a person must abide by.

Before I conclude the arguments against teleology it must be noted that I have not said that teleological arguments *per se* are wrong or misplaced, but only that teleolgical arguments of a particular type — which generate what Kant would call

'Hypothetical Imperatives' — are wrong. Hypothetical Imperatives have the form: 'you ought to act thus *if* you want to achieve such and such an end', whereas the type of imperative required to show acting justly to be necessary must have the form: 'act thus because this is the only way you ought to act'.

Having seen the inadequacies of the teleological arguments, let us now move on to other alternatives, the chief amongst which is essentialism, such as of Aristotle, Plato, Del Vecchio, Radbruch, and Hegel.

The essentialist argument states, in one way or another, that it is the very nature of man to be just. This belongs to his essence. Within the Western tradition the most formidable essentialist argument is that of Plato, although Plato does not use the language of essences. His account of justice is to be found in a number of works but chiefly in the *Republic.*[15] The inquiry is in the first Book,[16] and the exposition in the Fourth.[17] Justice, for Plato, is one of the four virtues, the others being wisdom, temperance and courage. Justice is the practice of virtue; and since everything in the universe has its own station and task, virtue is the right condition which enables each man to do his own task best, an end attained when the three parts of the soul, the reason, the emotions, and the appetites, are in their proper order, with reason dominant over the other two. In such a case the whole man is a free citizen to follow that activity for which he is best qualified by his nature. Justice, for Plato, is harmony, the performance by each thing of what is proper to it, while injustice is what follows from the denial of this principle. Plato insisted that justice is the same for the individual and the state.[18] The individual can attain harmony only in an ordered state. The rulers, the guardians, and the artisans in

15. Plato, *Republic*, tr. by B. Jowett, Doubleday, New York, 1960.
16. Plato, *Republic*, I, 351ff.
17. *Ibid.*, IV, 441ff.
18. *Ibid.*, 435ff.

a state must be in their proper order and practise their particular virtues: wisdom for the rulers, courage for the guardians, and temperance for the artisans. When they do so there is harmony.

What Plato is telling us is that the nature of our soul is such that if we wish to be harmonious with ourselves we must be just. Although this is tenable, the problem with his view, against which all egalitarian and modern thought rebels, is the assertion that the individual's task or station in life is (or ought to be) predetermined. The assertion of this view, as a natural law or theory, leads to casteism. If we take egalitarianism to be true, then the basic question remains: what is my task in life? If justice is to be determined according to my task, then in the absence of the answer to this question Plato's theory remains incomplete, although not wrong. For though we know that acting justly will lead to harmony, we do not know what task is to be fulfilled or achieved in being harmonious. This argument, therefore, can provide us with a good reason for acting justly, but not a sufficient one.

The egalitarian theme is followed more vigorously by Aristotle for the citizens (he did not count slaves as citizens). Aristotle was more interested in defining and classifying *what* is justice than in justifying *why* we should be just. On this latter question, he followed his teacher Plato faithfully. According to Aristotle, man by nature being a political animal will seek to establish the ideal state; also, man by definition being rational will seek to apply the rational principles of justice to achieve this ideal state.[19] We have seen earlier what problems the ideal state thesis poses. In *Politics*, however, Aristotle's arguments are not conceptual; they are empirical. He claims to derive these conclusions by observing the social organisation of other animal species and the history of mankind as known to him. As an empirical theory the thesis does not hold water, for although we observe that man is a political

19. Aristotle, *Politics*, tr. by B. Jowett, Carlton House, New York, 1960, bk. I, ch. 1-2.

animal, we also observe that quite often he builds very unjust states; and even though the defining essential characterisation of man may be in terms of rationality, he very often fails to be rational (hence man, in terms of Aristotle's definition). Clearly, empirical generalisations about man's social nature cannot provide (have not provided) sufficient motivation to build just states, nor have identificational characteristics, in terms of defining man as a rational being, provided sufficient clarity, since the question why I should act rationally still remains.

Although Aristotle defined man in terms of rationality, from the point of view of justice he identified them in terms of equality. This first principle of justice states that men are to be treated as equal. Such a definition of justice makes a major shift from Plato. Whereas in Plato justice was defined in terms of a subjective concern, in Aristotle equality is an objective value, which binds man to man. But how is such an objectivity to be sustained, on what basis can we say all men are equal, and how does this equality necessitate that I act justly? Aristotle does not attempt to prove or explain this. But evidently, insofar as justice is an objective value (applicable to all in the same way), it stands in need of justification. This is the question to which Gustav Radbruch addresses himself.

Radbruch saw clearly that justice is not a subjective but an objective affairs, and despite the legitimacy of individual morality it often demands a different end and hence a separate justification. He points to connections between the autonomous spirit and the jural reality, and views law as a value-related phenomenon of culture, a phenomenon which embodies the absolute values of justice.[20] This type of neo-Kantian theory faces a major problem: how is ethical relativism, expressed in laws, to be upheld

---

20. Gustav Radbruch, *Legal Philosophy* tr. by Kurt Wilk, 3rd edn., reprinted in *The Legal Philosophies of Lask, Radbruch and Dabin*, Harvard, 1950. References are to this edition, pp. 73-5, 107ff.

together with ethical absolutism, expressed as principles of justice? This, however, is not the problem we are concerned with here. A more serious problem that Radbruch's theory raises — and with which we are directly concerned here — is: how is the objectivity of ethical absolute principles of justice to be upheld? Having separated values from truth, autonomous spirit from jural reality, Radbruch loses the grounds on which he can rest his principles of justice as objectively true principles. Radbruch, like Plato, declares that justice has to do only with the good, not with truth.[21] But in some sense those who wish to hold that the principles of justice are objective also want to hold that they are true.

A significant attempt to get over the subjectivity of values is that of Del Vecchio. He asserted that justice inheres in the acknowledgement that the other may also be a subject and that recognising the subjectivity in others is in fact equivalent to recognising the objectivity in oneself.[22] Del Vecchio interprets objectivity in terms of inter-subjectivity. He tries to save the objectivity of his conception of justice by resorting to a kind of interpretation which is similar to the one Hegel gives of Vico's reliance on social history. Although social history may be objective in some sense, the mere interpretation of objectivity in terms of inter-subjectivity does not help, because any dualistic thesis which recognises the self and the other as separate does not *ipso facto* recognise them as equal. Although I may acknowledge the objectivity of others as part of my own subjectivity, in seeing them as objects I may still see them as inferior to myself in some sense — the master-slave relation, for example.

The mere fact of inter-subjectivity cannot establish equality between subject and object, and hence the truth of the proposition

---

21. Gustav Radbruch, *Legal Philosophy*, p. 91.

22. Grigorio Del Vecchio, *Justice*, tr. by A.H. Campbell, Edinburgh University Press, 1951, p. 78.

that in some essential sense all subjects or objects are equal. The truth of this proposition becomes self-evident only on the condition that the subject is identical with the object; since the subject is equal (identical) to itself, it is identical (equal) with others.

This is the line of thought that is explored by Hegel. It was also explored by Fichte, Schelling, Herder, and others influenced by Kant earlier. Although Kant did not put it this way, one can read into him that since the noumenal self stands apart from the phenomenal self (the ego), the noumenal self, like the thing-in-itself, is ontologically identical. Ontological monism, of course, is not peculiar to those influened by Kant. It is the central theme in Spinoza and of many pre-Socratic Greek thinkers.

Amongst the Western thinkers, Hegel's account of justice is one of the more explicit theories founded on ontological monism. In his *Philosophy of Right* he tells us: "The basis of right is, in general, mind; its precise place and point of origin is the will. The will is free, so that freedom is both the substance of right and its goal, while the system of right is the realm of freedom made actual, the world of mind brought forth out of itself like a second nature."[23]

In Hegel we find the full blossoming of the post-Kantian Enlightenment idea that will by its very nature is free and that the basis of justice lies in its freedom. To maintain that all wills are similarly free (and equal) one would have to accept the ontic unity of the wills, as Hegel does. One need not here get into the issue of whether or not the expressions of the will are only ideas, that is, whether idealism is necessarily connected with ontological monism. The thesis about the ontic unity of the wills (agents of actions in the universe) is independent of whether the world consists of only ideas, or only matter or both. The central question that concerns us is that given that the acceptance of

23. G.W.F. Hegel, *Philosophy of Right*, tr. by T.M. Knox, Oxford, 1977, p. 20.

ontological monism is necessary to establish equality amongst the wills, is the characterisation of it as free, necessary and sufficient to explain the basis of justice?

The answer is: it necessary but not sufficient. Even if my will is *ab initio* free and I can claim and protect my rights to freedom on that basis, what prevents me from claiming my rights to do injustice on the same basis? That is, does the fact that my will is free suffice to assert that freedom ought to be expressed only in doing justice? To assert this, something more is necessary than merely the fact of my freedom. To generate just actions from free actions, or alternatively to ground just actions in free actions, my freedom must be of a nature which is internally limited in certain directions, which allows certain paths and forbids others; otherwise the question remains: freedom as to what? and freedom from what? It must be noted that the question is not why man is free, for it has already been granted that it is the essence of man's nature to be free; but given that there is this fact of freedom, is it totally unstructured and non-vectorial? Or are there certain purposes, meanings (limiting factors) within which freedom can be sustained? If freedom is limited in certain directions, that is, if freedom is internally so structured that certain types of actions are permitted and others prohibited, this limitation on freedom stands in need of explanation. The issue of direction leads us back to the questions of teleology. Kant eventually came to this question in his Third Critique, *The Critique of Judgement*. The limiting condition on freedom of nature, Kant finds, is that 'nature does nothing in vain'; the purpose of doing, Kant suggests, is the achievement of beauty.[24] By nature Kant here means biological nature. He argues that the principle of causality cannot apply to biological nature. Where does man and his freedom stand in this scheme

---

24. Immanuel Kant, *Critique of Judgement*, tr. by J.H. Bernard, Hafner, New York, 1960, p. 222 (66).

of things? Insofar as he is a part of nature, does the limiting condition on freedom in nature apply to him too? Neither in the Third Critique itself nor later does Kant explore the implication of this Critique *vis-a-vis* man's freedom and its teleology in nature. The question is left unanswered.

In his *Philosophy of Right* Hegel relates the freedom of the self with how it manifests itself in the social modality—through the family, to the community and finally to the nation-state. The unfolding of an individual's freedom then turns out to be the unfolding of the ideal nation-state. The question whether the German nation-state that Hegel described to be the ideal is correct does not concern us here. Nor does the question: why must one stop at nation-state, why not proceed to the idea of an international community? Hegel had no place for International Law in his system. The issues that concern us here are: how does one show this sort of teleology to be necessary, and how does one limit the manifestation of free action within the domain of just actions? One would wish to argue that even if in an non-ideal nation-state the individuals have absolute freedom of some sort, must one make the teleological development of an individual necessarily dependent upon the existence of an ideal state? Cannot the individual realise through his free and just actions whatever teleological end(s) he is supposed to realise, independently of the social conditions? Moreover, insofar as Hegel makes the resolution of contradictions the basic reason for transformations, the fact that social progression will come to an end at a certain point (the ideal) raises serious problems about the process of dialectics. As noted earlier, similar problems are faced by Marxism — will the generation of the ideal state lead to its contradiction? In the final analysis, Hegel's theory is unable to provide satisfactory answers to these basic questions, and consequently to the question: why am I obliged to follow a certain teleology (of just actions)? In Hegelian terms, insofar as

I have a free will, what makes it necessary that it must unfold its freedom in one way (towards a family, state) and not another (towards renunciation, self-sacrifice)?

This incapacity to explain the modalities of freedom, in the Enlightenment and post-Hegelian theories, leads to a major crisis which becomes more evident in the existential literature.

The assertion that there is no inherent or natural direction towards which human freedom must lead humanity, and also the inability to show what necessitates the restriction of this freedom to do just actions, leads thinkers like Kafka and Camus to characterise the human situation as absurd, and others, like Kierkegaard and Sartre, to relate this freedom to dread and anxiety. Such existential literature in fact exhibits the failure of the Enlightenment to explain the purpose of human freedom and not necessarily the truth about human freedom and its teleology.

V

Let us then briefly recapitulate the major issues which have been problematic in Western thought and on account of which no satisfactory theory explaining the grounds of justice has been possible.

The first relates to the metaphysics of the self and of the community. Since a theory of justice demands that I follow such and such a principle, it becomes necessary to explain whether I have a nature which can follow these principles. Merely saying that I am rational will not do, because I am also irrational; nor will the assertion that I have a free will suffice, because the free will can be used to do both justice and injustice. It is, therefore, further required to show what should restrict my freedom to do justice. But this in turn requires a notion of a direction, a path, a teleology of the self, satisfactory theories about which are not available within Western thought. Questions about the nature of the self also arise from the point of view of inter-subjectivity, since principles of justice relate one person to another. One has, therefore, to know the nature of the entities who are the bearers of these relations. Do they in fact have a nature which can allow them to be related by these principles? Expositions of these relations show that one of the relations by which people have to be united is that of equality. But any dualistic theory, which shows I and the other, or I and nature or I and god to be separate, essentially loses the ground for equating the two (or more) as equals. As suggested earlier, what is required is ontological monism, but this is not a well developed line of thought in the West. In fact, for religious and economic reasons Western thought seems to have been hostile to this line of thinking.

The metaphysics of the community raises different sorts of problems. Just as one cannot make the doing of justice necessary for the ordinary person dependent on the existence of an ideal person, one cannot make the doing of justice in an ordinary society dependent on the existence of an ideal community. This is not to say that teleological arguments concerning the community are out of place. On the contrary, in the final analysis, working out the teleology of the community is just as significant as that of the individual, because no odd series of actions performed by a community can be said to be a just series. The notion of direction or path towards justice is again involved here, and consequently that of the internal restrictions on a community's freedom. Self-determination *vis-a-vis* a community has been dealt with in Western political and legal thought only in terms of what other communities may not do to a particular community, and not what a community *must* do for and by itself. Internal self-determination by a community in this sense is related to its internal self-realisation. Just as with reference to a person the question 'what is an ideal self-realised person?' demands an answer to the question 'what is a person?', with reference to a community the answer to the question 'what is an ideal self-determined community?' demands an answer to the question 'what is a community?' There seems to be a dogma in the Western political, economic and sociological thought that the question 'what is community?' can be bypassed; it is simple, its answer is clear and not so deserving of inquiry; only the question 'what is a person?' is problematic. This, in fact, is not so. The questions 'what is the self?' and 'what is the community?' are equally problematic. Any theory of justice which invokes or depends on the notion of an ideal community or Kingdom of Ends must simultaneously provide answers to the latter questions.

Questions about the objectivity or truth of the principles of justice, as we have seen, are not independent of the metaphysical questions concerning the nature of persons and what relates them as community. Hence any hope that there can be a metaphysically neutral epistemology which can establish the truth about people is like attempting to chase shadows F.S.C. Northrop, for example, seeks to establish the objectivity of the basic principles of law in the manner one establishes the objectivity of mathematical principles.[25] People, however, are not morally neutral entities like mathematical entities; they are agents of action who often demand total freedom from any rule-governed behaviour as a condition to express their subjectivity. Unlike mathematical entities people have a subjective side; hence they can speak up and deny that any objective rule governs them, something which mathematical entities cannot do.

The question of the objectivity of principles, as we have noted, is also related to the nature of compulsion on a person to act justly. Autonomous theories are in a better position to explain this compulsion or necessitation than heteronomous theories of the will. The 'free-will' theories, however, are not complete or satisfactory in themselves, in the manner explained.

---

25. F.S.C. Northrop, *The Complexity of Legal and Ethical Experiences*, Oxford, 1975.

In brief, we have here examined:

Positivism — the belief that the basis of justice lies in external compulsion, and found it wanting; because such a theory cannot distinguish between political (arbitrary or coercive) obligation and juridical obligation.

De-ontological theories — which base justice on free will and objective principles, and also found them wanting, because in the final analysis such theories are unable to explain why the free will must necessarily be constrained by certain objective principles, and what makes such principles 'objective'.

Teleological theories — which make the doing of justice necessary for the realisation of the ideal state, in this life or after; such theories are unable to explain the basis of justice sufficiently because the possibility of the ideal state itself needs to be proved first, and its contradiction shown to be impossible; also the necessity for a person to participate in the realisation of this ideal state needs to be shown (for a person can renounce the world, with his rational will).

Essentialist theories — such theories wish to make the doing of justice essential to man's nature, but in doing this they do not go beyond characterising man as 'free' or 'rational'. It has been argued that these conceptions by themselves are unable to show why doing justice is necessary.

It must be noted that only positivism has been totally rejected, as being inherently incapable of explaining juridical obligation, since it cannot even distinguish obligation from coercion or compulsion. Of the other theories it has been argued that they are on the right track, but do not go far enough and hence are grossly inadequate. It has also been tacitly suggested (but not explored) that an appropriate theory will need essentialism, de-ontology and teleology together, though not in any arbitrary combination.

These then are the major reasons why the basis of justice cannot be explained within Western thought, unless some very radical changes take place in thinking. Most of these radical changes, however, lead towards the Indian alternatives, which, in their complexity of thought, are better suited to explore the issues of the nature of the self, its teleology and that of the community. These alternatives, I assume, will not be sought by Indian philosophers and others till they have seen through (or wish to see through) the Western dogmas and their shortcomings. This paper, I hope, is a step towards unveiling these shortcomings.

5

Justice and Morality
Some Unresolved Issues Concerning the Unencumbered Self

Ramesh Chandra Pradhan

THIS paper is concerning the nature of the moral self which underlies the concept of justice understood in the framework of the liberal tradition. The idea of an unencumbered self, as Michael Sandel[1] has pointed out, is at the core of the Kantian-Rawlsian theory of justice. This idea has evoked arguments and counter-arguments regarding whether justice requires the concept of a socially and culturally burdened self at all. My argument in this regard is that a morally robust conception of justice requires the notion of self that is not only socially and culturally adequate but also is transcendentally rooted. That is the reason why the concept of a just society falls back on the morally transparent notion of an unencumbered self.

Justice and the Imperatives of a Moral Society

Justice, as understood in the social and political context, is the basic feature of a well-ordered and rationally developed society.

---

1. Michael Sandel, "The Procedural Republic and the Unencumbered Self", in *Communitarianism and Individualism*, ed. by Shlomo Avineri and Avner De-Shalit, Oxford University Press, New York, 1992.

As Rawls puts it, "justice is the first virtue of social institutions, as truth is of systems of thought",[2] thus implying that justice characterises the 'basic structure' of a society of rational individuals. He further says,

> While a political conception of justice is, of course, a moral conception, it is a moral conception worked out for a specific kind of subject, namely, political, social and economic institutions. In particular, justice as fairness is framed to apply to what I have called the 'basic structure' of a modern constitutional democracy.[3]

Thus justice as fairness follows as a moral imperative for a well-ordered society of the free and rational individuals. The moral imperative lies in the fact that the rational individuals must choose the fairest among the principles of justice that cater to the rational needs of everyone.

The most rationally acceptable conception of justice from this perspective is that justice is fairness, i.e., that justice consists in the fair adjustment of the rational interests of the individuals concerned. The two principles[4] of justice as laid down by Rawls provide the rational framework in which the basic rights of the individuals are taken care of in conformity with the moral demands of equality and freedom. The first principle states that "each person is to have an equal right to the most extensive basic liberty compatible with a similar liberty for others",[5] while the second principle states that "social and economic inequalities are to be arranged so that they are both

---

2. John Rawls, *A Theory of Justice,* Oxford University Press, Oxford, 1972, p. 3.
3. Rawls, "Justice as Fairness: Political, Not Metaphysical", in *Communitarianism and Individualism,* pp. 187-8.
4. Rawls, *A Theory of Justice,* sect. 11, pp. 66-7.
5. *Ibid.*, p. 60.

(a) reasonably expected to be to everyone's advantage, and (b) attached to positions and offices open for all".[6] These two principles constitute the very foundations of a politically just society that conforms to the imperatives of a moral society.

Justice as fairness thus presupposes the following moral facts:

1. The individuals constituting the just social order are moral persons.
2. The just social order is basically a moral order enjoining upon the participants to respect each other's freedom and equality in respect of all the basic or primary goods of the society.

It is to be argued, therefore, that the concept of justice has a moral justification so far as it aims at the first principles of a democratic order that makes everyone an equal partner in the original social contract.

The moral deduction of the concept of justice is deeply embedded in the contractual theory of Kant and Rawls insofar as they presuppose that there is an 'original position'[7] in which the moral persons agree to choose the principles of justice as the moral imperatives of a stable and rational social order. This choice is the free choice of the rationally reflective moral persons constituting the moral community under what Rawls calls the 'veil of ignorance'[8]. The veil of ignorance, as it is aptly called, screens out the empirical conditions of the interacting individuals and highlights their rational constitution as the freely choosing moral persons enjoying the autonomy of the Kantian 'Kingdom

---

6. Rawls, *A Theory of Justice*, sect.11.
7. *Ibid.*, pp. 17-22.
8. *Ibid.*, pp.136-42.

of Ends".[9] Given thus the moral autonomy of the community of the rational individuals, the choice of the principles of justice becomes inevitable on the part of the moral persons.

Thus it can be argued that the Kantian-Rawlsian theory of justice situates the concept of social justice in the broad framework of a moral society or community that is wedded to the universal and necessary principles of morality[10] concerning the freedom and equality of the moral persons. The twin concepts of freedom and equality are the basic moral concepts that make justice follow necessarily as a natural corollary. This does not mean that justice is not a basic concept from the political point of view; only it emphasises that the morally basic concept of an autonomous person is a *sine qua non* of the political concept of justice. Justice in the latter sense is deducible from the primary concepts of liberty and equality which belong to the moral realm.

Moral Persons in the Original Position

The idea of an original position, as Rawls posits it, has enormous potential in sharpening the concept of a moral person. Moral persons, according to Rawls, are situated in the original position which is a representational device[11] of showing how the rational individuals under the veil of ignorance behave morally. These individuals, men and women, of the rational community are ignorant of their particular social positions and their specific

---

9. Kant, *The Critique of Practical Reason*, tr. by Lewis W. Beck, New York, 1956 and also the *Groundsworks of the Metaphysics of Morals*, tr. by H.J. Paton, New York, 1948. See also Bruce Aune, *Kant's Theory of Morals*, Princeton University Press, Princeton, New Jersey, 1979.
10. *Ibid.*
11. Rawls, *A Theory of Justice,* Sect. 4. See also his "The Basic Liberties and Their Priority", in *Liberty, Equality and Law*, ed. by Sterling M. McMurrin, University of Utah Press, Salt Lake City, 1987.

personal interests[12] such that they remain identifiable as the bearers of the moral consciousness of freedom and rationality. Such morally conscious free and equal individuals in recognisable ignorance of their historical contingencies come forward to choose the principles of justice for realising a stable and inherently balanced social order. This state of ignorance is not a state of moral blindness[13] as regards the necessary and universal laws of morality: it is a state of conscious disregard for the contextual and contingent features[14] of the individuals themselves. In this respect the original position is not a hypothetical empirical situation, nor is it an imagined state of a pre-political society, but is the absolutely unconditioned state of the rational community that is morally conscious of its unique autonomy — a state very much like Kant's 'Kingdom of Ends.'[15]

The original position thus presented is a moral position that is necessitated by the fact that the persons involved as the parties are moral persons. If the persons concerned would have been non-moral or morally blind, no choice of the principles of justice would have been possible. Since such persons would have all the details of their personal idiosyncratic life, they would be none the less blind to the fact that they are moral persons and thus would cease to be worthy of justice. They would in fact have no knowledge of the distinction between the just and the unjust and between what is morally right and what is wrong.[16] Thus in Rawls' argument there is a Kantian presupposition that only

12. Rawls, *A Theory of Justice,* sect. 24.
13. Amartya Sen argues that the veil of ignorance leads to blindness of some sort, See Sen, "Equality of What?", in *Liberty, Equality and Law,* pp. 139-62.
14. Rawls, "Kantian Constructivism in Moral Theory, Rational and Full Autonomy", *Journal of Philosophy*, LXXVII, No. 9, (1980), pp. 515-72.
15. *Ibid.*
16. *Ibid.*

morally autonomous persons can make a moral choice. The contractual requirement of choosing for everybody and thus representing every rational individual[17] makes the task of the rational self enormously important though complicated. This is the reason why Kant makes it very clear that rational individuals are equally the representatives of the rational will. This impersonal will is the extreme model of what Rawls calls the full autonomy[18] of the rational individual. Thus both Kant and Rawls, though differently, emphasise the fact that it is the rational will that underlies the system of justice that can be built for all conceivable human societies.

Kant's constructivism in the theory of justice entails the fact that the moral principles presupposed by the just social order are not a matter of intuitive grasp but are rather the legislative constructions by the rational will.[19] They are brought into being by the moral subjects themselves. The moral persons are the autonomous beings and are not the accidental creations of a moral sovereign. Therefore they are the autonomous source of morality itself. For Kant the moral will is *sui generis* and self-legislative. It creates its own moral standards which are of the character of the Categorical Imperative. In this sense it is made clear that the moral persons and their moral will make enormous difference to the actual historical world of the ordinary individuals engaged in political and economic activity. The real partners in the actual society depend very much on the ideal conception of themselves as the harbingers of justice into an otherwise unjust world. Kant did realise much before Rawls that it is the original conception of man as a rational being that leads to the idea that there could be a just society at all. Rawls' idea of original position is a rehearsal of the Kantian notion of the world of the rational

17. *Ibid.*
18. *Ibid.*
19. Kant, *The Metaphysical Elements of Justice,* tr. by John Ladd, Bobbs-Merrill Company, Inc. Indianapolis, 1965.

will.[20] Without the conception of the original position it is difficult to arrive at the idea of justice as fairness.

The history of the actual societies shows that persons are imperfect in their actual moral life and that their actual sense of justice suffers from imperfection. This makes one think that the actual history has no hope of providing the true sense of justice along with the principles of justice as the latter follow from an ideal conception of man. That is why Rawls says that justice depends upon the conception of the moral persons who can take responsibility for the morally stable society of free and equal partners. This requires a sense of autonomy as a moral and rational being. This is possible only under ideal and non-historical conditions. The more the conditions are decontextualised and made ahistorical, the better the conception of a moral person in a moral society. And this facilitates the possibility of justice.

The notion of the original position thus accentuates the difference between the actual and the ideal conditions of the society. It also marks the difference between the necessary and the contingent in the social behaviour of the people. The contingent and the hypothetical is distinguished from the necessary in moral and social life because it is the latter that is the background of the conception of justice. In the original position the contingent facts of life are bracketed or kept out of action for the reason that they are a hindrance to the conception of ourselves as moral persons. The veil of ignorance is precisely meant as the screen to put out of action the contingent facts about the persons concerned. The necessary facts about the persons which pertain to their rational will and their sense of justice make the persons choose the principles of justice as a matter of moral necessity. Thus the original position on which

---

20. Kant, *op. cit.*, See also Rawls, "Kantian Constructivism in Moral Theory", *Journal of Philosophy*, LXXVII, (1980), pp. 515-72.

the concept of justice depends so much is not a mere abstraction from the actual society nor is it a pointer to a hypothetical situation which the individuals might have occupied. The original position is the ideal conception of the human society which is the very basis of morality and justice.

The Necessity of the Unencumbered Self

The idea of a moral person in the ideal original position leads to the idea of the self that is unencumbered in the social and historical sense. The idea of a detached or unencumbered self follows from the fact that in the original position the rational individuals are disinterested[21] in each other's context-specific interests. Such persons are cognitively disinterested in what the specific plans of life each individual is pursuing including his own. They are, however, in full cognitive command of the total rational plan of life worthy of the human beings as such. This includes the pursuit of the free choice of the ends of a rationally satisfying life of rights and liberties, duties and obligations, and the primary goods of income and wealth. There is a systematic gradation of the primary goods the priority being accorded to the basic liberties.[22]

The pursuit of the above plan of life would not be possible if there is no rational noumenal self[23] as Kant would say. The noumenal self is the non-empirical metaphysical self that is the background of the empirical self that pursues its social goals in the actual historical world. In the absence of a metaphysical self no conception of the moral self-embodying the moral will is possible. This Kantian urge for the noumenon has its justification in the fact that the moral will itself demands that the noumenal world alone is the seat of all moral actions. The historical world is not denied

21. Rawls, *A Theory of Justice*, sect. 4.
22. *Ibid.*, sect. 15.
23. Kant, *Critique of Pure Reason*, tr. by N.K. Smith, Macmillan, London, 1929.

but it is emphasised that it itself is not enough and must be transcended at a higher level. The persistent demand for transcendence is ingrained in the very concept of a moral person. That is why it can be said that the historical world does not fall apart from the moral world, rather it is integrated into the latter in the sense that actual moral actions take place in the historical world itself. Besides, the actual world derives its sense or meaning from the moral world which is itself autonomous. In this framework morality is independent of the empirical world as it cannot be derived from the latter. But the empirical world is unintelligible if there is no noumenal moral background.

Rawls' original position under the veil of ignorance does have the Kantian urge to defy the empirical facts about the moral persons. This is reflected in the denial of empirical information about the persons' personal and other social interests which do not directly flow from the rational nature of theirs. This refusal to cognitively endow the self with empirical interest in the world is the first step towards the conception of the unencumbered self. This does not mean that Rawls' moral self is an abstract entity cut off from the social world. It is in fact in the historical and social world but yet it tries to go beyond it to comprehend a wider view of the community as a whole. In this wider view does lie the sense of justice as fairness. Rawls maintains, however, that

> The veil of ignorance, to mention one prominent feature of that position, has no metaphysical implications concerning the nature of the self; it does not imply that the self is ontologically prior to the facts about persons that the parties are excluded from knowing. We can, as it were, enter this position any time simply by reasoning for principles of justice in accordance with the enumerated restrictions.[24]

---

24. Rawls, "Justice as Fairness: Political, Not Metaphysical", in *Communitarianism and Individualism,* p. 203.

This is only to dispel the doubt that there could be any self which is ontologically prior to the social facts about the persons concerned. But Rawls has left no one in doubt that we enter the veil of ignorance just to make available to us the awareness of the self being unencumbered by the morally irrelevant social facts. The reflective self choosing the principles of justice is unencumbered or unburdened of the socio-cultural facts of the contingent kind. This is in a sense a defence of the Kantian noumenal self though in a less metaphysical garb.

Michael Sandel has, however, a different version of the Kantian-Rawlsian account of the unencumbered self. According to him, this self is a transcendental self that denies itself a role in the community and in history at large. This leads to a refusal to concede any of the social facts to the self which constitute the self being a person. Sandel writes,

> To imagine a person incapable of constitutive attachments such as these is not to conceive an ideally free and rational agent, but to imagine a person wholly without character, without moral depth. For to have character is to know that I move in a history that I neither summon nor command, which carries consequences none the less for my choices and conduct.[25]

Thus, according to him, a characterless self is a mere metaphysical abstraction which lacks the basic moral sense which comes from the 'constitutive attachments' that make the social self. Sandel is therefore critical of Rawls' apparent denial of these empirical facts about the moral persons.

Rawls in fact would agree with Sandel that a socially truncated self emptied of all attachments and loyalties is a mere metaphysical abstraction which will be incapable of moral

---

25. Michael Sandel, "The Procedural Republic and the Unencumbered Self", in *Communitarianism and Individualism*, p. 23.

choice. He would further concede that the moral persons are very much involved in society and history. But he would deny that the social self as it is found with all the empirical details is the best representative of the moral self. The moral self has an edge over the empirical self as it can choose the principles of justice and commit itself to the demands of a just society. This itself entails that the moral self has a deeper sense of justice and duty which the empirical self lacks.

It is not that the empirical self is denied or that it is reduced to a shadow as Sandel claims, since there is a virtual concession to the fact that a social role is granted to the moral self in Rawls' moral theory. Rawls is particularly sensitive to the socio-economic involvement of the moral persons though he agrees that these involvements are in accordance with the highest-order[26] interests of the moral persons. The principles of justice, besides, limit the interests of the moral persons so far as the rational plan of life is concerned. Thus Sandel's argument that "the liberal ethic puts the self beyond the reach of its experience, beyond deliberation and reflection"[27] does not hold good. The self is very much the focus of the moral experience and the deliberative reflection of the rational self. It is another matter that the moral person makes a deliberate distinction between the non-moral experiences of a person and those of the justice-seeking reflective persons. It is to the latter that Kant and Rawls draw our attention.

To view the self of the moral person as left in the lurch "between detachment on the one hand and the entanglement on the other"[28] is to view it in an improper light, since the unencumbered self is not in such a precarious position. Rawls'

---

26. See Rawls, "Kantian Constructivism in Moral Theory", p. 525.
27. Sandel, "The Procedural Republic and the Unencumbered Self", p. 24.
28. *Ibid.*, p. 28.

theory of moral self takes into account the facts of the social life and yet searches for the higher rational order that gives meaning and value to the former for all that it seeks to deliver is the moral foundation for the social life. The unencumbered self is not a self-creative principle in the Hegelian sense, but is a rational and legislative self in Kantian sense. That brings order and harmony into an otherwise chaotic state of nature. The self transcends nature only in a moral sense, that is, in order to make the latter ethically meaningful.

Limits of Communitarianism: Why Procedural Justice is not Enough

The alternative to the conception of the liberal form of justice as fairness is the idea that justice is communitarian, that is, justice lies in the moral institution of the state. The communitarian form of justice has its advocates[29] who see the best realisation of justice in a community which is elevated to the status of a moral person.[30] But can the state embody the rational will except in a perverted sense?

The argument of the communitarian is that the community precedes the individual in the sense that without the community the individual is a mere abstraction. The community makes an individual rather than the other way round. From this it has been claimed that the community in the form of a state becomes the source of morality and also of the political ideals of freedom and justice. In this sense the individual is moral to the extent it obeys the dictates of the state and is free as long as it is an organic part of the state. The liberal concept of justice is made the subject of abstraction and of ultimate denial as it is viewed

29. See, Amy Gutmann, "Communitarian Critics of Liberalism", Alasdair MacIntyre, "Justice as a Virtue: Changing Conceptions" and Charles Taylor, "Atomism" all in *Communitarianism and Individualism*.
30. C. Taylor, *Hegel,* Cambridge Univrsity Press, Cambridge, Part IV.

to be egoistic and atomistic in character. Charles Taylor, for example, has rejected atomism in the conception of justice while favouring what he calls the justice in the shape of communitarian decisions. He writes,

> If realising our freedom partly depends on the society and culture in which we live, then we exercise a fuller freedom if we can help determine the shape of this society and culture. And this we can only do through instruments of common decision. This means that the political institution in which we live may themselves be a crucial part of what is necessary to realise our identity as free beings.[31]

Thus, according to him, our own identity as morally free persons depends upon the rationality of our civilisation and society as such. No person is free *qua* a person but as part of a whole society. So, according to Taylor, "an anarchist society not an available option",[32] since anarchism is the enemy of the freedom of the individual as it is of the state.

Taylor's argument suffers from many limitations from the individualist point of view. The individualist could argue that the collective existence of the state is a construction rather than a metaphysical discovery. If the state would have been ontologically prior to the individual themselves, then freedom and justice could have been written into the state itself. But that is not the case since state has remained imperfect throughout history. It is the collective agreement of the morally conscious individuals which has led to the existence of a moral community. The community has as much moral and rational capacity as the individuals themselves. Thus the primacy of the individual cannot but be accepted as a moral datum.

---

31. C. Taylor, "Atomism", in *Communitarianism and Individualism*, p. 47.
32. *Ibid.*, p. 48.

Besides, the primacy of the rights and the liberties cannot be denied since to sacrifice the supremacy of the individual is to bargain for the tyranny of collectivity. The collective reason in the sense of the Hegelian universal reason[33] is a myth as it lends to divinise the collective will and mentality to determine and delimit the sphere of individual freedom. To collectivise morality and freedom is to empty it of all content.

The individualist liberal philosopher does not advocate, however, the plain absurdity that the society is an artificial creation of a group of individuals. It is in fact the case that we find ourselves already in a society and civilisation just as we find a family into which we are born. Thus our selves are already as a matter of fact encumbered in many ways. Our loyalties, attachments and plain relations with other humans make it obligatory on us to seek moral and political life in the society itself. But this itself does not cancel the fact that the individual persons themselves matter so far as their basic liberties are concerned. The basic liberties have a moral primacy and so the principles of justice arise out of a moral necessity. Besides, the civilisation in which we are born does not create the moral necessity itself; it only acknowledges the *a priori* character of the principles of justice.

The burden of the civilisation extended too far will extinguish the individual's moral worth as the encumbered self found in history is incapable of realising its moral worth. The burden of history has to be cancelled in the ideal world of the moral persons. This can be done for the purpose of raising the individuals to the rational level by dropping what is otherwise acknowledged to be contingent. Rawls' original position as argued already throws a challenge to the communitarian myth of the state as a moral entity. The state is derived from the individuals' search

---

33. Taylor, *Hegel*, Part IV.

for a community of fellow citizens agreeing on the fundamentals of justice and freedom.

To conclude: the liberal theory of justice as fairness defended in this paper is not a theory of procedural justice alone, i.e., not a fomalistic doctrine. It is a substantial theory of justice that aims at the realisation of a rational social order. The rational order is intended to be made concrete in the real world of the concrete individuals. To some extent justice is a matter of the formal structure of the society but beyond that it is a matter of serious concern of any rational society. The aim of relating justice to the unencumbered moral persons is to build a bridge between the lawless freedom of the natural man and the morally obligatory duty of the moral persons to protect freedom. Freedom is the substantial moral basis of justice.

6

The Original Position and the Concept of a Person

Bijoy H. Baruah

I

DE-ONTOLOGICAL liberalism may be described as a theory about the primacy of justice amongst other political and moral ideals. This theory is synoptically captured in the slogan that the right is prior to the good. Justice is brought to a society — society conceived as composed of a plurality of persons each with his or her own aims, interests and conceptions of the good — when it is governed by principles which do not themselves presuppose any particular conception of the good. And what justifies these principles is not their contribution to the maximisation of social welfare or promotion of any other good, but rather their conformity to a moral category prior to that of the good and independent of it — namely, the concept of right. Thus, moral primacy is assigned to justice in the sense that the rights of individual citizens cannot be sacrificed for the sake of any other political or social goods, values or goals.

If the moral primacy accorded to the value of justice is not derivative upon any conception of the good, what constitutes the fundamental primacy of the principles of justice, which in turn would account for the unqualified moral primacy of justice? What, in other words, is the ultimate ground of justice if it has moral precedence over other values such as our particular aims, interests and conceptions of the good? In order to ensure that moral primacy of justice is both secure and non-coercive, it would be necessary to derive the principles of justice from something other than the multiplicity of competing and circumstance-dependent aims, interests and ends adopted by human beings.

It is precisely this question of the foundation of justice, or the derivation of the principles of justice independently of any valuable ends of human life, that inevitably drives the de-ontological liberal to seek an answer in a highly specific theory of the person or conception of the self.

Kant, the greatest of classical de-ontological liberals, povides the justificatory locus of justice in his account of the nature of the human subject. As a subject possessed of a will which can be exercised freely, the human person is an agent of autonomous action. It is this autonomy of the will, or the capacity to exercise it freely, which is fundamental to the dignity and worth of human beings. What makes any of us a human subject at all is not the particular aims, interests and conceptions of the good which we decide to adopt and pursue, but rather the capacity to think and act autonomously which sustains such decisions.

On the de-ontological view Kant exemplifies, there is a pure primary capacity to choose the ends of life that defines our moral personhood. And since the value of this capacity is morally prior to any particular end it is employed to affirm, what really matters about the human person is also similarly prior to any ends adopted by the person. Additionally, saying that the right is prior to the good corresponds to the assertion that the human subject is prior to its ends. In short, the de-ontological assignment of absolute priority to justice is to be understood by reference to, and as paralleled by, its assignment of absolute priority to the subject.

Following the footsteps of Kant but without treading on

mushy metaphysical grounds of noumenal reality, John Rawls offers us *A Theory of Justice*[1] that articulates the modern temperament of de-ontological liberalism. There is, on the part of Rawls, an explicitly Kantian attribution of absolute moral primacy to justice in the following passage:

> Justice is the first virtue of social institutions, as truth is of certain systems of thought. A theory, however elegant and economical, must be rejected or revised if it is untrue; likewise laws and institutions, no matter how efficient and well-arranged, must be reformed or abolished if they are unjust. . . . Being first virtues of human activities, truth and justice are uncompromising. (*Ibid*., pp. 3-4).

Rawls is also explicit in attributing foundational primacy to justice:

> We should . . . reverse the relation between the right and the good proposed by teleological doctrines and view the right as prior. (*Ibid*., p. 560)

It is because he shares the Kantian view that what really matters about we human beings is our capacity to set, pursue and revise our own conceptions of the good that Rawls advocates the regulation of society by principles of justice that do not depend upon any particular conception of the good. Persons have a 'highest-order interest' in protecting this capacity and hence it is crucial to justice that no exception be made that may adversely affect the full and equal exercise by any person of this capacity freely to determine how she should live. In short, moral personhood consists most fundamentally in a person's capacity freely to choose her ends, and any just social order is that which is so organised as to accord privileged respect to this feature of personhood.

---

1. John Rawls, Cambridge, Mass, Harvard University Press, 1971.

II

That the human subject as an autonomous chooser of ends is the locus of moral worth, or what is most worthy of respect in our treatment of human beings, is a substantive or first-order ethical view, and one which Rawls believes to be the cornerstone of a theory of justice. As a substantive ethical position it is no different from that of Kant's ethical theory. But in the case of Kant there is a definite second-order, metaphysical conception of the human self which grounds the first-order moral claim that human beings have an unconditional right to be treated as members of the 'Kingdom of Ends'. The underlying second-order theory is that human beings, *qua* rational agents, partake of a noumenal realm beyond space and time. The rational self is a noumenal self, and only as a noumenal self can it be beyond the realm of causally determined nature and be a truly free agent.

A question therefore naturally arises whether there is, and there must be, an analogous second-order theory of the human self, an underlying philosophical anthropology, that constitutes a foundational account of the human person, which is presupposed by Rawls' first-order ethical view. Understandably, Rawls does not allude to any apparently unintelligible metaphysical framework that construes human beings as dual-aspect beings, who are at once part of nature and yet capable of transcending the limits of nature. Nevertheless, there seems to be some general metaphysical, second-order theory of the person, concerned with the essential nature of human subjecthood, that supports the first-order theory of moral personhood in the case of Rawls as well.

There indeed is a very specific set of views about the self which are evident in the way Rawls pictures the relation between the human subject and its ends. The moral priority accorded to the self *qua* a free determiner of its life-ends is paralleled by, and explained by reference to, the corresponding assignment of a metaphysical priority. The self has its essential unity or identity, from the metaphysical point of view, prior to its choice of, and attachment to, its life-ends. It is the absoluteness of this mataphysical priority that accounts for the absoluteness of the moral priority.

There is not any explicit acknowledgement on Rawls' part of his commitment to any second-order, metaphysical theory of the self as the ultimate basis of his substantive ethical view. But there are certain passages in *A Theory of Justice* that seem to have a metaphysical rather than moral connotation, and to which attention has been drawn by Michael Sandel, a foremost critic of liberalism, in his *Liberalism and the Limits of Justice*.[2]

Sandel's claim that Rawls must be committed to a metaphysical conception of the self is based upon Rawls' emphatic assertion of the priority of the self over its ends:

> . . . the self is prior to the ends which are affirmed by it: even a dominant end must be chosen from among numerous possibilities. . . . (Rawls, *op. cit.*, p. 560)

The unity and identity of the self cannot be constituted by its chosen attachment to the ends because the self is antecedently there to exercise its choice of ends. As Rawls admits:

> The main idea is that given the priority of right, the choice of our conception of the good is framed within definite limits. . . . The essential of unity of the self is already provided by the conception of right.
>
> (*Ibid.*, p. 563).

What this ontologically antecedent unity and identity of the self means, according to Sandel, is that no amount of conditioning of the human individual by her surroundings, values and goals can constitute her true identity. For her unity and identity, her sovereign agency, is independent of such circumstances and

2. Cambridge University Press, 1982.

guaranteed in advance. Thus, not to assign absolute priority to the right over the good would not just be wrong on the substantive level. It would rather be a metaphysical contradiction — contradication of our essential nature as persons. Rawls makes this clear in the following:

> What we cannot do is express our nature by following a plan that views the sense of justice as but one desire to be weighed against others. For this sentiment reveals what the person is, and to compromise it is not to achieve for the self free reign, but to give way to the contingencies and accidents of the world. (*Ibid.*, p. 575)

In other words, the human subject's sense or sentiment of justice as the first virtue is not only reflective of the moral fact of its autonomous agency that determines its own ends. It also underscores the metaphysical fact that the subject is individuated antecedently to any end it decides to adopt.

This metaphysical conception of the self as having its unity and identity prior to its projects and goals is held to be embedded in the imaginative construct of the 'original position', which is the fulcrum of Rawls' argument for his theory of justice. If, as Rawls thinks,

> . . . the circumstances of justice obtain whenever mutually disinterested persons put forward conflicting claims to the division of social advantages under conditions of moderate scarcity. (*Ibid.*, p. 128)

Then presumably the parties to the original position would think of society as a cooperative venture for mutual advantage. On Sandel's view, to regard society as primarily a system of cooperation implies viewing its members as already (asocially) constituted individuals when they enter into it for their mutual advantage. The metaphysical import of this is that we are distinct persons firsts and only later do we enter into a societal or communal framework and engage in cooperative activity. We are, essentially and primarily, mutually disinterested distinct individuals. Hence the relationships we form with one another by sharing certain common interests and ends cannot be integral to our constitution as separate selves.

There is, thus, a distance between who a person is and what she values as her life-end. But what is the consequence of this distance between self-identity and the self's engagement in the world? Sandel has the following remark to make on it:

> One consequence of this distance is to put the self beyond the reach of experience, to make it invulnerable, to fix its identity once and for all. No commitment could grip me so deeply that I could not understand myself without it. No transformation of life purposes and plans could be so unsettling as to disrupt the contours of my identity. No project could be so essential that turning away from it would call into question the person I am. Given my independence from the values I have, I can always stand apart from them; my public identity as a moral person 'is not affected by changes over time' in my conception of the good. (p. 62)

But the actual experiences of human moral and political life furnish evidence contrary to what the Rawlsian position depicts. There are abundant examples of human situations where the self is constitutively attached to its ends and circumstances, and cases where one's sense of oneself is torn apart by conflicting desires of aims, both at intra-subjective and inter-subjective levels.

In short, given the conception of the person as metaphysically asocial or antecedently individuated, it rules out the possibility of developing constitutive attachments to the community. It also fails adequately to acknowledge the idea that the creation, inhabitation and maintenance of a communal framework might be integral to one's identity or personhood.

There appears to be a similar criticism of Rawls' position by MacIntyre.[3] MacIntyre's critique also highlights the asocial individualism of Rawlsian liberalism and the emotivist conception of the self of which the Rawlsian self is a new version. The detachment of individuals from the facts of their social existence — which is how Rawls conceives of people in 'the original position' where they are to find themselves under the 'veil of ignorance' — is taken by MacIntyre to imply that Rawls is committed to the emotivist assumption that those facts are extraneous to the individual's real identity. It is Rawls' commitment to the emotivist conception of the person, the conception that moral agency is comprehensible independently of, and detachable from, the natural and social endowments and the value commitments of the particular individual, that is held to underlie Rawls' reason for advocating the use of the 'evil of ignorance' for the articulation of a theory of justice.

But the emotivist conception of the self is unsatisfactory in that, according to MacIntyre, it lacks the logical resources that are needed to make sense of human personhood and rational moral agency as real possibilities.

III

If we are to pause here for a critical review of the anti-liberal criticisms of the Rawlsian theory of justice by Sandel and MacIntyre, we would have to scrutinize the implications of 'the original position' and 'the veil of ignorance'. The question is whether the hypothetical construct of the original position can justifiably be interpreted as presupposing an unacknowledged ontological hypothesis, as Sandel's critique does.

The metaphysical reading of this hypothesis is not incontrovertible. For one could argue that the structure of the original position only reflects Rawls' substantive view that

3. Alasdair MacIntyre, *After Virtue*, Duckworth, London, 1981.

social justice categorically requires that we regard our fellow citizens as free and equal. It does not embody the further claim that one's identity as a person is metaphysically independent of their roles, character traits and life-ends at any particular time. Drawing any ontological import out of the picture of a person as a free and equal citizen portrayed in the original position would surely be unwarranted if the original position is interpreted as no more than a dramatic device argumentatively deployed in a political theory so as to drive home the point that, when thinking about social justice, we must refrain from letting our deliberations depend upon our knowledge of what our natural and social endowments and our value committments really are.

The imaginative construction of the original position is not so much to be conceived as a conceptual device to find an Archimedean point *from* which a substantive moral theorising is supposed to begin, as it is to be understood as that *to* which moral theorising inevitably leads in order to determine the parameters of social justice. More importantly, the conception of the person modelled in the original position is only the conception of a citizen with freedom and equality as its in-built features: it is, strictly and fully, a *political* conception drawn out from the available resources of the public political culture. The political conception of the person as citizen need not presuppose the validity of any metaphysical or comprehensive doctrine of personhood. The political person represented in the original position is not erected out of an unencumbered subject, a shadowy self detached from all its ends. Presumably, the idea of the person as a free and equal citizen is entirely non-metaphysical, and it would therefore be quite consistent with whatever conception of personhood one upholds at the metaphysical level.

In short, the hypothesis of the original position, being exclusively part of the argumentative structure of a political theory, does not permit it to be interpreted as embodying an essentialist conception of personhood. For the person as citizen is not, or at least it need not be, the person *as such*.

The political conception of the self is restricted to the domain of the political, and it is latent in the public political culture. It would therefore be wrong to view Rawls as holding that the individual, *qua* a member of the political community, has ontological priority over society. The status of the individual as a citizen does not entail anything about its ontological priority or otherwise in relation to society.

The above line of defense against the anti-liberal critics is developed by Rawls himself in some of his later writings.[4] He stresses the point that justice as fairness is 'political not metaphysical' — the qualification here being intended as an argument to block off Sandel's charge that the Rawlsian theory of justice presupposes an incoherent metaphysics of personhood. In his own words:

> we adopt a conception of the person framed as part of, and restricted to, an explicitly political conception of justice. [And] persons can accept this conception of themselves as citizens and use it when discussing questions of political justice without being committed in other parts of their life to comprehensive moral ideals often associated with liberalism, for example, the ideals of autonomy and individuality
>
> — *Philosophy and Public Affairs*, 14.3, p. 245

In other words, the self-conception involved in the public, political sphere is to be distinguished from, and can co-exist with, quite different self-understandings and interests in other, non-political areas of life. Political self-understanding and self-identity are not

---

4. See for example, his "Kantian Constructivism in Moral Theory" in *Journal of Philosophy*, 77, 9, pp. 515-72, "Justice as Fairness", in *Philosophy and Public Affairs*, 14, 3, pp. 223-51 and "The Priority of Right and Ideas of the Good" in *Philosophy and Public Affairs*, 17, 4, pp. 251-76.

to be seen as inevitably spilling over people's self-understanding and self-identity involved in contexts beyond the political.

The political conception of justice is viewed by Rawls as "a moral conception worked out for . . . the basic structure of a constitutional regime" (*P and PA*, 17.4, p. 252), that is for the central political, social and economic institutions which fit together into one unified system of social cooperation. Further,

> the political conception presents itself as a reasonable conception for the basic structure alone; and . . . it is formulated not in terms of any comprehensive doctrine but in terms of certain fundamental ideas viewed as latent in the public political culture of a democratic society. (*op. cit.*)

The original position thus represents the individual subject as a moral agent that specifically fits into the structural organisation of society's political institutions. It models our culture's understanding of people as citizens.

IV

Rawls' 'political' move does seem to have adequate countervailing effect upon the arguments of his critics. But by making this strategic move of sharply demarcating the sphere of the political from that of the non-political and restricting the matters of social justice to the former, he seems to have created a new problem that makes questionable the fairness of the theory of justice as fairness. The new problem is whether it is plausible to think that people who are deeply committed to particular values or pursuits of life in the non-political areas, such as religion and art — pursuits which may not themselves accord highest priority to the values of individual freedom or autonomy — can none the less shift wholeheartedly to an understanding of themselves as citizens that does accord absolute priority to these values.

Such a possibility would require the person to be

schizophrenically tied up with mutually conflicting values. At its worst, it would be a painful internal cleavage for them whose private non-political commitments seriously clash with the publicly available political conception, and who are nevertheless ultimately swayed by the latter because of its overriding primacy. Is this desirable at all?

A sharp separation between the political and the personal, between public and private morality, in the life of every individual is likely to affect the meaningful integrity of our lives. For our commitment to the political value of autonomy, required of us as citizens, may necessitate us to suspend or bracket some of our non-political or personal commitments which shape our identity. If citizenship is designed as a cloak we must put on for the sake of our political identity even at the cost of suppressing our most significant non-political identity, then such a design may be suspected to be 'unfair'. It means that the exclusionary political concept of justice as fairness may itself be unfair.

To conclude with a tilt towards a non-exclusionary perspective, I allude to some remarks of Gandhi. To Gandhi, the idea of keeping politics separately from some other most serious concerns of life, especially religion, is inconceivable. For him there is no independent political identity that does not allow to be permeated by religion. For religion provides the moral basis to human activity as such, to the service of mankind. So he says:

> For me, politics bereft of religion are absolute dirt, ever to be shunned. Politics concern nations and that which concerns the welfare of nations must be one of the concerns of a man who is religiously inclined, in other words, a seeker after God and Truth. For me, God and Truth are convertible terms. . . . Therefore, in politics also we have to establish the Kingdom of Heaven.[5]

5. *Young India*, 18.6.1925, p. 214, quoted from R.K. Prabhu and U.R. Rao (eds.), *The Mind of Mahatma Gandhi*, Navjivan Publishing House, Ahmedabad, 1967.

It is clear from the above that the Rawlsian concept of justice constrained by the limiting notion of citizenship would be, not just far too restrictive, but deeply fractured and, perhaps, symptomatic of modernity's self-image.

7

Karma and Social Justice

Sarat Chandra Panigrahi

Karmavāda or the doctrine of 'as you sow, so you reap' assumes that the moral order is inviolable. Human achievements and failures, prosperity and adversity, happiness and sorrow are explained by appeal to this doctrine. Needless to say that varied issues, such as the logical status of this doctrine, its applicability to human situations and its bearing on free-will and justice have been the butt of wide ranging controversies. I shall attempt to show that the idea that the *karma* doctrine runs counter to the notion of social justice is unsound. It will be argued how the idea of social justice is not only compatible with the *karma* doctrine but it gets corroborative support from the latter.

The *karma* doctrine, which presupposes a moral order, stipulates that as are the actions, so are the consequences. No virtuous action goes unrewarded and no vicious action goes unpunished. The present status of the individual with the attendant experiences of pleasure and pain are the moral consequences of the past actions. The important aspect of the doctrine is the notion of rebirth which is nothing but a conceptual extrapolation in order to explain away the apparent anomalies in the action-reaction nexus. The present life span of the individual may not be long enough to bear the fruit of the actions in the past. A future life is postulated wherein the reincarnated individual lives the residue of the reactions. Pleasure and pain come as a form of natural reward or punishment for an individual. This introduces to us the notion of natural justice which provides a broad canvas against which the concept of social justice is rendered significant.

If the *karma* doctrine is to be accepted in letter and spirit, then the discrimination in respect of one's birth, dispositions and consequent actions are to be traced to the actions in the past. If this be the case, the prosperous people should be allowed to prosper because they have been born fortunated by their past deeds and the poor and tormented should be allowed to suffer as they are so destined. It is only through suffering that they make the requital of the past *karma*s. In what follows, it will be seen how the foregoing criticisms betray the misconceptions of the proponent.

Another resulting conception of the *karma* doctrine is that, it indirectly supports *varṇāśrama dharma* which divides human community to different classes as brāhmaṇas, kṣatriyas, vaiśyas and śūdras and considers some castes as privileged or higher castes and others as under-privileged belonging to lower castes. Thus there appears to be a contradiction in the ideas of social justice ane the karmic order according to which the individual differences are predetermined by birth which is also determined by their past deeds. According to some again, idea of *guṇakarmavibhāga* which is an innovation of the *Bhagavad Gītā* is also based on the karmic order. The *Bhagavad Gītā* says, *cāturvarṇam māyā sṛṣṭam guṇa karma vibhāgasaḥ*. That is, 'I have created the four castes on the basis of to *guṇa* and *karma*'. It is held that this social stratification is determined by the difference in action and quality which ultimately falls back upon the moral desert of the individuals.

The idea of justice, particularly social justice, is highly controversial in view of the diverse standpoints from which the subject has been investigated upon. The objective here is neither to consider the alternate standpoints of the Economist, the

Jurist, the Political theorist or, for the matter, of the philosopher nor to propose a formalistic or legal or juridical definition of social justice. The principal objective is rather to enquire into the logic or criteria of social justice. In other words, we have to analyse the conditions that would be responsible for a just society or, for that matter, an unjust society.

The ordinary and traditional view is that a society is just when it dispenses justice to its members considering everyone's due. But it is difficult to decide what exactly is one's due. Should we take into account the *worth* or capacity of the individual, or should justice be meted out considering the *need* of the individual members ignoring their merit or should we take into account the principle of equality, i.e., equal opportunity for all members. Each one of the considerations is crucial and yet controversial. It may be held[1] that man's due or right is that which is his, by virtue not merely of the law or the prevailing principles, but by valid moral principles. Thus a society is just if it accords its members what is their valid moral deserts. According to this view, social justice consists in the apportionment of good and evil, rewards and punishments, jobs and other privileges in accordance with the valid moral principles. This argument sounds quite plausible, for what could be more obvious than that a society is just if it dispenses what is just to its members? But the difficulty lies in deciding what constitutes the justness in the society. It has to be made clear whether there are universally just principles for all societies. Moreover, whether justice is to be defined distributively or retributively in accordance with the valid moral principles seems to depend on the moral principles turn out to be valid. What exactly is the basis of these moral principles which can regulate social justice. The difficulty with this criterion is that it might lead to a confusion of right-making and just-making principles. This might coerce one to accept

1. William K. Frankena, "The Concept of Social Justice" in Richard Brandt (ed.), *Social Justice*, Prentice Hall, N.J., 1962, p. 3.

what is right (morally valid) as always socially just, or at least just.

Mill draws a distinction between a just society and a good society. In this regard, the question is, what are the pre-requisites of a just society, or a good or right society? According to Mill, the society must distribute good and evil in certain ways rather than maximise the quantitative balance of the one over the other. Thus he distinguishes between principles of justice and such other principles of morality as generosity and beneficence. For him, the criterion of justice would be balancing responsibility with right. Justice implies something which it is not only right to do and wrong not to do, but that which some individual person can claim as his moral right. That means, social justice is to be governed by certain norms or rules. The core idea of justice is that every duty implies its correlative rights. Thus according to this view, society is just if and insofar as it does to its members that which it ought to do. But Mill does not clearly spell out what exactly is the principle which constitutes the basis of the distribution of rights. Of course, his consideration is utility. But Mill only offers a formal definition of social justice. He only says that society to be just must have rules and act on them. But he does not clearly say what the rules should be.

Justice, individual or social, is connected with the idea of distribution. That means it centres round the question of distribution of opportunities as well as responsibilities. It has been stipulated that the ideal justice must be based on the principle of equality. It is not possible, however, to met out similar treatment to all similar cases. Hence as D.D. Raphael[2] points out that matters of justice should not always be identified with moral considerations. Frankena[3] holds that this principle is to be revised. That is, justice consists in treating persons

2. "Equality and Equity", *Philosophy* Vol. XX no.1, 1946, p. 5.
3. *Op. cit.*, p.10.

equally, except as unequal treatment is required by just-making consideration. To say that justice lies in treating people equally is not to say that identical treatment is to be given to every individual. When society distributes land to landless people and the electricity facility to undeveloped villages, it is treating them *differently* and *yet equally*. Does it then mean that social justice, and for that matter, equality consists in distributing goods among people according to their need? In that case the need of two professors, two carpenters or two military persons may not be equal. Moreover, the question still remains what considerations are relevant to the justification of inequalities or dissimilarities? Mill, Hart and Raphael seem to take the utilitarian consideration in the distribution of justice. Raphael contends that justice consists in protecting the interest of the individual members. This criterion includes in it the claims of desert and equality. Frankena offers a criterion of social justice in the following way:

> A just society, then, is one which respects the good lives of its members and respects them equally. A just society must therefore promote equality, it may ignore certain differences and similarities but must consider others; and it must avoid unnecessary injury, interference or impoverishment — all without reference to beneficence or general utility. The just society, then, must consider and protect the good life of each man equally with that of any other, no matter how different these men may be, and so it must allow them equal consideration, equal opportunity, and equality before the law.[4]

It is clear from the above discussion that the consideration of social justice is without any prejudice to the recipient's degree of moral goodness or moral desert. Vlastos also says that merit is

---

4. Frankena, *op. cit.*, pp. 19-20.

not the criterion of justice.[5] By merit, he understands any valuable equality. Social justice does not pertain to the consideration of individual excellence or good quality. These qualities may be required for other purposes but so far as the requirement of social justice is concerned, merit is not the necessary condition of distributive justice.

II

What then is the criterion of justice, particularly social justice? It might be argued that an action is just only when it produces maximum utility to the members of the society. Society has to adopt rules, according to this criterion, for distribution of justice. But the rules which a society adopts may not be perfect. When we think of adopting rules considering the question of utility it may not be necessarily universal one. The idea of justice cannot be universal or impartial if anything is claimed to be just on the ground of someone being born to a particular community or other. Social justice will be devoid of significance if it allows discrimination of caste, creed and colour, etc. On the other hand, when equality of treatment is demanded simply on the ground that one is born as a human being, then one cannot draw a line of demarcation between justice and injustice. It has already been pointed out that principle of equality does not mean that everyone must be treated on equal footing. If *A* is a musician, *B* is a teacher and *C* is an engineer, then the principle of equality does not mean that all these persons must be treated identically. The principle of equality does not mean that all these persons must be given identical-treatment. It is neither possible nor desirable to give equal treatment to all in that manner. The statement 'all men are born equal' means that having been born as human beings they are all equal. That, however, does not mean that social privileges can be distributed equally irrespective

---

5. Gregory Vlastos, "Justice and Equality" in Brandt (ed.), *Social Justice*, p. 45.

of the efficiency and merit of the persons. On the other hand, there cannot be social justice at all if equal opportunity is not granted to all the members of the community. In other words, discriminatory treatment is not justified either on legal or on moral ground. This is now the crux of the problem, and solution to the impasse cannot be found so easily.

The doctrine of *karma* offers a solution which, to my mind, seems to be a cogent solution. According to the *karma* doctrine, what is most important is to consider the speciality of the agent in giving him equal treatment. This speciality, according to the *karma* doctrine, is the desert of the individual. According to Nathan, this is the most popular idea of justice since:

> The most popular group of senses of 'just' comprises those on which the value of man's attributes depends on his deserts of desert-dependent senses of just.[6]

This idea seems not only to be the most popular sense of justice, but is the universal idea of justice. Justice demands that everybody must get his due, even the devil. This is a non-criterion endorsing sense of justice as Nathan would put it. It is not the law-abiding sense of justice, as we have already seen that merely law-abiding criterion does not bring justice. Justice cannot be enforced, or even social justice cannot be meted out in confirmity with certain values or ideals only. The minimum requirement of justice is that each one must get what he deserves. Again what he deserves cannot be decided by any means other than the desert of the individual. We consider someone's demand to be just only when we see that the demand is proportionate to his worth, and not to any other consideration. The *karma* doctrine contends that rewards and punishments for actions are neither awarded nor inflicted upon. They are earned by the individual. In this sense, the doctrine avoids all sorts of conflicting considerations. This, according to some advocates of the doctrine,

---

6. N.M.L. Nathan, *The Concept of Justice*, Macmillan, 1971, p. 9.

constitutes the foundation of morality.[7] No doubt, the karmic idea of 'due corresponding to worth' is the foundation of the moral life, but that does not mean that the idea of social justice is to depend on any moral principle. The problem here might be to ensure the worth of the individual. Again, the pertinent question is, whether the 'worth' we are talking of is the moral worth of the individual? The 'worth' of the individual, so far as social justice is concerned, is the efficiency of the individual or the merit of the individual which is to be taken into account in dispensing social justice. 'Worth', 'efficiency', 'merit', etc., of an individual ultimately fall back upon the karmic consideration. That, however, does not mean that distribution of social justice is bound to relapse to past activities (*saṁskāras*). The real implication of the doctrine is its progressive aspect, rather than its regressive aspect. The progressive aspect consists in its emphasis on self-effort (*prayatna*). In other words, *karmavāda* appropriates the prosperity or suffering of an agent of action to the nature and character of his self-effort. This is a sort of 'effort-deterministic system' which in no way contravenes the idea of meeting the minimum needs of the individual. That is exactly the reason why there is no scope for any racial or other discrimination in the conceptual framework of the doctrine. Rather in making the individual responsible for his own actions, *karmavāda* leaves scope for individual growth to earn special privileges available in the society. Individual effort along with the sense of responsibility being central to the *karma* doctrine, it is free from the onslaughts of the critics. It is again significant to note that the social model propounded in the *Bhagavad Gītā*, as mentioned earlier, stands on the solid foundation of karmic idea of *effortism* and individual responsibility.

The *Bhagavad Gītā*, which recommends the division of human community to four castes depending on quality and

7. N.C. Padhi, *Karma and Freedom*, Upagupta Publications, Cuttack, 1986, p.181.

action, is also corroborative of the karmic model. It is clearly evident that the social model offered by the *Gītā* does not rest on the rigid classification of human beings. Rather, the model is dynamic insofar as it provides enough scope for the development of the worth or efficiency of the individual. With this social structure there is scope for a śūdra to acquire the qualities of a brāhmaṇa. On the other hand, the brāhmaṇa can be reverted to a śūdra for his evil deeds. The idea of social justice itself is not rigid one as it varies from society to society and time to time. However, one ideal model cannot be proposed as no social model is sacrosanct or absolute. The minimum requirement is that while dispensing justice to the individual members, the worth of the individual, determined by quality and action, is to be taken into account. It is significant that *karma* doctrine, in its prospective or positive aspect constitutes the foundation of the social model offered by the *Gītā*. The progressive aspect of the doctrine lends enough scope to the individual to develop his worth without discrimination of any sort. The retrospective aspect of the doctrine which accounts for the present in terms of his past deeds, is only a warning for refraining from being indulged in evil deeds, which might ultimately debar the individual from enjoying privileges due to him. However, this version of the doctrine should not be misconstrued as recommending certain moral principles nor should the doctrine be viewed as a constraint on the path of the distribution of equal (not exactly identical) opportunity to the members of the community. It should not, however, be thought that a double standard for social justice, is proposed here. What is meant is that though it is the duty of the society to provide minimum equal opportunity to the individual members with a view to allowing every individual to grow up to the social expectations, it is the social responsibility on the part of each and every member to develop his worth through self-effort in order to enjoy the privileges that is due to him. To my mind it is the quintessence of social justice. Negligence of this aspect might lead to social chaos and degeneration of the collective psyche.

8

Retribution and Criminal Justice
Some Conceptual Problems

Mahasweta Chaudhury

SOCIAL justice is based on the concept of social balance between rights and duties. When other people are affected by our action we face the question whether the action would be *just* to them. In other words, is our action (say smoking in a public place) just or it violates the right (of having clean air) of others? The question of maintaining the balance between rights and duties become crucial when someone's rights are invaded. The exercise of my freedom should be limited by the right of others. If I violate someone's rights I *deserve* to be punished — no matter if the punishment does me any good or not. One earns a punishment (as a student earns a grade in her examination) for one's wrong-doing. It is the duty of a society to provide because it has taken a stand on behalf of certain rights and cannot forsake them. Kant has championed this notion of punishment as retribution or price for the wrong-doer to pay. He defines justice as 'the aggregate of those conditions under which the will of one person can be conjoined with the will of another in accordance with a universal law'. "If legal justice perishes", says Kant, "then it is no longer worthwhile for men to remain on this earth."[1] Just as

1. Kant, *The Metaphysical Elements of Justice*, tr. by John Ladd, pp. 100, 102.

moral laws and moral rights are universal and hold irrespective of its utilitarian consequences so too is the propriety of punishment. Although Kant recognised that legal statutes may not always be of moral worth, he believed nevertheless that we owe them obedience while trying to change them. There is a moral imperative to punish wrongdoing, just as there is moral imperative not to tell lies. While we cannot create a perfect world consisting of virtue and happiness going together, we should deprive the evil-doers of happiness, they must not be allowed to benefit from their deeds, because that would be unfair to the innocent.

Laws and penal systems are means that a civil society has chosen to vindicate its commitment to the basic rights of individuals. Criminal justice consists of making the offender pay the appropriate price. Examples for Kant are death for murderers and castrations for rapists.

The above is known as the retributive account of punishment which justifies punishment as a price for infringing upon someone's rights in society. Indeed it sounds closer to the notion of justice as a restoration of balance in society than any other account. Punishment here is meant for the *individual* himself not for educating *others* by treating him as a means. There is also a third account that punishment is meant not for others but to educate/reform the wrong-doer himself. The retributive theory although apparently close to the concept of justice as a balance between rights and duties unfortunately plunges into many conceptual problems contrary to the dictates of criminal justice.

Any theory of punishment needs to reconcile two of our opposite intuitions; namely:

(i) deliberate and intentional infliction of injury is wrong.

(ii) a wrong-doer deserves punishment.

To reconcile these two contrary intuitions is specially difficult for retributive theory which claims to consider the guilty not as a means but as an end in itself. It needs therefore a justification for inflicting suffering on the guilty, which otherwise we regard as a wrong action. Why again does the guilty deserve punishment? Does it bring any good to him or does he owe it just as such? There are several philosophical questions related to the issue which have no easy answers.

In a recent paper Richard Burgh[2] has argued that even the strongest arguments in favour of retribution fail to give a justification based on principle of justice. He concludes from that: We should look for an alternative theory upon which our concept of the criminal law can be based. I shall examine Burgh's analysis with which I agree to a great extent and clarify some further points in the issue of retribution which is not considered by the existing literature. My analysis leads to reject retribution as it fails to give a satisfactory account of punishment without violating the principle of justice (like Burgh). My own conjecture is that retribution does not serve the purpose of treating the guilty as an individual by conferring exactly proportionate 'just'(?) punishment. Therefore it amounts to no more than retaliation or revenge which surely cannot be the aim of any theory of justice (unlike Burgh). The other alternative is to opt for the utilitarian view of punishment which (is even worse) treats the guilty as a means to fulfil social cause. I also disagree with the middle line of justification between these two that punishment can be justified for the good effect on the guilty himself. There is no deterministic law of criminal behaviour to establish that.[3] What we have are only statistical laws which cannot settle the issue decisively.

Richard Burgh's line of argument attemps to undercut the

---

2. Richard Burgh, "Do the Guilty Deserve Punishment?" *The Journal of Philosophy*, April, 1982.
3. See A. Grunbaum, "Freewill and Laws of Human Behaviour", *American Philosophical Quarterly*, October 1971, II, Sec. A & B.

neo-Kantian type of arguments revived by Hart, Rawls, Morris and Murphy. The fundamental doctrine of retributive theory is that the guilty deserves punishment because he received undue benefit by his offense; therefore he has to pay the just price only through punishment. The balance of justice can only be restored in this way. In other words, justice is the equilibrium of benefit and burden. Punishment takes away the unjust benefit the guilty has extracted through his offense. So the equitable distribution of benefit and burden which existed prior to the offense can be restored by the imposition of punishment.

There is a tacit assumption underlying in this kind of argument for punishing an offender — that he is the one who originally disturbs the equilibrium of moral *status quo*: therefore he deserves punishment. The 'prior to the offense' state of affairs is not considered here at all, but that may be relevant to the context. For example, the character of the victim or his action may have extracted some unfair benefit, which the present offender tried to counter-balance by committing an offense which is injurious to the victim. A common tactic used by Agatha Christie in her crime novels was to find out the victim's history and personal character which helped finding out the guilty. In those cases 'restoring the balance' picture would not hold good, and the offender, for example, the murderer of a blackmailer would not be any less guilty. He would indeed be guilty but for a different reason, (not for upsetting the balance of justice) namely taking law into his own hand, (in which he does not have any right whatsoever to punish that person) instead of referring it to the office of justice.

A second assumption here is about the nature of law. Laws are to be obeyed, it is assumed, because otherwise the equilibrium of benefit and burden will be destroyed. This assumption is unwarranted involving several difficulties. Firstly, what if laws are not moral? In other words, it is not inconceivable that there may be laws which are not just and therefore some people may feel that they are better be violated. Rebels against a military or totalitarian regime violate existing laws. But they may have a rationale which is more acceptable than the absurd assumption that the rebels should be punished because they disturbed the equilibrium. Or, if we take the cases of non-violent civil disobedience of Thoreau or Gandhi who were ready to face the punishment for disobeying an unjust law — the absurdity of the assumption is even clearer. They have overriding reasons to convince that the 'prior to offense' state of affairs was unjust, and unbalanced. Therefore, it sounds ludicrous that punishment of the people participating in civil-disobedience is justified to bring back lost equilibrium of burden. Surely these law-breakings do not extract any 'unjust benefit' which should be restored by punishment. On the contrary they tried to restore the tilted balance of social justice by undergoing all the accompanying hardships of law-breaking. So compared to them, other people who did not participate in the law-breaking cannot be particularly described as carrying the burden of abiding by the law.

Secondly, if certain laws are repeatedly violated, then they may well be reconsidered as to their moral worth. For example, the notorious salt-tax imposed on Indian people for British salt or the levy imposed on tea in America which led to the revolution are extreme cases which provoke violation for their intrinsic unfairness. Kuhn describes in his celebrated scheme of 'paradigm change', when an existing theory is repeatedly refuted, then it is time for it to go and be replaced by a 'revolution'. The repeated violation of those social laws cannot be considered as an attempt to extract unfair benefit and therefore be encountered with punishment as a just retribution. The existing literature on retribution has not considered this point of the status of juridical law as not unviolable.

Before probing into the further assumptions of the retributive theory, an exposition of the arguments will be helpful.

The general structure of the theory is based on the thesis

that the offender deserves punishment because justice demands so.[4] "In committing an offense the offender forfeits his right not to be made to suffer."[5] Therefore the principle of distribution can be considered as a necessary condition of punishment.

Whether the principle of distribution is a necessary or sufficient condition, Burgh rightly indicates some other principles for retribution which I shall call (1) reciprocity condition and (2) proportionality condition. (1) Punishment should be restricted only to the deserving (the guilty). That means it is a necessary condition for all punishment that it should be inflicted only to those who have unbalanced the equitable distribution of justice by taking an undue benefit through their wrong-doing. Otherwise it will not be compatible with the principle of justice. But this condition is already not a sufficient condition, because it is not only necessary that the guilty be punished, but also that he is justly punished in the fair degree. So we need (2) the further condition that the guilty be punished only in proportion with the degree of his offense, not more, not less. The underlying notion is that the guilty does not deserve punishment in an unnecessary degree but only in a degree proportional to the 'gravity of the offense he committed'. The reason behind it again is compatibility with the principle of justice. Any amount of punishment in excess to the degree of offense is tantamount to be inflicting injury to an innocent person and therefore unjust.

Before examining these conditions let us first ask the question why at all the offender deserves punishment, if infliction of suffering on others is regarded as wrong? A standard retributive answer is that having rights generally entails having duties to honour the same rights in others. So, if these duties are not fulfilled (for example by committing the wrong) then the rights

---

4. See Hart, "Prolegomena to the Problem of Punishment", in *Punishment and Responsibility*, New York, Oxford, 1968.

5. See Burgh, "Do the Guilty deserve punishment?".

cease to exist. Burgh has competently argued against this dubious reason by citing cases where a person may violate another person's right (e.g., of free speech) but that does not mean he loses his right (to free speech). So violation of right does not constitute forfeiture of rights, it cannot serve as a sufficient basis for punishment. Besides this, there is an assumption here that it is possible to counterbalance a set of duties with a set of equivalent rights. But this is not so well-defined. The punishment for cheating should, according to this argument, be that the guilty be cheated himself, which is absurd and not morally acceptable to anyone. And it is not clear what set of rights would be equivalent to the offense. There is always a chance of either overdetermination or underdetermination which definitely is contrary to the notion of justice. No one including the retributivists even would welcome the notion of either unjustly overpunishing the guilty or the other alternative of punishment being not sufficient for the gravity of the offense committed. Moreover there are certain natural rights which are not always matched with a set of duty. It is not clear what kind of duty is not fulfilled by a starving man stealing food or money to buy food. Or, it is not justifiable that an inmate of burning house should not be saved because he did not save other inmates of the house risking his life.

There is another argument held by Hart and others based on the notion of voluntary choice in alternatives open to the guilty by fair distribution. That means the culpable guilty is aware of the option open to choose and the price he has to pay for each. . . . "The pains of punishment will for each individual represent the price of some satisfaction obtained from breach of law."[6] Retributivists like Hart think that "The price is justly extracted . . . because within this framework the individual is given a fair opportunity to choose between keeping the law required for

6. Hart, "Legal Responsibility and Excuses", in *Punishment and Responsibility*, *op. cit.*, pp. 44-7.

society's protection or paying the penalty by being punished."[7] The tone of this analysis implies vindication of retributive punishment in terms of forfeiture of the wrong-doer's right not to be made to suffer. Burgh has belaboured to show that even if Hart is correct, the argument does not establish that giving a fair opportunity to choose does necessarily justify infliction of pain to anyone who does not choose the alternative that guarantees one not to suffer. It is indeed a better situation than no opportunities at all. But what if the other alternative is unacceptable for moral or other grounds? For example, if a man is asked either to tell a lie (or kill a person or do some other wrong) for the sustenance of an existing government or suffer a torture, he is indeed given 'a fair opportunity to choose' — but a conscientious rebel or a patriotic leader may have overriding moral ground not to choose to obey that command. Surely punishment in these cases cannot be justified as 'paying the penalty' for society's protection: The consequence of considering Gandhi's, or any other rebellious leader's punishment for civil obedience to be the just price for the 'satisfaction obtained from breach of law' — would not be acceptable to anyone including the retributivists. Secondly, when we say 'fair opportunity to choose', it refers to an existing structure of law and its violation. Indeed there is a fair chance between options. The person is free either to obey the law or face the penalty, but he is nevertheless not free to choose the law within a certain framework. The existing law may be unfair on moral basis and therefore one may have superior reasons for breaking than obeying it. It is not inconceivable that there may be (and contingently it is true as well) social laws which are unjust. People are not free to choose the laws and in the above cases, they may regard obedience to these laws as morally wrong and breaking it as right. The retributivists cannot give a rational account for punishment in similar cases of civil disobedience in its different forms like non-

7. Hart, "Prolegomena", pp. 22-3.

payment of tax, strike, boycott, sit-in, etc. Only because a person is given a fair chance either to give away the name or whereabouts of an anti-establishment rebel friend and accept a prize or otherwise face a penalty — does not justify his beating only because he knew the penalty for doing so. The positive aspect of deriving a benefit contrasted to the penalty cannot describe the punishment to be at the dictate of justice.

Some other line of argument in this connection may be phrased as follows: that it would have been rational for the offender to have chosen such laws for himself which are the most preferable ones in a scale of hierarchy. So it is not necessary that he in fact should be given the opportunity to choose the law. Burgh mentions Rawls describing this kind of possible antecedent position of choice as 'original position'. The guiding principle here is known as 'rationality principle' in social sciences. It claims that a rational person (like the culpable offender) acts in such a way as to maximise the most desirable preference and minimise the least desirable preference. This principle is argued by many as false in social sciences.[8] It can be shown at least not to operate in case of moral choice. To quote Burgh

> An example might be the rapist. Could one show that it would be rational, in the original position, for him to choose laws prohibiting rape? Certainly not, because given his attitude toward women, it is quite possible that, in the original position, it would be rational for him *not* to choose such laws.[9]

This kind of problem does not let one to argue for forfeiture of right of the guilty to be made not to suffer on the basis of his 'rational' choice.

---

8. Karl Popper is one of them.
9. Burgh, "Do the Guilty Deserve Punishment", *Journal of Philosophy,* April 1982, pp. 201-2.

So far whatever is discussed is an attempt to show that the reciprocity condition cannot be satisfactorily fulfilled. This is (as I have said following Burgh's line of argument) the necessary condition of retribution. The result is tantamount to say that it is problematic to claim that all cases of punishment can be justified on the basis of just extraction of price in response to wrong-doing: So the picture of justice being an equilibrium between benefit and burden or duty and right does not necessarily capture all cases of punishment being rightly deserved by the offender.

Let us next see the more complex situation arising from the sufficient condition of punishment namely the proportionality condition. As we have seen earlier, retribution demands not only that the guilty deserves punishment but also that he deserves it only in proportion with the gravity of his misdeed. Otherwise punishment will not be in compatibility with the principle of justice. The main line of argument in favour of this claim rests on the notion of wrong being an unfair advantage of benefit that the wrong-doer has acquired in contrast to others who are carrying the burden of self-restraint by not committing the crime. Punishment, on this account, takes away the benefit by imposing a burden. In this way the original state of affairs of equitable distribution of benefit and burden is restored. There are several assumptions underlying this account which I shall like to clarify and show that these difficulties eventually lead to the refutation of the retributivist thesis. Before going into that discussion let us see what this notion of unfair benefit may mean.

Burgh classifies the 'possible candidates' for benefits as (1) the ill-gotten gain; (2) not bearing the burden of self-restraint; (3) the satisfaction from committing the crime; and (4) the sphere of non-interference which results from general obedience to the particular law violated (e.g., each person benefits from property laws, so far as his own property is concerned). It is clear that the fourth benefit the offender receives before he violates the law whereas the first three benefits he receives by committing the crime. We can discuss the theory of punishment held by Herbert Morris and Jeffrey Murphy in this connection.[10] The strength of Morris's analysis lies in the claim that it can generate a scale of punishment according to the degree of gravity of the crime. Thus retribution can be shown on his account, to be compatible with the principle of justice. Crimes, Morris claims, can be ranked in terms of their seriousness. The idea is this: each law prohibits some kind of crime and thus creates a sphere of non-interference: These spheres of non-interference can be graded according to value. For example, the sphere defined by homicide laws are graded higher in the hierarchy of value than laws defined by traffic laws. Crimes violating a law in a sphere of higher value would be regarded as of more gravity. Murder is defined in terms of life, therefore it is more serious crime than shoplifting, which is defined in terms of property. Punishment also can be justified accordingly in terms of the value of the benefit the guilty removes. Thus the punishment for murder should be much more severe than punishment for shop-lifting. The degree of punishment therefore is compatible with the principle of justice because, Morris claims, that on this account we cannot only explain why the offender deserves the punishment but also make punishment fulfil the (sufficient condition) proportionality condition, which means the guilty deserves punishment only in the right degree in conformity with the gravity of his crime.

Jeffrey Murphy describes the benefit in terms of the renunciation of the burden of self-restraint. Burgh[11] has criticised this account sufficiently, yet I would like to add a few points from

---

10. H. Morris, "Persons and Punishment", *Monist*, LII, 4 (Oct. 1968), and J. Murphy, *Retribution, Justice and Therapy*, Boston, Reidel, 1979.

11. Burgh, "Do the Guilty Deserve Punishment", *op. cit.,* pp. 207-8.

a different perspective. In very Kantian tone Murphy claims that nobody should profit from his wrong-doing. Natural justice prohibits that. But the criminal does profit by not carrying the burden of self-restraint. Therefore he deserves punishment for restoration of the original balance between benefit and burden. The argument can be expressed as follow:

> Nobody should profit from wrong-doing
> Whoever profits from worng-doing deserves punishment
> The criminal profits from wrong-doing
> The criminal deserves punishment.

Now, even if we grant Murphy his analysis — the best it can explain is to give a justification of punishment on the basis of equitable distribution of benefit and burden. This analysis or the previous one given by Morris cannot give any criterion for deciding the degree of gravity of different crimes — namely whether robbery is more or less serious than rape. The fact remains then that we cannot escape the possibility of punishing the guilty by an arbitrary standard. It cannot explain the degree of punishment deserved. This consequence is definitely against the principle of justice. Of course, this kind of analysis can preserve the proportionality condition by requiring that less grave offences should be matched with less severe punishment and more grave ones with more severe punishements and so on. But the theory however does not say how this hierarchy of offences and the parallel scale of severity of punishment be generated from it. Burgh has examined and criticised this view. I propose to clarify a few assumptions behind it.

I. The reciprocity condition assumes that the offender has upset the equitable distribution of benefit and burden by violating the law and therefore he deserves punishment. This requirement needs moral laws to be consistent with all juridical laws. What if juridical laws are not moral? In other words, it is not inconceivable that there may be laws which are not just and therefore some people may think that they are better be violated. For example, segregation laws or some unfair tax-imposition. Rebels against a military or totalitarian regime violate existing law (A paradigm example of an absurd unacceptable law is the present law of Khomini that women should cover their head); but they may have a rationale which is more acceptable than the assumption that all rebels should be punished because they disturbed the equilibrium. Kant of course tries to vindicate all legal constitutions even if they are made by a despotic government.[12] "Public law laden with injustice must be allowed to stand, either until everything is of itself ripe for complete reform or until this maturity has been brought about by peaceable means; for a legal constitution, even though it be right to only a low degree, is better than none at all. . . ." Again he maintains about rebelling against a tyrant that "it is in the highest degree illegitimate for the subjects to seek their rights in this way. If they fail in the struggle and are then subjected to severe punishment, they cannot complain about injustice anymore than the tyrant could if they had succeeded."[13] It is surprising to find such emphasis on the superiority of law in Kant who upholds the notion of natural right of the individual to be supreme. He speaks of moral law to be internal and higher and juridical law to be external sanction, but nevertheless justifies punishment for any law-breaking, no matter whether these are on moral ground or not.

II. As I mentioned earlier, if certain laws are repeatedly violated, then instead of imposing punishment, they may well be reconsidered as to their moral worth. For example, if there is a law (I refer again to the notorious

12. Kant, *Perpetual Peace*, Appendix I, fn. 1.
13. *Op. cit.*, Appendix II.

Salt-tax imposed by the British Government on the Indian people) which is violated by the majority — then the punishment as retribution becomes trivial and ludicrous. The country-wide law-breakers of the salt-movement overfilled the jails in such an absurd extent, that the law lost its importance. The repeated violation of a juridical law cannot be maintained as an attempt to extract unfair benefit and therefore be encountered with punishment as a just retribution. On the contrary, the law in question needs to be revoked. Any retributive theory has the burden to account for such cases.

III. Another important notion in the retribution theory is that of benefit (profit) and burden. In the fourfold schema benefit may be regarded firstly as an (1) 'ill-gotten gain' of the guilty as a point of advantage over the other members of the community. This interpretation is not adequate. The term 'benefit' or 'profit' is misleading and difficult to judge due to the lack of decisive criterion. The actual circumstance of a crime may be very complicated for various factors to decide whether the guilty gains anything by it, many a times it is conceivable that the offence committed leads to disadvantage for the guilty and he gains nothing by it but shame, mistrust and dishonour, financial loss including a dismissal from the job. Many offences look so unprofitable compared to the sufferings and risks the offenders take that the acts look irrational. So we need other criterion than 'gain' or 'profit' to characterise an offense. Does that advantage (2) lie in not bearing the burden of self-restraint? The assumption here is that the offender does not bear the burden of self-restraint whereas other people are all carrying that burden. Why should not committing a crime be a burden to carry; unless we presume everybody as potential criminals? It may very well be natural disposition of many people not to commit a crime. This is most probably true. So it is quite natural for them not to commit a crime. In that case they do not need to carry any burden of self-restraint to do so. On the other hand, committing a crime may lead to mental-physical tension for the guilty, often amounting to unbearable condition which can be described as a state of burden. So, instead of not bearing the burden, he may, on the contrary, start bearing a state of burden by committing the very act of crime. (3) The 'satisfaction' feature can be also developed from this. The offender's motive may have been to find a kind of satisfaction from the offence, but that may not necessarily follow from the actual performance of it. Instead of feeling satisfaction, he may feel remorse, self-hatred, etc., or nothing at all. The latter is possible in case of hired or professional criminals, whereas any crime impulsively performed for emotional reasons may give rise to the other extreme of violent emotional disturbance which is very far from 'satisfaction'. If punishment is the fair price extracted for the wrong-doer — there is no distinction made between the two different kinds of offenders performing the same kind of crime. What I want to emphasise is that only the nature of the wrong and not the nature of the guilty enters the discussion of the retributivists. But the notion of gain, profit, burden, satisfaction involve a reference to the subject, without that, the analysis is inadequate. Moreover, the benefit-burden mechanism of retributive theory assumes that all individuals have the same potentiality of extracting 'benefit' or 'profit' out of the offence for carrying the burden of self-restraint for not committing the crime. But different individuals may benefit differently by the same act of offence. To some, as I said earlier, it may be mechanical, e.g., hired professional criminals, to some it may give an absurd ecstatic feeling for doing something they think 'right' for

> some crazy reason. There may be some others who may not have 'benefited' at all — carrying the evergnawing burden of guilt and misery to such a great extent after the offence that the benefit-burden schema works just inversely for them. Dostoyevsky's Raskalnikov is a paradigm example. To be compatible with the principle of justice, the notion of retribution as a price for the crime is thus not enough if we only take the crime into consideration without reference to the criminal and the 'prior to offence' state of affairs.

Another line of approach (as maintained by Morris and Murphy) assumes that it is possible to compare 'rights' and 'duties' of one both qualitatively and quantitatively. Justice demands that an offender should repay his debt which he owes by his offence exactly in proportion by the punishment he deserves. It would have been a nice scheme, if it is possible to determine the degree in which the original balance has been destroyed. But unfortunately this is not an easy task and it may not be possible at all to give a satisfactory criterion for each case. Murder or robbery may be more straightforward cases (not so easy if they involve complex psychological or ideological factors like black-mailing, provocation or robbery for a benevolent motive), where the damage or loss can be determined in more or less precise ways. But cheating or forgery, even threat or breach of trust are offences which may cause complicated and long-drawn repercussions on individual victims. It is difficult in these cases to determine the exact proportion in which the punishment is justified to 'extract its just price'. There is always a chance either to underpunish in which case it is not just retribution, or overpunish, in which case it leads to the worse situation of inflicting injury on an innocent person (so far the punishment is in excess to the original wrong he has done).

Another way of interpreting the benefit-burden is in terms of the strength of the inclination to commit a crime. "The stronger the inclination, the greater the burden one undertakes in obeying the law." "That means the greater the inclination one has for committing a crime, the greater is the advantage to be achieved by committing that crime. Hence it deserves more severe punishment than a crime for which one has less strong inclination. Burgh has shown very competently that according to this analysis tax-evasion should be more severely punished than murder because most of us have stronger inclination to evade tax than committing a murder. No sensible persons, not even the retributivists, are ready to accept such absurd and counter-intuitive consequences. So this interpretation also fails to give a satisfactory account of retribution.

We thus face a problematic situation in any attempt to account for a justification of punishment as retribution. Reciprocity as such is not a sufficient condition to be compatible with the principle of justice, because we surely do not want the guilty to be punished without reference to the degree of gravity of his offence. If we include the condition of proportionality for providing an account of punishment only in conformity with the seriousness of the wrong done—we face even greater a difficulty. There is neither a further criterion for comparing different kinds of crimes for their gravity nor is it possible to have a general rule for judging different kinds of crimes and penalty in different circumstances. Not only is it difficult to judge the various kinds of crimes (for example, questions like why murder is a graver offence than robbery, or if murder is worse than rape, are not easily settled), but the effects of punishment on different wrong-doers also are difficult to determine. There is always a chance of overdoing or underdoing it. The same physical infliction of punishment may have different effects on different people and also on the same person on different occasions. One night's jail or very slight physical assault may shatter someone's personality to a damaging degree whereas severe physical torture may not be of any effect to a seasoned criminal. So the possibility of depriving the guilty of the appropriate degree of benefit which he extracted by wrong-doing is thereby excluded. Punishment may be either excessive or meaningless in these cases, and thus violate the demand of justice. Other kinds of punishments like imposition of fine or depriving the guilty of some right or privilege (like taking away some license or permit) may have different effects on different people. More public exposure to court or police custody may damage the self-respect of a certain person to severe humiliation whereas some cool premeditated crime may be anticipated by the criminal for such contingency and in spite of the punishment, thought of as paying for some other consideration. So, punishment would be trivial in the case where, for example, a robber knew he would get 10 years if he is caught and does not mind taking the risk because compared to the punishment, the 'benefit' to him is overwhelming. Different cases of penalty therefore should be examined differently; there is no general rule to judge them all by the same standard. The result leaves us with no way to justify punishment specially by the retributive theory.

Recently a revival of retribution from slightly different standpoint is found in Nozick.[14] He claims that retribution can best be understood as different from revenge. The former is (1) public, (2) for a wrong done, (3) not personal, (4) not related to emotions except from satisfaction of justice being done, whereas retaliation is (1) private, (2) for an injury, (3) personal and may not be for any wrong done, (4) has an emotional overtone. He further maintains that the guilty, by virtue of his wrong-doing become disconnected from the correct value of life. Punishment reconnects him with the correct value. So retribution is not just retaliation but it has a positive message to the guilty by showing how far he has 'flouted the correct value'. Punishment, he thinks, can be justified as a message or attempt of communication

---

14. Nozick, *Philosophical Explanations*, Harvard University Press, 1981, in the chapter on value, section III, Retributive Punishment.

with the guilty. So, this theory is treating the guilty as an end in itself, not a means to teach others. The aim of punishment is not just to deter him for future crime, but rather to rehabilitate his own values. It does explain further why the conscientious objector or the civil resister does not need any punishment, because the people who disobey laws in these ways do not 'flout the correct value' therefore do not need any message of reconnection with correct value.

Nozick's version of retribution claims to be a compensation for the victims. It is "appropriate to let the penalty be the maximum of the amount of disutility the victim reasonably could have been expected to undergo, and the amount of disutility the perpetrator would (reasonably be expected to?) undergo from the same act". The important role punishment plays is communicative of a message to the offender. The criminal is intended to realise that he is intended to realise why he is punished. There are difficulties in the retributive matching. First of all, it is not always possible to match every heinous act. It is not possible beforehand to know all the possible ways of brutality or meanness of a criminal act. How to achieve an appropriate matching means of conveying the message to the guilty that 'you have done exactly this!' No civilised jurisprudence can cope with all the possible mean ways of committing crimes. We do not have any way exactly to know what kind of punishment is the right price for a particular act. Punishment therefore is bound to be arbitrary. Moreover, imposing a 'fine' for a certain kind of crime, or depriving the guilty of a certain privilege amounts to putting a price tag for a certain crime which may vary in kinds and details from one case to another.

It is assumed here that if an act to wrong, the most effective way to show that is to do exactly the 'same' thing to the wrong-doer or the very similar one. Surely we cannot do exactly the 'same' thing to the offender (or even similar). Or if the robber returns the goods, is he considered any less guilty in that case?

The robber cannot be robbed or the rapist raped, even if punishment is meant for their moral improvement. To kill the murderer for connecting him to correct values is absurd, but that kind of conclusion follows from Nozick's theory. Secondly, even if it is possible to do the same thing to the guilty to make him realise his lost value, how does it show him that he is wrong? The underlying assumption is that the punished person will realise his fault when similarly wrong act is done to him. This assumption is unwarranted and based on another assumption, namely, that the guilty is *not* aware (or correct value) of what he is doing; and only through punishment he can be *made* aware of the gravity of his deed. But the condition of being responsible[15] excludes the possibility that the wrong-doer is not aware (the awareness may vary in degree of course) of what he is doing and the possible bad consequences of his act. "Punishment does not wipe out the wrong," Nozick says, "the past is not changed, but the disconnection with value is repaired." It breaks the guilty's 'anti-linkage' with correct value by its restitution. But at the same time he says that some people like Hitler deserve to die in punishment for their action. According to Nozick, retribution is consistent with determinism. So even if a neurophysiologist would find something in Hitler's brain-mechanism to say that he was causally determined to do everything that he actually did, Nozick can nevertheless make him responsible for what he did because Hitler flouted the correct value (even if caused to do so). So far, so good. But if Hitler (or some other criminal for that matter) is caused to perform heinous crimes, how can any punishment (however severe it is) be enough to reconnect him to correct value? If he is 'caused' to do that, punishment would not be of any help in restitution of value. Secondly, crimes of the type Hitler had committed cannot be matched with any conceivable kind of punishment adequate enough to convey the message of

---

15. Nozick's $P = r \times H$ formula explains punishment is a function of degree of responsibility and the magnitude of the crime.

repairing correct values from which he is disconnected. And as I said before, death sentence cannot convey anything for the wrong-doer's realisation and reconnection of values. As such, punishment is no use there. So, however intuitively clear it may be, it is not so obvious that Hitler deserved to die (even if we ignore the possible deterministic explanation of his behaviour) — as Nozick claims, at least not from his theory of retribution.

I shall briefly sum up my observations about Nozick's views of retributive punishment as follows:

1. The difference between revenge and retaliation is not rigid, the common feature between the two is more fundamental than the seeming differences. A penalty is inflicted in both cases for a reason (a wrong or an injury) with the desire that the other person know why this is done to him, and know that he is intended to know.

2. Punishment as reconnection of correct values has unwarranted assumptions like (i) The guilty was not aware of the 'correct value' *before* the wrong-doing, or (ii) The guilty becomes aware of 'correct value' *after* the wrong-doing. (i) and (ii) are not necessarily true. As I said before, (i) is excluded by his equation $P = r \times H$. (ii) is linked with (i); if a person is responsible, he is aware of what he is doing, so the question of his being aware of it after punishment does not arise. Sometimes punishment may on the contrary damage the sense of value and self-respect of a person. There is no golden rule about it. For some seasoned criminal, crime may be mechanical, punishment may not mean anything to them.

3. Everybody belongs to the community of some 'correct value'. That means it ignores the possibility of difference of correct value for different cultural and sociological factors.

4. Punishment is the only effective mode of communicating with the offender. Why other modes of measures would not do? Nozick's answer is that a saintly figure or an inspiring example of right would not be enough because by those the offender is not being responsive to the specific wrongness. I do not see why the 'specific wrong' has to be emphasised for regaining correct values. Without referring to a 'specific wrong', one can be taught about the general way of correct value, but that may sound more like reforming or educating the offender (less like retribution) which is contrary to Nozick's non-teleological retributive theory.

The upshot of all these discussions about possible defenses of retribution is to show that they fail to give a satisfactory account of punishment in compatibility with the principle of criminal justice. The absence of a philosophical justification may lead one either to look for an alternative theory of punishment, or to say that punishment as retribution cannot do anything to the offender but retaliation in response to his wrong act. If punishment amounts to nothing but a form of retaliation, I think we should rather give up the institution of punishment than stick to a principle contrary to the dictate of justice.

9

Justice-based Morality and the Gender Question

Shefali Moitra

JUSTICE-based morality is one of the most prevalant views upheld by recent and contemporary analytical philosophy. Great names like Kant and Rawls are associated with this tradition. Justice-based morality is also referred to as right-based morality; it could just as well be called principle-based morality. Justice, rights, principles, equality, reciprocity are presupposed as values in this mode of morality. These values could very well be the presuppositions of any other system of morality. What would differentiate one moral system from the other would be the way these values are interpreted. When we are talking of justice-based morality we are talking of a substantive theory of justice and not merely of its procedural aspect.

We shall begin by stating some of the salient features of Rawls' theory of justice as expounded in his article 'Justice as Fairness' and in his book *A Theory of Justice*. Rawls speaks from within the Western individualist tradition — where every man is a self-seeking atom who may or may not have altruistic tendencies as well. All relations between individuals are seen as either heirarchical or contractual. The individual self is identified as totally separate and distinct from the other and not as a phenomenal centre that defines itself in relation to others. As a result we have either self or other. That is to say that the individual-self is not seen as a relational self whose identity is a product of interaction with others.

Justice-based morality professes to be gender neutral in relation to self-identity. It is held that women do not differ from men in their capability of choosing rational goals in their self-interest and also in their choice of reasonable means for the achievement by those goals. Furguson explains the position of justice-based morality *vis-a-vis* women in the following way,

> . . . if men and women make different choices as to how to develop what economists call 'human capital', that is, their skill and abilities, including their formal education and job training, this is due not to innate gender prejudices and skills (e.g., that men are more competitive and aggressive and women more nurturant and submissive). Rather it is the realistic options that society and individual circumstances provide.[1]

What follows is that there is no gender bias in the justice-based theory itself. Any sexism associated with it is caused by the way it is implemented. The social options for men must be extended to woman so that they can compete on equal terms. In addition,

> Men will be persuaded to overcome their sexist attitudes when they see that women can do men's jobs as well as women's, and will stop treating women as inferious.
>
> (Furguson, p. 95).

Feminists working within the framework of justice-based morality try to identify areas of marginalisation and silence in respect of women and seek more and more opportunities to include women into the mainstream decision-making procedure.

---

1. Ann Furguson, "A Feminist Aspect Theory of Self" in *Women, Knowledge and Reality*, ed. by Ann Gerry and Marilyn Pearshall, Unwin Hyman, Boston, 1989, p. 95.

Here the emphasis is on inclusion into an already existing social structure without questioning whether the mainstream is already biased or not. They do not, for instance, wonder why and how a liberal state can permit a pornography industry that sexually objectifies women, thus legitimising male violence over women (Furguson, p. 93). Traditionally woman is taught to behave as the inversion of man or as his complementary. According to feminists supporting justice-based morality these role models need to be changed to bring about 'equality', 'justice' and 'reciprocity'. For this, where necessary, many feminists prescribe some amount or psychological counselling to make women more assertive decision-makers. In this way feminist philosophers see feminist theory as an extension of traditional philosophy. Problems relating to sex and gender conducive to formalisation are included by them in philosophy while those emotive, sentimental, existential problems which resist formalisation are bracketed and excluded as personal and private not fit for philosophical treatment. Abortion for instance, has been translated into a problem of personal identity and included into philosophy whereas the experience of mothering has till date been denied inclusion. Feminist philosophers working within the liberal tradition see their project as transient. In future, after all sex descrimination is identified and eliminated philosophy will be reinstated to its staus of glorious neutrality. Janet Radcliff Richards, who works within the justice-based morality framework, thinks that feminism is not about women but about social justice. She writes,

> feminism should not even regard itself as a movement to *support women who suffer from injustice*. . . . Feminism is not concerned with a group of people it wants to benefit, but with a type of injustice it wants to eliminate.[2]

---

2. Emphasis in original, *The Sceptical Feminist: A Philosophical Enquiry*, Penguin, Harmondsworth, 1982, pp. 17-18.

Richards uses John Rawls' theory to assess and correct feminism.

Perhaps the most distinguishing feature of John Rawls' theory of justice is that all human beings are seen as rational maximisers. We all want to assure that we achieve or procure an optional share or utilities/welfare/entitlements available. To achieve the goal of our choice we decide on certain principles rights and duties. The choice of principles may not always be on ethical grounds, they may as well be chosen for self-interested reasons. Once the principles are agreed upon exceptions cannot be made, not even if they go against our best interest in the future. Here the principle of morality is a commitment to principle without which one would not have the right to challenge anybody else. We can clearly see that Rawls' commitment to principle is a form of mitigated Kantianism. A mixture of principle and contract.

Many may not be aware of the heterogeneity of feminist theory. Amongst feminists there are conservatives, liberals and radicals. Rawls' theory of justice in particular and justice-based morality in general have been criticised severely by radical feminists. The criticisms have taken different forms and the alternatives suggested are also various. Some criticisms are off the mark, some are not very well argued. Nevertheless an alternative voice is definitely articulating itself which needs to be addressed with due importance.

There are three major areas where the justice-based theories are vulnerable to feminist criticism. It has been argued that the sex/gender divide which plays an important role in all practical decisions has been ignored, secondly, the idea that human beings are all by nature rational maximisers is incorrect, thirdly, justice-based morality is a *status quo* morality. These three criticisms seem legitimate and serious enough to threaten justice-based morality. That does not mean that justice, equality, reciprocity are being rejected as ethical values. The criticisms are two-fold; one regards the definition/explanation of these values and the other is the observation that either important values are being ignored or devolved resulting in the improverishment of morality. Unlike liberal feminists who see feminist theory as an extension of existing theory the radical feminists question existing philosophy. They do not keep philosophy uncriticised and see women as a problem; for them philosophy also needs critiquing.

We shall now take up each of the feminist objections separately. It has been alleged that the sex/gender difference has been ignored by justice-based morality. We know that the biological differences between male and female are known as sex differences. In addition to these natural differences there are certain cultural differences projected on male and female members of human society. Common among these constructions are the construal or masculine identity which is generally constructed as assertive, objective and rational. Side by side feminine identity is commonly constructed as emotive, intuitive and submissive. These culturally constructed identities are gender identities as contrasted with sex identities. Constructions vary from culture to culture. Therefore all forms of masculine gender identity are not identical nor are all forms of feminine gender identity. Moreover all forms of gender identity do not always sit well with each member who falls under the projections. Gender differences are as important as sex differences. Gender differences change but there will be no future when there will be no gender difference, since gender and culture go together. All we can work towards is a gender difference which is not oppressive and heirarchical. Whenever a rational choice is made by man or by woman the choice is deliberated through a masculine or feminine psyche. Feminist philosophers have tried to explain the genesis of the white male psyche which is also the culturally projected masculine psyche for all industrial and post-industrial societies.

The two principal authorities are J. Gardiner and Nancy

Chodrow. They have closely examined the orthodox, psychoanalytic account of the emergence of individual identity of an adult male and adult female. Orthodox thinkers like Freud, Jung and Lacan have modelled their explanation of the emergence of adult identity on adult man's gendered relation to woman. A male is generally nurtured by a female and 'taught' to gain his identity in a negative fashion by learning not to be a woman, that is not to emulate the female gender identity of mothering, care, sentimentality, adhocism and so on. The female, by contrast, establishes her gender identity by asserting her bonding with her mother. Gardiner and Chodrow thus trace the origins of gender identity to early childhood. They disagree with Freud that Phallus is a universal a historical power embodied in man and that there is a universal lack in every woman which is expressed in the way she expresses herself. They see this explanation of masculine/feminine identity as an outcome or a form of patriarchy. Patriarchy has many forms. Patriarchy positions man and woman in different superior and inferior social positions and grants different meanings and values to them. Patriarchy affects all aspects of social and interpersonal life.[3] Sandra Harding calls patriarchy an organic social variable which is not merely an effect of other primary causes.[4]

The way male-identity is constructed by Freud has important implications for all human relationships and not only heterosexual relations. Freud postulates an either/or investment of libidinal energy. The energy is directed either towards one self or it is directed towards an other resulting in an either/or binary opposition. The recognition of such an opposition is fundamental to the Western analytic tradition. Having separated the self

---

3. Elizabeth Gorez 'Philosophy' in *Feminist Knowledge: Critique and Construct*, ed. by Sneja Gunew, Routledge, London, p. 150.
4. Sandra Harding 'The Visibility of the Sex/Gender System' in *Discovering Reality*, ed. by Sandra Hàrding and Merrill B Hintikka, D. Reidel Publishing Company, Dorderecht, p. 312.

from the other the ethicists keep searching for methods of reconciling egoism with altruism.This was what Sidgwick's *Methods of Ethics* was all about. The same problem has recurred in Rawls. A recurrent tendency which results from this self/other opposition is to either ignore the other or to make the other into self. Sexism, recism, casteism are all results of such behaviour. A common response, which has mostly come from post-modernism, is that all binaries are heirarchy supporting. From here the post-modernist passess through a few quick steps to the conclusion that reason itself or more specifically two-valued logic is to be blamed for this. The consecutive steps taken by them, are, all binaries are heirarchical, e.g., black/white, male/female, good/bad, mind/body and binary thinking is the result of two-valued logic, therefore two-valued logic is heirarchy perpetuating. Though widely accepted and influential, this piece of post-modernist argument is pretty convoluted. What is at fault is neither two-valued logic nor reason, but reason coupled with power. Reason coupled with power is heirarchy producing.

The argument by which masculine values are projected as neutral, universal human values and females are required to conform to them are projected by power groups. By virtue of this power values projected as human values are rationality, objectivity, impartiality, assertiveness whereas values such as emotion, intuition, care sentiment are seen either as disvalues or as values which need to be purified by reason like rational sentiment, or prudential care, or rational emotion or so on. So values with which women feel comfortable with are systematically ignored or transformed not by reason *qua* reason but by a form of rationalisation to fit the man-human ideal. Certain features of masculinity are universalised as if they are representative of both sexes. On the other hand woman, femininity and their characteristics have been rendered invisible, incapable of representation and thus outside the philosphical or theoretical realm.

The radical feminist response to this process of deciding what is relevant to philosophy and what is not is that in the name of being rational and gender neutral what is actually happening in philosphy is that male values are upheld and the feminine is neutralised. Theoretically in a matriarchy the reverse could have just as well happened. Feminine values could have been universalised and masculine values neutralised. Historically, however, this never happened.

Carol Gilligan argues that women have a different style of moral reasoning than men. When presented with moral dilemmas women tend to find a contextual solution while men formulate abstract principles. Women, rather than men, play the role of mothering, therefore they are more inclined to care oriented ethics, concerned with life preservation, place keeping, social acceptability.[5] Two approaches to a fable will help bring out the type differences Gilligan is suggesting between masculine adjudication and feminine adjudication, arguably the difference is caused by a gender difference. The story goes that a porcupine needs shelter and enters a mole's hole. This inconveniences the mole considerably. Now the question is what would be a moral solution to the problem? Justice-based morality would sanction answers like:

(a) The porcupine has to go definetely, it is the mole's house.

(b) Send the porcupine out since he was the last one there.

The sactioned responses of care oriented ethics would be like:

(c) Wrap the porcupine in a towel so that he does not incovenience the mole.

(d) The mole should help the porcupine find a new house.

---

5. See Carol Gillegan, "Remapping the Moral Domain: New Images of Self in Relationship", in *Mapping the Moral Domain*, ed. by Carol Gilligan, Janie Victoria Ward, Fill Mclean Taylor, Bitty Bridige, Distributed by Harvard University Press, 1988.

(e) Both of them should work together to make the hole bigger.

In the justice-based set of alternatives rights and justice are adjudicated in the isolation as in an I *versus* Thou situation. Whereas in the second set of alternatives rights and justice are determined in relation to others. That an identical situation can be seen in two or more ways and that arguments can be tailored for all alternatives shows that there is no one rational solution. It is not that one set of the above solutions are rational therefore moral and the other set emotion-based therefore immoral. The more the different groups in society are negotiating the more the need to listen to alternative voices is emerging. Apart from the masculine-feminine debate, we are quite familiar with the problems of many monolithic societies having now to bargain with immigrants or other cultures. The feminist criticism of justice-based morality on this account is that it poses to be or aspires to be gender neutral but fails and is deemed to fail. Because their objectivity is not objective enough. Had they been fully objective they would have acknowledged the plurality in society.[6] Even if justice-based morality did attain full objectivity it would be inadequate because all human beings are not means/ends calculators, there are many other aspects of a human self that have to be acknowledged. The prevalent rights-based moral theories, like that of John Rawls is monolithic and too simplistic to be able to capture the pluralism of human goals and aspirations.

We shall now pass on to the second group of ciriticisms forwarded by radical feminists against Rawls' and other justice/right-based theories. Radical feminists argue that we are not always rational maximisers and all our moral choices are not always rational choices. The rational maximiser theory overlooks the way people, especially women, make existential choices. For

6. See Rae Langton, "Beyond a Pragmatic Critique of Reason" in *Australasian Journal of Philosophy*, Vol. 71, No. 4, December 1993, p. 382.

most women their choices are gender defined and socially engineered. Had all women been rational maximisers then a number of educated wealthy women would not have remained silent when abused or battered: or those who could afford higher education would not go in for a less paying career, or women who are economically independent would not choose a life which is less rewarding and involves deferring to a husband (see Furguson, p. 100). One could continue arguing in a Rawlsian vein by saying that a woman who makes these choices must be gaining something worth her while, be it a form of social security or some (dubious) form of virtue, or some other gain which she perceives as her end and that those choices help her to succeed. But that would lead to a further question, does any rationalised principle pass for a rational principle? Does being rational mean doing the appropriate thing required by a given role or status or does it mean something different, something bigger? I would expect being rational meant being capable of standing away from a given situation, of being capable of being objective or detached enough to evaluate the situations itself. Not only to evaluate the most rational option within a situation but to evaluate the situation itself. A related point has been made by Langton. She makes a difference between *being appropriate* and *being in the interest of an individual*. Certian behaviours, will for example, maximise the benefits the slave can achieve as a slave. These are behaviours which are considered appropriate for the slave. To make such choices would constitute a good strategy if a slave wanted to remain a slave but it would not be in the interest of the slave, because it is no one's interest to remain a slave.[7]

This brings us to the third observation made by the feminists against justice-based morality, especially of the Rawlsian type. Such morality is designed to maintain a *status quo* system of morality which has no built-in mechanism for systemic change. By being insensitive to other voices these systems are change

7. See Langton, *op.cit.*, p. 378.

resistant. The only change that is morally sanctioned is change that does not threaten the *status quo*. Given the fact that justice-based morality is being prescribed for a heirarchy ridden, competitive, individualistic industrial society where the division between the bargainers is that of the powerful and the powerless, and where empowerment means delegation of power according to existing power norms; there a process of homogenisation on the terms and conditions of the most powerful is bound to take place. The radical feminists point out that the problem is not that men have all the power and are manning all the power positions and women want to invade the power positions by being included in the power game. The question, as they see it, is how to change the entire power game of justice-based morality (where contracts and competitions are rules of the game) to a model of morality based on a symbiotic mutual adjustment where equality is not on exclusively masculine terms or exclusively feminine terms and where adjustment of goals is not on the basis of bargaining.

10

Markets, Democracy and Social Justice

Kamala Kanta Panda

It has been conventionally believed and conveniently asserted in most of the academic circles that market economy stands for democracy and economic growth whereas socialist economies bring about equalitarianism in the political system.[1] The distinguished Yale political scientist Charles E. Lindblom in his influential work, *Politics and Markets: the World's Political Economic Systems*, was of the opinion that

> It is in communist provision of . . . some degree of equality in the distribution of income and wealth that the communists claim to approximate the humanitarian vision . . . seems undeniable. On these fronts communist systems have to be credited with greater accomplishments, on the whole probably greater than those of the polyarchies (capitalist democracies).[2]

During the 1960s, 1970s, and 1980s a good number of research studies have indicated that economic equality in socialist

---

1. See, Kamala Kanta Panda, "Socialism and Market Economy in cross-national Perspective", in S. Mukherjee and S. Ramaswamy ed., *Political Science Annual, 1996*, New Delhi, 1996.
2. Charles E. Lindblom, *Politics and Market: the World's Political Economic System*, New York, 1977.

economies was greater than those in the market-oriented economies. Paradigm builders like Lydall (1968) and Pryor (1973) have stated in their works that the socialist economies are more equalitarian than market economies at comparable levels of development.[3] They assert that social justice could be better ensured in socialist systems. However, a number of cross-national studies have challenged these ideological assertions. They indicate that "for reasons not wholly understood, political democracy has been unable to exist except when coupled with market". Whereas all democratic political systems are market economies, not all market economies are necessarily democratic. There are good theoretical reasons to believe that market economies can stimulate economic growth better than socialist systems. It is argued that by accelerating the pace of reforms process, economy of a political system would be in a better position to achieve more and sustained growth rate which, in turn, could reduce poverty by the trickle down effect of the economy. An accelerated growth rate, they argue, would ensure better social justice. Economists like Professor Jagadish Bhagawati have been arguing that to achieve more growth rate that would have visible impacts on poverty and social justice, the structural adjustment programmes need to be pushed to a higher gear. But one has not to overlook the fact that in a political economy like India having more than 40 per cent of the population below the poverty line, and more than 80 per cent being confined to the rural areas, the dislocation cost of reforms could prove to be costlier than one can imagine. An increase in the national income does not necessarily lead to equilibrium in the social and economic process. Concentration of national income in the limited upper layer of the social system automatically results in the growth of a psyche of depravity

3. See, Harold Lydall, *The Structure of Earning*, London, 1968; Frederic L. Pryor, *Public Expenditures in Communist and Capitalist Nations*, Bloomington, 1977.

among the marginalised majority. It creates political uncertainty, a climate of hunger, and cumulative inequity in the political economy.

Referring to the very existence of hunger, Professor Amartya Sen said that hunger in the modern world is more intolerable than past hunger not because it is typically more intense but because it is now so 'unnecessary'. During his presidential address at the American Economic Association on 7 January 1995 in Washington D.C., Professor Sen said,

> The contemporary world suffers from many new as well as old economic problems including, among others, the persistence of poverty and deprivation despite general economic progress, the occurrence of famines and the widespread hunger, and threats to our environment and to the sustainability of the world in which we live.

He said that hunger could be better combated both by a healthy

> functioning economic system to provide people with regular means of income and survival, and a social security scheme to provide compensatory entitlements when employment rewards are inadequate.[4]

Elsewhere, he had commented that

> I sometimes consider whether there is any way of making poverty terribly infectious. If the privileged could catch poverty from the poor they meet in the street, I don't doubt at all that poverty would be eliminated with remarkable speed.

The comment seems to be a simplistic one. Why should the political elites of the day make 'poverty terribly infectious'? And for what, and for whom?

---

4. See, Amartya Sen's views in *Times of India*, New Delhi, February 22, 1988.

It is not definitely hunger but the consciousness of a relative inequality in income distribution and sense of an acute deprivation that could make hunger 'infectious'. In a motivated political economy, areas of priority of the ruling elites would be for the creation of a psyche of acquiescence, and not for 'entitlement'. Such a political economy could never be converted into a productive political process that could ensure social justice for the weaker, marginalised majority. Scholars like Nagel (1974), Mueller and Seligson (1987) have conclusively proved that income inequality is a major determinant of political violence especially when accompanied by rising levels of economic development. While cross-national studies by Cutright, Kuznets, Jackman, Paukert, Adelman, Ward, Morris and others have shown that inequality tends to decrease as the level of development increases, it is not always so. While some of the nations like Taiwan, Singapore, Costa Rica, and South Korea have experienced greater amount of equality in their political systems as a result of their economic growth, it is not so in case of Mexico, Argentina, Brazil, and Philippines. Growth, equality, democracy, social justice and an enlightened public policy have to move simultaneously. There is a crucial linkage between patterns of representation and process of redistribution of national income. Cutright argues that "Political structures that facilitate access by the masses to the elite will decrease inequality." High levels of constitutionalisation and participation in a system could be measured by the extent to which the system has extended the modern concept of citizenship to all segments of population.

During the 1990s, the concepts like 'new world order' and 'international governance' gained much momentum as part of the 'new thinking' to deal with the issues of globalisation and structural adjustment programmes. The liberalisation of economy was considered to be the only solution to ensure a balanced growth of economy and a just and equitable world order. The basic aim of the globalisation and liberalisation of economy was to integrate economy of the developing countries with the world economy. Some of the researchers and paradigm builders considered globalisation to be the result of the world technological transformative process. The fact that it is not the result of a natural process has been well-documented, among others, by George Rosen in his book, *Western Economists and Eastern Societies* (1985).

Since the publication of Francis Fukuyama's article, "The End of History" in the journal *National Interest*, in the summer of 1989, there has been a tendency among the policy-makers and social scientists to be 'more open' to the notion of market-based development strategies and 'non-class' democracy.[5] The other developments in the field of international politics, i.e., Desert Storm, Fall of the Berlin V all, break up of the Soviet Union, ethnic developments in Yugoslavia, landing of the American troops in Somalia, and the systematic devaluation of the United Nations as a peace-keeping organisation, have contributed to the popularisation of the concepts like 'globalisation' and 'democracy' in liberal capitalist forms. It was widely publicised that the failure of the Soviet experiment in the late 1980s, and other developments thereafter, has provided 'a death certificate' for socialism and socialist values. Under the liberal democratic framework, socialist values and normative practices of the political system were made subservient to the economic development dialogues. The role of the state to meet the basic needs of its entire citizenry was minimised. Democracy was reduced simply to an image associated with rituals. The political systems under the market economy in the developing world were left with little rooms for the adoption of more compassionate development policies with beneficial social contents for their poor. The Japanese thinker, Eisuke Sakakibara, referring to the debate

---

5. See, Francis Fukuyama, 'End of History', *National Interest*, Vol. 16, 1989, pp. 3-18; same author, *The End of History and the Last Man*, New York, 1992.

on 'end of history', said, "After fifty years the normal process of history has started to move again and what we are witnessing is not the end of history, but a fresh start." He said that two versions 'progressivism'—communism and capitalism—have suppressed the most important process of history: interaction and accommodation between diverse civilisations. Peter F. Drucker, Clarke Professor of Social Sciences and Management at Claremont Graduate School, California, said that

> Communism is dead, socialism is on its way out, and capitalism is not far behind. No one knows just what shape post-capitalist society will take but there is a good chance that in the process some Third World countries will transform themselves quickly into economic powers.

Similar views have been expressed by internationally renowned economist, Walt W. Rostow. He said,

> What they may not realise, and I have argued this since the late 1950s, is that the most powerful underlying force at work in the world arena is the diffusion of effective power away from both Washington and Moscow. That has been accompanied by a growing interdependence economically and politically, in the contemporary world.

With the collapse of the Soviet Union, the American administration became more interested in the market economy in the developing economies. It was considered to enhance American national economic and security interests. In fact, the National Endowment for Democracy, a foundation created by an act of the Congress in 1993, spent more than $ 725 million on democracy related programmes in fiscale 1995 to advance democracy abroad.[6]

---

6. See, Peter F. Drucker's books: *The End of Economic Man*, *The New Society*, *Landmarks of Tomorrow*.

The emerging concept of 'new international order' was popularised by President George Bush during his address to the Joint Session of the Congress. President Bush said that the concept of new world order promises

> a world quite different from the one we have known, a world the rule of law supplants the rule of the jungle, a world in which nations recognise the shared responsibility for freedom and justice a world where the strong respects the weak.

The ideological pressures of the 'new world order' with its commitments to liberal democracy, has provided the authoritarian states with an alibi for concealed authoritarianism with a human rights dimension of democratisation process.[7] The liberal democracy, with Milton Friedman's dictum of Free to Choose as the guiding spirit, became the guiding doctrine of the developing countries in the 1990s. In India, since 1991, the Government of India has adopted the polity of liberalisation. More and more sectors of economy have been made open to the international competitions. Public sectors have been neglected and multinationals have been invited even to the consumer sectors. This has negatived the very basic philosophy of the state. The profit motive has replaced social commitments. I am reminded of what Professor J.K. Galbraith once said,

> Restraints on competitions and the free movement of prices, the principal source of uncertainty to business firms, have been principally deplored by university professors on lifetime appointments.

---

7. See, Noam Chomsky, *Deterring Democracy*, New York, 1992. Discussion on 'low intensity democracy' by Barry Gills and Joel Rocamora, in *Low Intensity Democracy*, University of Sheffield Papers in International Studies, no. II, 1992, p. 39.

Democracy, Markets, and Growth

Individual freedom is the core value that has guided both market economy and democracy over the decades. Whereas one can cite a number of theoretical reasons to show that market economies can stimulate economic growth better than socialist systems, one is not always certain about the linkage between growth and social justice. The debate between market and democracy is still an inconclusive one. Addressing the Tenth Annual John Gaus Lecture at the American Political Science Association 1995 annual meeting in Chicago, Professor Lindblom said,

> One difficulty may be that we-meaning people all over the world — have actually tried the market in many of its possible forms, learning greatly from both its flaws and merits; but we have not yet tried democracy, only distant approaches to it. That criples us when we try to compare the two.

It is possible to present oneself as an anti-market but I don't think any informed intellectual is prepared to be known as an anti-democracy professor of political science.

Although a good number of works have been conducted on the relationship between markets and democracy, no serious study has yet been undertaken on market-impacts on democracy.[8] Professor Lindblom said,

> it does not seem that political science has sufficiently explored market impact on democracy, often leaving the field to those economists who tell us, simplistically, sometimes even dogmatically, that democracy cannot survive without help from the market.[9]

---

8. See, Robert Lane, *The Market Experience* (1991).
9. C.E. Lindblom, "Market and Democracy-Obliquely", *Political Science and Politics*, Vol. 28, no.4, December 1995, pp. 684-8.

Both market and democracy are complementary methods of popular control over elites in a political system and are tied.

Regarding the relationship between democracy and growth, there is also no conclusive evidence. Mr. Lee Kuan Yew, Singapore's leader for many years and one of the most successful policy-makers, told an audience in the Philippines in 1992,

> I do not believe that democracy necessarily leads to development. I believe that what a country needs to develop is discipline more than democracy. The exuberance of democracy leads to indiscipline and disorderly conduct which are inimical to development.

For many years Indian policy-makers have strongly stressed democracy to be responsible for the slow growth of the country. This theme is also advocated in case of the East Asian States — South Korea, Taiwan, Singapore, and Hong Kong. A much-cited study of Taiwan, by Robert Wade of the Institute of Development Studies of Sussex University states that Taiwan was successful in managing its economic affairs partly because "it was spared popular pressure to intervene unintelligently".[10] Although most of the scholars support this proposition of conflict relationship between democracy and economic growth, this proposition is not universally accepted. In some studies democracy appears to promote growth, in others to retard it. Professor Mançur Olson of the University of Maryland, a leading analyst of the economic weakness of democratic government argues forcefully that democracy is far more conducive to long-term economic growth than dictatorship, even of an apparently benevolent kind. He says that regard for individual rights is necessary for lasting democracy, and that regard for exactly the same rights is also

---

10. See, Robert Wade, *Governing the Market: Economic Theory and the Role of the Government in East Asian Industrialisation*, Princeton, 1990.

needed if there is to be any lasting commitments to security of property and enforcement of contracts.[11]

Often we have been told that with the collapse of Marxism as an ideology and of communism as a political system, there is no other way but to move into a society where liberal capitalist philosophy dominates. I do not delude myself with the idea that we are anywhere near the 'End of History'. Like every concept, the concept of liberal democracy in the post-capitalist phase will not be same as liberal capitalist democracy. Drucker supports this view.[12]

Since early 1990s, there has been a systematic attempt in the developing countries to import the American pattern of liberal democracy. It has been consistently advocated that liberal capitalist democracy can alone ensure new 'international governance' and a just social order. Scholars like Robert Dahl, Howard Wiarda, Irving Kristol and Robert Packenham have been critical of the American approach towards democracy. Howard Wiarda said,

> I doubt that democracy US style can be exported. There are alternative legitimate routes to power in Latin America besides election, and democracy itself often is of tenuous legitimacy.

Packenham wrote,

> The chances of liberal democracy in most Third World countries in the foreseeable future are not very great; and the chances that the United States can be effective in advancing the cause of democracy through positive actions are probably even smaller. The attempt to promote liberal constitutionalism is often both unrealistic

11. Mancur Olson, "Dictatorship, Democracy, and Development", *American Political Science Review*, September 1993.
12. See, Peter Drucker's book *The End of Economic Man*.

> from the point of view of feasibility and ethnocentric from the point of view of desirability.

Irving Kristol says that

> strong cultural tradition, certain strong cultural attitudes are necessary for a system.

Robert Dahl was very critical of the American approach to democracy particularly in the Central American systems. He said,

> Much of the debate over Central America has been based on what increasingly appears to be a faculty assumption. That the region's no-democratic regimes can all be converted into democracies by means of American assistance, guidance, and intervention.

Growth and Social Justice

The concept of social justice has acquired a new connotation in the context of globalisation and liberalisation of economy. John Rawls' theory of social justice is often referred to as the only solution to the problems of a liberal capitalist society. Rawls in his famous work, *A Theory of Justice*, said,

> It is these inequalities, presumably inevitable in the basic structure of any society, to which the principles of social justice must in the first instance apply. . . . The justice of a social scheme depends essentially on how fundamental rights and duties are assigned and on the economic opportunities and social conditions in the various sectors of society.

He is interested to develop a conception of justice that can provide a standard by which the distributive arrangements of a society could be assessed. Rawls is more concerned with the legal protection of freedom of thought and liberty of conscience, competitive markets, private property in the means of production and the monogamous family. Writing on the heels of a period of intense political questioning, a period when the Civil Rights and Black Liberation movements, followed by anti-Vietnam war agitations that challenged the basic postulates of the American liberalism, Rawls was more at home with the neo-classical economists. His emphasis on market-maximising behaviour was to prevail over social norms and ethical values. It does not provide for an efficient social arrangement through which goods of society could be justly distributed among the members of the society. It neither ensures a social scheme of equal access to economic opportunities and social conditions in various sectors of the society nor it can guarantee quality of being fair and just in social relations of human beings. Rawls' preference for class inequality concept would lead to the growth of an inequality of power and concentration of wealth in some limited sectors. Within the limited scope of the present paper, it is not possible to provide a critical assessment of Rawls' theory of social justice by leading theoreticians like C.B. Macpherson, Milton Fisk, Richard Mill, Thomas Nagel and Norman Daniels. Rawls' theory is, thus, an apology, at best, for the theory of liberal democratic justice.[13]

The concept of social justice, as I look at it, implies an egalitarian, non-exploitative society that always stands for basic needs to its citizenry. Both welfare capitalism and centrally planned socialist systems have been criticised for their failure to create a socially just political order. Whereas welfarism has resulted in the fiscal crisis, slow economic growth, and loss of moral and ethical values in society, the socialist economies have failed to ensure Marx's vision of a non-exploitative society. To

---

13. See, my paper, "Structural Adjustment Programmes and Africa Development Strategy". Presented at the International Conference on India and South-south Cooperation, India International Centre, February, 15-17, 1996.

rely on the market economy to meet the basic needs of a system often creates a politically dangerous situation. This has not been refuted even by Professor Milton Friedman, the leading economic philosopher of the Free to Choose doctrine. In an article in Praxis, he said that a non-market device of a minimum guaranteed salary should be provided to all workers to enable them to satisfy their basic needs. However, this measure should be accompanied by the removal of all social security and any protection for the rights of workers.

I know that a universal theory of social justice has not yet evolved either in the Western liberal philosophy or in the socialist and communist doctrines. However, certain basic ingredients of the concept of social justice have already been projected through the international human rights documents and national constitutional documents. The basic aim of social justice is to remove the imbalances in the political, social, and economic life of the people and create a just society.[14] The subordination of social justice to markets in the developing countries has resulted in the emergence of politics as a self-perpetuating power doctrine, not as a conscious, critical and creative participation of it in the structural interactions. Politics is neither a basis of a legitimised monopoly for coercing others, nor a realm of projection of unconsciousness and unresolved personal complexes. These ideas of people like Max Weber and C.G. Jung are responsible for the sharpening of the inherent contradictions in the state structures. The market-based development process, structural adjustment programmes, and consumerist culture have created a psyche of restlessness.

The basic policy of a political system is to assist in the self-actualising process to fulfil the inner requirements of an individual for its continuous moral growth. According to Michael

---

14. See, N.R. Madhava Menon (ed.), *Social Justice and Social Process in India*, New Delhi, 1988.

Oakeshott, the state, as a corporate enterprise association, should try to achieve, not 'benefits' or 'satisfaction', but creation of conditions under which an individual can fully exercise its duties and responsibilities. "The supreme test of all political institutions and industrial arrangements", said John Dewey, "shall be the contributions they make to the all-round growth of every members of society". An emphasis on profitability and market efficiency provides an amoral grounding to politics. The total dependence on market economism creates crises of ethnocide, ecocide, and authoritarianisation of political and social process. It dilutes the democratic and liberating role of the nation-state as well as the question of equity between and within nations. In his report on Our Creative Diversity in 1995, President of World Commission on Culture and Development, Javier Perez de Cuellar said that the economic approach was probably not the best way to solve development problems, the cultural issues had also to be addressed. He said that cultural dimension of development had to be emphasised with human beings at the very centre of development dialogue.

In his address to the World Summit for Social Development, the United Nations Secretary-General, Boutros Boutros-Ghali said that the goal of the constructive social integration is a 'society for all' in which citizens feel that the state is responsive to their needs; one that promotes "development consistent with justice for the individual, harmony among groups and social cohesion". An healthy economic growth, not growth *per se*, is seen as

> essential to successfully meeting the challenge of peace and security, the challenge of human rights and responsibilities, the challenge of democracy and the rule of law, the challenge of social justice and the reform and the challenge of cultural renaissance and pluralism.[15]

15. *Towards a New Asia* (Report of the Commission for a New Asia, 1994), p. 39.

The question of empowerment of people is central to both social justice and growth. The 1993 Human Development Report emphasises that market should serve people instead of people serving markets. Further,

> both state and market should be guided by the people. The two should work *in tandem* and people should be sufficiently empowered to exert effective control over both.

Market, Third World, and Social Justice

During the Davos Conference of the World Economic Forum in February 1994, the Prime Minister of India, Mr. P.V. Narasimha Rao emphatically stated that the collapse of the communist model had established the primacy of the market forces. Liberalisation of trade and pursuit of policies to allow an unfettered movement of international finance, technology, and entrepreneurship to move across international frontiers, had been considered to give strong impetus to economic growth and poverty alleviation programmes. The then Indian Finance Minister, Dr. Manamohan Singh emphasised during all his budget speeches (1991-6) that the key element of the Indian structural adjustment programmes had been to give top priority to strengthening anti-poverty programmes. However, after the publication of the National Sample Survey Report in 1995, there has been a number of serious debates on the incidence of poverty. Regarding the faces of rural poverty, it has been found out that more and more people have gone below poverty line since 1989-90. From 33.67 per cent in 1989-90, it has increased to 41.72 per cent in 1992-3. Similarly, during 1989-93, the share of top 30 per cent in the field of national consumption has gone up whereas share of bottom 70 per cent in the areas of national consumption has gone down. The price rise of essential commodities has gone up whereas the governmental statistics regarding national inflation has gone down. In one of the editorials in a national daily, it was stated that

> What such an economy cannot conceal is the structural settlement of islands of prosperity in a sea of poverty. Politically the government of the day is obliged to borrow increasingly to expand social security programmes. It ends up with borrowing more to repay loans and is left with shrinking budgets to found what it had borrowed for.

The external debt has touched $ 100 billion. There has been a decline in the gross saving rate from 24 per cent in 1990 to 20.2 in 1994. In a country where 80 per cent people depend on agricultural economy in the rural sector there has been no meaningful state intervention to remove rural backwardness. Mahatma Gandhi once said,

> Our cities are not India. The city people are the brokers and commission agents for the big houses of Europe, America and Japan. The cities have cooperated with the bleeding process that has gone on for two hundred years.

Rising unemployment, debt service ratio, political corruption, privatisation of public sector economy and declining law and order situation have deeply affected the social justice programmes in India.

Many China watchers like Professor Thomas Gold believe that the market-Leninism of China would not be in a position to take it too far. It is growing into a 'disintegrating dynasty'. Social conditions in the rural China is deteriorating everyday. The situation is not different in the Latin American countries. During the 1970s, Brazil with its growing growth rate and export-oriented economy, was considered to be the 'Country of the future'. 1970s was a 'miracle period' for Brazil. After it became a part of the globalisation in the 1980s, its 'miracle period' gave way to the 'period of lost decade'. The situation in Africa is fast becoming more alarming day by day. The African political system is facing today a continuing conditions of scarcity, frustration, criminalisation, ethnic violence, and extra-constitutional growth. Complex and contradictory trends are becoming more and more pronounced in different crisis sectors. Alcohol-related deaths in Russia has gone on increasing because of "despair caused by economic hardships because of market-oriented reforms". Likewise, corruption in China has grown to such a proportion that President Jiang Zemin has warned that it threatened to ruin the Party itself. In India, the issue of corruption has affected the very foundation of the political system itself.

Toward a Just Social Order

It has been observed that extreme poverty and income disparities often exist along with rapid increases in GNP and other indicators of growth. Some critics regard it as a deep disappointment or a 'moral outrage'. The trickle-down theory and Kuznet's inverted 'U' theory of income distribution has not been very successful in checking the growth of internal colonies. The real development of human beings invloves much more than what is often referred to as economic growth. As market economy is concerned with a limited upper layer of population, it fails to initiate a sense of empowerment among the marginalised majority.

Economic growth by itself does not lead to the domocratisation of society. Neither it strengthens its institutional processes, nor it automatically creates a linkage between growth and social justice. This could only be possible if the infrastructural forces of social democracy are committed towards egalitarian ethics. A just governance is multi-dimensional. Apart from targetting of resources efficiently, coordination of conflicting objectives, and the management of deep societal cleavages, the ruling elites in a system ought to have credibility and commitment towards social justice (See, Mansbridge, 1980; Habermas, 1989; Wuthnow, 1991).

Since 1950, the political and economic policies of India have failed to evolve what Professor V.R. Mehta calls a new faith in the capacity of the democratic structures to cope with the socio-economic issues facing the country. He said,

> the economic and political developments in the country have, in fact, not only tended to increase economic disparities and inequalities but have also created ominous links between those who control economic power and those who control political power.[16]

Social justice in a system is the product of social construction of difference, concentric patterns of political and intellectual acquiescence, and the language of political economy. It cannot be achieved through what Michael Ignatieff refers to as 'bureaucratic transfer of incomes among strangers'. A proper and meaningful policy planning process has to be evolved to integrate the concept of social justice with the political economy dialogue. Indeed, what we need today is a new approach, a comprehensive alternative development, and an integrated vision of the people-oriented social justice concept.

16. V.R. Mehta, *Ideology, Modernization and Politics in India*, New Delhi, 1988, p. 7.

11

Social Justice and Development
A Multilingual and Multicultural Perspective

Debi Prasanna Patnaik

SOCIAL Justice is viewed differently from different disciplinary perspectives. Some say that as it deals with rights, duties and justice, it is a legal concept. Some say that as it deals with the nature and structure of a state within the framework of which social justice is to be seen, it is a political concept. Some say that as social justice can be established only through equal distribution of goods and services within a society, it is an economic concept. There are yet others who feel that as it deals with attitudes and behaviours it is a psychological concept and some who believe that as social justice is grounded on an ethical framework it falls within the philosophical domain. Like the proverbial seven blind men looking at an elephant we are all groping in the darkness.

Our perspectives of development is equally bizarre. The way adjectives are used does not only restrict the meaning of development, but makes nonsense of it for example, physical development, social development, cultural development, rural development, regional development, women's development, agricultural development, industrial development, economic development, political development and development of a people. All these usages tell us something about the scope of 'development' while confusing us with the utter vagueness and contrary meaning.

Some believe that growth is development while others believe that growth with justice is development. Some believe that without seeing development in its three dimensions, physical, mental and spiritual, one cannot properly apprehend the meaning of the term. The development theories built by the West, who are in a state of blissful ignorance of the 'other', are inadequate to explain the problems of the Third World. If in a society poverty, unemployment and inequality have increased, "it would be strange to call the result 'development' even if the *per capita* income doubled".[1]

Language inequality is a symptom of socio-political inequality. State formation around unitary and binary symbols is found wanting. Political structures are crumbling down both in the erstwhile USSR and Europe. Alternatives have to be searched in the Third World precolonial experience. It must be recognised that the Indian sensibility as representative of Third World Sensitivity is a counter to the Western sensibility.

The world is multilingual with 5000 languages. India with its 1652 mother-tongues according to 1961 census and with about 3000 mother-tongues listed from the beginning of the census is representative of countries in Asia, Africa and Latin America. All these countries are lumped together by the developed countries and are called the Third World. These countries not only accepted the appropriation of the 1st and 2nd world status by the developed countries, but also accepted their Third World status. Another thing common among these countries is their colonial past. These countries were colonised by one or the other of the developed countries. In fact, their so-called development is due to the exploitation of the colonies.

Looked from the post-modern perspective, colonialism has always returned in new garbs. First of all it came with the explicit

1. Dudley Seers in *Economic Development of the World,* ed. by Todero, p. 61.

purpose of civilising the natives. About the time when the fraud was exposed, they wore a different garb. They came to develop the undeveloped Third World. When development, no matter how it was defined, ceased to make sense, they have now downed the mantle of protecting our environment. Whether it is to civilise, to develop or to protect, the purpose is the same-exploitation.

European Nation States were formed around unitary symbols. One language, one religion, one culture and, in its extreme manifestation one party and one leader defined the Nation State. The colonies tried to build themselves after their colonial masters. During the Indian freedom struggle Gandhi pleaded for linguistic reorganisation of States and the Congress accepted it. In Gandhi's scheme of things this was only a step towards *grām svarāj*. But the elite leaders of India did not know how to manage diversity. While one group pleaded for Hindi another pleaded for English. In the English *vs* Hindi debate the issue of languages of India got a decent burial. They tried to build a country around unitary symbols, one language, one anthem and one flag.

During the freedom struggle poets everywhere sang of the State as well as the Centre. Thus, the Kannada poet said, you are the daughter of Bhārata Mātā, O mother Karnāṭak (*bhārata jananīya tanujā tu. jayatu karnāṭaka mātī*). The Oriyā poet sang of Utkal Jananī as well as Bhārata Mātā. The Bengālī poet eulogised mother India while singing of *sonār bānglā*. As the states favoured the majority language, the minor and minority languages were marginalised. Even the states came under tension as protagonists of Hindi and English fought a bitter battle.

In most multilinguist and multiethnic countries of the world, state formation has assumed grave proportions. The Centrist State is found unsuitable to meet the aspirations of its diverse population. The Federal State, which represents power sharing between the national and the regional elite, is equally unsuitable. An alternative is provided by Gandhi's *grām svarāj*. Another alternative is provided by Lohia's 'Four Pillar State'. Although the tensions created drag us inexorably towards the *pancāyat*s, we are far away from the Four Pillar State in India.

India has never been a single political entity prior to the advent of the British. Kingship as well as democracy have remained side by side. And yet India as a single culture area has been recognised from time immemorial. Visitors, be they Chinese, Greek, Persians or Arabs, have referred to India. The cultural miscegenation has resulted in India being a single linguistic socio-linguistic and semantic area in spite of having languages belonging to four language families. These cultural factors are not taken into consideration while planning for education or for development.

The First and the Second World are manufacturers of theory and the Third World is the consumer. Let us look at language for illustration. For the First and the Second World one language is the ideal and the norm. Bilingualism is a quantum jump insofar as it is 100 per cent achievement over one. Thus languages are grudgingly acknowledged to accommodate European countries like Switzerland. Anything over and above is considered absurd. For the multilingual countries the reverse is true. Many languages are the norm. Thus languages represent a restriction in the choice of language use. Two languages are a handicap and one language is absurd. A political scientist in those countries can justifiably ask a question, how much plurality can this culture tolerate! But if such formulation is made by a political scientist in a Third World Country, he would not be worth his salt as a social scientist. Here the formulation would just be the reverse, how much uniformity can this culture tolerate?

Once many languages are dubbed as muddle headed thinking, the Third World is faced with a dilemma. Search is on to find a solution as close to the monomodel as possible. In Paraguay, Guarani is the language of 90 per cent of the population and yet the colonial language, Spanish, is the state official language.

This can be compared with Kaśmīrī which is the mother tongue of the large majority, Hindus and Muslims, but is sacrificed on the altar of Urdu. The search took a different dimension when a state language was created based on the majority language, as was done in Indonesia. It can be compared with the attempt to create a national/official language based on Hindi. Several factors worked against it in India. First is Hindi chauvinism which excluded Urdu on the one hand and mother tongues such as Maithilī, Māgadī, Braj, Avadhī and Bhojpurī on the other. Even creation of intermediate standards like Pādī and Rājasthānī was looked with suspicion. Secondly, although the constitution differentiated between state language Hindi and the official language Hindi, the Hindi chauvinism sought to blur the distinction between the two. Instead of moving towards the enhanced registers, it sabotaged all activity which could have been initiated under Article 351. It is strange but true that not a single programme has been initiated under Article 351 during the last fifty years. All initiatives by non-Hindi organisations were gegged by Hindi chauvinists. Yet another dimension is the adoption/imposition of Kiswahili in parts of Africa. This can be compared with the role of English in India, excepting for the fact that it is the language of the 'creamy layer' among the Indian intellectuals. Instead of 200 years of promotional activities by the British and 50 years of such activities by their minions, English is the language of less than 4 per cent of Indian population. Another dimension is provided by the Three-Language Formula in India, which is adopted in some African as well as Latin American countries. The 'Three-Language' formula does not provide for the mother tongues different from the state official languages, for classical languages, for languages of proximate communication and for foreign languages (other than English), and is restricted to secondary education. Yet the New Education Policy of 1986 and its modified version of 1992 has nothing to say about languages. They refer us back to the 'Three-Language' formula of 1968 as though no development has taken place between 1968 and 1986. In the first ever policy document written by me for the Government of India, I had stated that the 'Three-Language' formula is a strategy and not a goal. After discussions with me the then Education Minister, Professor V.K.R.V. Rao and the Education Advisor, J.P. Naik permitted it to stand as policy. But as time passed and Bureaucratic Reports were developed, this consciousness was dimmed and we continued to pay homage the 'Three-Language' formula and sabotaged all constitutional provisions about education, beginning with primary education. In any case, external allegiance and internal sabotage has been our policy in the field of education and culture.

The developed countries have never taken to multilingualism with good grace. Even bilingualism was considered subtractive before 1961. In 1961, Wallace Lambert, the Doyen of Western research in bilingualism, changed his line and from then bilingualism earned respect. The fact that in 1991 Harvard University Press brought out a volume entitled *Bilingualism and Multiculturalism* is symptomatic of the attitude of the developed world towards multilingualism. The American socio-linguist Fasold concludes that "there is a definite relationship between linguistic uniformity and economic development".[2] But he is reluctant to concede the same connection with linguistic diversity.

The word 'development' is used in so many senses that it appears meaningless. Its faces are seen in expressions like social development, economical development, political development, urban development, rural development, tribal development, development of the girl child, slum development and so on and so forth. There was a time when development was measured in terms of GNP and GDP. This was given up in favour of PIQL.

---

2. Fasold Ralph, *The Sociolinguistics of Society,* Oxford, Basil Blackwell, 1984.

Even that is given up in favour of a new set of paradigms developed by the World Bank and the UN.

In order to understand development, one has to ask a number of questions. If poverty, hunger and inequality persist even if the GNP doubles, can we really call that development? Where children are denied access to real learning because they are denied the right to learn in their home language, where the imposition of a foreign language leads to semilingualism and underachievement, can that be called development? If a child is out of tune with her environment because she cannot name the things in it neither in her home language nor in her school language, how can she live in unison with her environment? Is this what we call development? If we create a machine which travels 20,000 miles per hour and bypasses space to visit outer space, but makes the neighbour a stranger, is this development? Questions like these need to be answered in order to understand development. These answers need to be viewed in the context of observations such as

> In the developing countries, the problem relates mainly to improving reaching conditions, especially in basic education. In developed countries, more attention is paid to achievements and to ways of ensuring a higher level of knowledge for all.[3]

That there is no language planning in India is acknowledged by the NEP 1986. The Programme of Action of 1986 says,

> The decision about language policy and development of languages are taken at various levels — Central and State Governments, universities, Boards of Secondary/School education, etc. Consequently there is no uniformity on the language policy followed in education. (p. 170)

---

3. Franqoise Caillods (ed.), *The Prospects of Educational Planning, International Institute of Educational Planning*, UNESCO.

It further says,

> the National Policy on education, 1986, has reiterated in respected languages the policy elaborated in the national policy on education, 1968.

Our regression from 1986 to 1963 speaks for itself.

The place English enjoys in the country can be traced back to the impulsive outburst of Jawaharlal Nehru in the Indian Parliament. This is continuation of Macaulay's famous words of 1813 which says,

> No Bengalee who undergoes this education has any respect left for anything Hindu. If your aim is to produce a whole generation of young people who are not just ignorant of their identity and their heritage, but have in fact, a positive contempt for it, then they must not be taught Sanskrit, the language of the powerful heritage and the unique Indian identity and they must be taught English and through that the western 'values' so that the Indian youth naturally respects the 'modern'.

Jawaharlal, in his search for modernity was unwittingly caught in the English snare. In his commitment to science and technology he forgot that science is universal, but technology is culture sensitive. While through a borrowed language one can assess a lot of borrowed technology, appropriate technology develop only when science interacts with society-science cannot interact with society in a foreign language or a borrowed language. When Satyen Bose of the Bose-Einstein statistics fame told me that "if a person cannot teach physics in his/her mother tongue, it is not because he or she does not know his/her mother tongue, but because he/she does not know Physics", immediately I could not relate it to the long thinking shadow of Macaulay. But over the years things have become clear to me. That English is a major factor in the social divide between educated/uneducated, urban/rural, elite/masses can easily be perceived. That it is the support system for the consumeristic mini sector of society and is the single important factor of social inequality in India is to be seen to be believed. Through English the information rich becomes richer and the information starved becomes pulverised. It is most unfortunate that any statement about English is perceived either as pro or anti. It is forgotten that English as a supplement is a strength while as a substitute it is debilitation. The clamour for pre-primary and primary English is to be seen in this light. That it results in anomie, alienation and culture perception blind spot is noticed only when it is too late.

It must give you an example of a multilingual. I give you my example. I speak Oriyā in my family and in the intimate circle. I am speaking before you in English. Most of my professional writing is in English. I use Sanskrit for prayer or as an entry into the indigenous knowledge systems. I use French for research and Bengali for aesthetic pleasure. I use my broken Kannaḍa and broken Hindi for proximate and distant communication within the country. I can understand Āssamese, Marāṭhī and Gujarātī. The roles of languages have been fixed by me and any alteration is likely to lead to disastrous consequences. Where we go wrong is when we compare my partial language register with a monolingual user of a language. While a monolingual uses his/her one language (may be with differing dialects, styles and registers) meet the demands of his/her universe of discourse, I use different languages. We go wrong in our assessment of performance as we are insensitive to the nuances of multilingualism.

I must give you another example of a multilingual. An Oriyā boy married to a Tamil girl speaking English at home living in the Bengālī surrounding of Calcutta brings up his children with a Hindusthānī *āyāh* and a Gurkhā security man. The children grow up with six mother tongues and their life is enriched as they grow up in viewing the same fact from different perspectives.

I would like to give you an example of language loss. This is the story of a Korean family in USA. The children of the family went to English schools which resulted in a break of parental input into the child's education. As time passed, the Korean of the children got rusted. Korean is a language with layers of honorifics. Loss of some of these leads to showing disrespect to elders. It is at this time that the grandfather of the children decided to come for a visit. As he did not know English, the father decreed that the children speak to their grandfather in Korean. The children tried their best. But their Korean without proper honorifics angered the grandfather. He gave a dressing down to his son as he was not bringing up the children in proper Korean tradition. The father transferred his anger to the children by hitting them with a stick. Thc next day somebody saw the stick marks on the kids. They were taken into protective custody and the parents were arrested. Nobody noticed that language is at the centre of this family drama until a socio-linguist reported it.

One of the gravest dangers to multilingualism is the call for joining the main stream and national integration. These are euphemisms for assimilation. As we ask the tribals to assimilate, the Hindi chauvinists expect the other Indian languages to assimilate. The beneficiary is English which poses itself as the neutral language and the language of equal difficulty for all Indian languages. It is strange but true that most anti-Hindi persons are anti-mother tongue.

The fulcrum on which a multilingual and pluricultural society is balanced is recognition and respect for the different. It is necessary to understand that it is not the recognition but the non-recognition of identities that leads to national disintegration. If we reject national integration, then its alternative must be structural incorporation of entities in a larger whole, be it language, ethnicity or identity.

Today modernisation is equated with westernisation and globalisation. Modernisation excludes everything indigenous and traditional. Globalisation excludes everything local. As societal change must relate to continuity, globalisation must relate to localisation. Tagore was a great Indiạn as he was a great Bengālī and he was universal man because he was a great Indian. There can be no globalisation without localisation and there can be no localisation without globalisation. One does not exclude the other.

After an overview of the situation one can say that although some economists are now talking about non-economic factors, their use in economic planning and development is a long way off. Whether it is the Theory of Melting Pot, Salad Bowl, or Distant Stranger, or call for National Integration or joining the Main Stream, all these are euphemism for assimilation. The world has not learned anything from the American experience, where 200 years of experiment with the melting pot resulted in the pot melting leaving the identities in tact. The Indian experience is different. As Professor R.P. Das, discussing about temple art, puts in,

> As the Indian consciousness of any time irrespective of the region, is a complex web of many strands, so also is the symbolism of temple art — a simultaneous and complementary balancing of many traditions.[4]

Whether one looks at languages, ethnicities, religions, cultures, one finds the 'simultaneous and complimentary balancing of many traditions'. Unless the difference is given due recognition and respect, the clash between uniform developmental planning and multiform realities of the grass-root will destroy mankind and social justice will remain a far cry.

---

4. R.P. Das, "Symbolism in Temple Art", submitted to Lalit Kala Akademi for the National Seminar — Rereading Indian Art, 1996, Jan 10-11, Calcutta.

12

Social Justice and Preferential Treatment

Rama Chandra Majhi

THE violent protest against government policy for reservation for the minority in the past indicates that certain sections of our society consider preferential treatment to the minority unfair.[1] The growing discontent makes it pertinent to look at the issue more closely than ever.

A member of the minority is preferred in admission to educational institutions and employment over a more qualified member of the non-minority. By reserving a number of seats in educational institutions and jobs for the minority, the state or an institution of the state denies the members of the non-minority equal access to those goods.[2] It is possible that a less qualified applicant from the minority be selected from quota while a more

1. I have not considered women's right to preferential treatment. It seems that women's problems are different from minorities groups. Women are not a minority. The privations and the kind of discrimination the minorities suffered in the past are not the same with women. Their cause needs to be vindicated by independent considerations.
2. For my purpose, educational privileges and jobs are goods of a society which are to be fairly distributed among its members. It becomes the responsibility or the obligation of the state to see that there is just distribution of those goods.

qualified general applicant may not be selected. The general applicant would have received the good had it not been for the reservation policy.

Article 16 of the Constitution of India confers a citizen a right to equal access to the opportunities. This specific right is based on a more general legal principle which is expressed as follows:

> Every citizen of a state has a right to equal treatment before law with regard to the rights conferred and the obligations imposed by the state on its citizens.[3]

Further, this legal principle is based on the formal principle of equality.

Those who are the same in the relevant respects ought to be treated similarly with regard to those respects; or, those similarly situated should be similarly treated.

The formal principle appears to be violated when a member of the minority is accepted or hired over a member of the non-minority where both equally qualify. The principle also seems to be ignored while keeping exclusively a number of jobs for the minority. The state has an obligation to see that the principle is not violated. Reservation policy transgresses this principle according to the perception of the non-minority. The discontent ensues primarily from such a perception.

On the other hand, the minority has been victim of centuries of exploitation and segregation in the form of untouchability. Social goods, cultural goods and material wealth has been largely inaccessible to its members while the non-minority benefitted from their miseries. An unfair amount of goods of several kind accumulated with the latter. In brief, there is an unfair distribution of wealth in the society. The state policy of preferential treatment just takes away this injustice. If the

3. Article 14 of the Constitution of India reflects this general legal principle.

minority is not given an edge, then the injustice suffered will not be mitigated.

Here is then the dilemma for the state — if the state adopts the policy of preferential treatment, then allegedly it is unfair to one group and if it doesn't, then it is unfair to the other. I argue that preferential treatment is justified and that the objections against it fall short of conviction.

Besides the objection from the violation of the principle of equal protection before law, there is an objection that preferential treatment breeds discrimination against the minority in educational institutions and workplaces.[4] Some members of the minority though bright but less qualified than others get into educational institutions and workplaces. However, they fail to compete with the non-minority. This entices one to think that the members of the minority are inferior and are not as good as the other. Allegedly distressing is the fact that a member of the minority may be influenced by such circumstances to believe himself as inferior. He may think that he got to his place because of the quota. The purpose of the preferential treatment is to bring the minority to the level of the society and to close the disparity and wipe out the discrimination. However, preferential treatment doesn't appear to serve its purpose. Scheduled castes and scheduled tribes become an inferior caste with low potentiality. A member of the minority is looked down upon as a 'quota man' in workplaces.

Preferential treatment striving to improve the lot of the minority, may cause discontent to the non-receiving group. The misperception that the minority is an inferior group and the

---

4. A version of this argument is made by Charles Murray. Murray's essay is on racial discrimination. However, the concerns he expresses and the arguments he places are equally applicable to the problems of the minorities in India. Most of the articles I have relied upon are relevant to the current problem of this paper though they deal with the problem of racial discrimination.

derision that someone is a quota man ensues from such a discontent. But justice must be upheld in the face of discontent and misperception. Preservation of justice has far greater value than these unwarranted discontent. The goal is to provide compensatory and distributive justice to that group which was denied of its rightful claims to the goods of the society.

Lissa Newton argues that preferential treatment doesn't seem to uphold justice for it denies the non-minority the right to equal protection before the law. She thinks that preferential treatment doesn't serve political justice. She distinguishes two senses of justice, moral and political. She doesn't say much about what moral justice is except that moral justice brings everyone under its umbrella irrespective of citizenship. About political justice she says:

> [Political justice] is the condition which freemen establish among themselves when they "share a common life in order that their association bring them self-sufficiency" — the regulation of their relationship by law, and the establishment, by law, of equality before the law. Rule of law is the name and pattern of this justice; its equality stands against the inequalities of wealth, talent, etc. — otherwise obtaining among its participants, who by virtue of that equality are called 'citizens'.[5]

Her argument obviously raises the issue about the right of the non-minority — their right to protection before the law. However there is an implication of her argument which has devastating consequences. If we just stick to political justice, that is, justice obtained by conforming to the law, as she says that we should, then the value of social justice is lost.

The history of the Blacks and the Jews express the conflict between social justice and Newton's idea of political justice. The Blacks of the American society were denied of human rights,

5. *Ethics*, Vol. 83 (1973), p. 308.

were bought and sold like cattle. Jews in Germany were exterminated for silly reasons or for no reasons. These inhuman activities did not happen in just societies though the Blacks or the Jews didn't have rights to protect them under the laws of those states. Some important elements of justice are missing there. The Blacks and the Jews have a right to be treated with dignity as fellow members of the society, though the political system didn't recognise their rights. Moreover, they were denied many other human rights. Human rights are those valuable commodities without which a society fails to be a just society.[6] The acknowledgement of injustice perpetrated to Blacks and Jews, shows that the core sense of justice is fairness, not the Newtonian sense of political. Rawls offers such general conception of justice in the following principle:

> All social values — liberty and opportunity, income and wealth, and the base of self-respect — are to be distributed *equally* unless an unequal distribution of any, or all, of these values is to *everyone's advantage.*[7]

This principle and other principles of justice which are special case of it are the guidelines for the design of the institutions of the society which confer rights and assign responsibilities to its people. These are the principles that free and rational persons concerned to further their own interests would accept in an initial position of equality as defining the fundamental terms of their association. A society satisfying these principles of justice comes as close as the society of the said hypothetical situation. Any political or social arrangement of a society is just if it reflects

6. See Wasserstrom's article "Rights, Human Rights and Racial Discrimination", *Journal of Philosophy*, Vol. 61 (1964), also in James Rachels (ed.), *Moral Problems*, 1979, Harper & Row Publishers, New York, which explicates the significance of the human rights.
7. "Theory of Justice" in *Reason and Responsibility*, p. 570 (emphasis added).

these principles. It is this conception of justice which makes the cruelty to Blacks and Jews unjust. It makes social segregation and forced poverty of the minority in India unjust.

There are some utilitarian arguments which attempt to justify unequal distribution of rights and liberties. There are good reasons to discard an argument for unequal distribution of rights and liberties from consideration of maximum utility for a society. First, utilitarian considerations are excluded from the society Rawls conceives of, because there is no good reason to opt for maximum aggregate utility for all when every member in this society is interested to further his own happiness which may turn out to be less according to utilitarian principles. Second, there is possibility of losing valuable rights and liberties if they come in conflict with utilitarian principles.

II

Justice demands that the minority should have been treated equally in the past because there was an unfair distribution of goods or rights to claim those goods. But the claim of a present member of the minority to preferential treatment, who is not subject to discrimination, can be justified only if a connection between the effects of the injustice to his group and his present condition is established.

George Sher points out that groups are not sorts of entities that can be wronged like individuals.[8] Assuming that groups can be wronged, he says that it is not clear how preferential hiring of its individual members could be a proper form of compensation for any wronged group that did exist. This is a problem of assigning a property to a class from every member of the class having that property. It is obvious that such an assignment is

8. Robert Simon also makes the same point in "Preferential Hiring: A reply to Judith Jarvis Thomson", *Philosophy and Public Affairs* 3, no. 3 (spring 1974): 312-20.

wrong since the fact that every member of a class is hungry doesn't make the class hungry. In this sense a group cannot be compensated by compensating its members and George Sher is right about it. But it is not necessary to think that preferential treatment is intended for the group or the class — *the minority* as opposed to its individual members. Its is directed towards the individuals of the group. The group comes to the picture because it indicates who are its members. That a group is wronged is to be understood as that the members of the group are wronged. That the wronged group deserves compensation has to be understood as that the members of the wronged group deserve compensation.

In practice, in contrast to what Shcr says, institutions in a legal system are conferred with rights and duties. They are also punished for wrong-doings and compensated for the injustice suffered. The idea behind the recognition of institutions as legal or social subjects is that they can affect the people in the society in several ways by their policies and decisions. The judiciary has a paramount interest in regulating the activities of such bodies. Further, the benefits an institution gets and the losses it suffers affects the individuals related to it. The judiciary regulates the conduct of the individuals indirectly by rewarding or punishing an institution.

Consider again about the grants of the University Grant Commission. If Sher is right, institutions receiving grants from the Commission will not make sense. Equally it doesn's make sense if Indian Railways compensates a company for the damage to its goods during transportation. But it seems that it make sense to recognise the claims of such institutions.

In a society at large, groups are like institutions though the former are not as organised as the latter. Nevertheless, the beliefs, the attitudes and the life shared in common by the members of a group generate actions which are like the implementation of policies and decisions of an institution. The objection that some members of a group may not share the common beliefs and attitudes is ineffective if he doesn't opt out of the group or is indifferent to the workings of the group. Usually most of them passively receive the privileges the group has. It is plausible to say that a group can be a privileged one. Equally it is possible that a group can be wronged. When a thirsty innocent *harijan* is punished for drinking water from the public well of a village and sometimes a whole *harijan bastī* is set ablaze because of such silly reasons, the violence is directed towards the group. It makes sense to say that the group has suffered like we say that an institution has suffered a loss.

One way to compensate a wronged group is to redress every member of the group. For example, like the cash settlement of the Union Carbide to the group of victims, the state can open schools or provide infrastructure facilities for the development of the group. Another way is to go for a Reservation Policy which offers limited opportunities which can be used by limited number of people individually. Yet those opportunities are open to every member of the wronged group provided that one qualify for it. Only those who deserve the opportunity will get it when opportunities are limited. Since everyone in the group has access to the opportunity, the compensation is for the group.

Given that the minority suffered injustice in many ways, it needs to be shown that preferential admission and hiring are the most effective ways of compensating the wronged one. Sher claims that there are better ways like providing equivalent amount of same sort of goods or cash settlement to the discriminated individuals for the past privations. But there are good reasons in favour of preferential admission and hiring. Jobs are wealth of a society like other economic goods. However jobs have an advantages that other economic goods cannot provide. Simple cash settlement or making food, good housing preferentially available is not enough for past privations of social segregation, lack of self-esteem and poverty. Education and jobs will mitigate the evils of social segregation and bring up self-esteem of the wronged ones in a more effective way than those goods can since a person is judged on what he does in a society.

III

It may appear wrong to single out an individual for a benefit by virtue of belonging to a group in India where Article 15 of the Constitution protects an individual's eligibility to public opportunities irrespective of his caste, religion, sex or commitment to any ideology. Such selections can be justified only if the members of a such a group are lacking those kind of goods that demand compensation and the name of the group is a convenient way of finding the recipient. Lacking of those goods is not a characteristic of being of a particular religion or being of a particular sex. The caste is only an indicator of the under privileged. The need for the caste is restricted to allocate the benefits by identifying the individual by caste.

So far the argument is mainly for the compensation for the individuals discriminated against. But further argument is required to show that hiring of a present member of a wronged group, a member who has not been subject to discrimination, is justified. Such an argument is developed by Judith Thomson.[9] The main idea is that though a current member is not denied employment and education, it is very likely that he has been deprived of other sorts of goods which justifies compensation for him. In spite of the facilities available to the current generation of the minority, they fail persistently to compete on equal terms with other groups in educational achievements and in employment. This shows that past discrimination has lasting effects. The back-log of reserved jobs shows that the effects of discrimination has run deep in our society. They fail to compete with others on equal terms.

---

9. See Judith Jarvis Thomson's "Preferential Hiring", *Philosophy and Public Affairs* 2, No. 4 (Summer 1973): 364-84.

The concept of a minority individual's failure to compete on equal terms with others can be explained by a simple example of an athletic event — marathon race. Think of a person who is malnourished, chained for years with no hope for change in his lot in future. This dispirited man is allowed to compete with other fortunate, well trained athletes with a belief that the competition is free and fair and open to all. This less fortunate one is not competing on equal terms with others. Let his condition be improved by offering nutritious food and training prior to the competition. The athlete still lacks the ability to compete with others on equal terms. We cannot restore his lost ability. But we can compensate for that.

The purport of the above example and the current problem is the same. Sher thinks that preferential treatment can be justified on the ground that the minority applicant would have got the job had it not been for lack of competitive edge. Further, the general applicant, like the normal athlete, seems to have gained from the original discrimination. By offering the job to the minority applicant that much qualification of the general applicant is taken away from him on which he seems to claim the job. This strategy overcomes the allegation of violating the right to protection before the law. Further, the objection that the general applicant is asked to bear an unfair share of the burden of the society is no more convincing.

However, the counter factual argument that the minority applicant would have got the job, had it not been for the effects of the original discrimination is problematic. An individual's achievement, be it education or getting a job, broadly speaking, is dependent on two important factors — environmental conditions and individual's efforts. Some of the environmental factors are good nourishment, proper accommodation, good educational facilities and competitive situations. It is not that individual's effort is not influenced by all these factors. However, there seems to be a positive and significant contribution of an individual's own making towards his achievement. There is no reliable criterion to determine the minority applicant's individual effort that would have contributed to getting him the job. Justice demands that compensation be made only when the injuries are not of his own making. Moreover, just compensation for the lost ability requires that only enough compensation be made in each individual case since situation may vary in each case.[10] For instance, the case of an affluent and highly educated minority becomes less persuasive for redress. The proposal seems to be theoretically intractable and preferential treatment turns into an impractical social policy.

A more effective way to argue for preferential treatment is that the ability to compete with equal terms is lost by positive contributions of circumstances which is shown by the fact that most of the members of the minority lag behind in competition and which resulted in not getting enough admissions in educational institutions and placement in jobs. The circumstances resulted primarily from discrimination of the minority. The state has an obligation to make policies to compensate for that in such a way that it will take away, after rational considerations, what seems to be the likely effects of that discrimination. Preferential treatment aims at achieving this general goal of the state.

In order to appreciate the strength of the above argument we have to go back to Rawls' theory of justice. The theory requires that wealth be distributed equally unless unequal distribution is to everyone's advantages. Jobs and human resources like talents are wealth of a society like any other kind of wealth since they are products of wealth and can generate wealth too. In order to ascertain if there is a fair distribution of wealth at present we have to go back to the hypothetical situation in which everyone is equal and see if that situation would have generated some hypothetical agreements of which the present society is the result. For the

10. Sher reluctantly admits these lacunas of his position.

simplicity sake, assume that the wealth of the hypothetical society is divided into four equal parts and there are two members, Madan and Hari, who are equal in every respect. In such a situation, both share the wealth equally which is fair. However, two parts of the wealth goes to Madan and one part goes to Hari. Subsequently, both try to acquire the last part of the wealth. They use their existing wealth and effort to gain the wealth. Here, assign an arbitrary value to each one's effort. This results in Madan acquiring some further wealth in the form of talent. Hari also acquires some talent. Both acquire the minimum talent to be eligible for the rest of the wealth, but Madan's talent is higher than Hari's talent. Now it will be unfair if Madan gets the rest of wealth though he has higher talent because there will be unequal distribution of wealth. Some inequality will be justified, for example, the difference in their talent which may be due to their individual efforts. But their existing wealth without talent is still unfairly distributed between them which Hari wouldn't have consented to. Nor he would have agreed to subsequent arrangements to acquire the rest of the wealth if he thought that he wouldn't have a chance to get it. When Madan gives away his right to his wealth to Samir and Hari gives his right to Gopal, in this case, Gopal's right to the rest of the wealth though he is less qualified than Samir, depends on Gopal's inherited right. Such a position is in accordance with Rawls' theory of justice and the principle of equal protection before the law is sustained because Gopal and Samir are unequally situated now. Similar considerations make a minority applicant's right to the job conspicuous.

Perferential treatment is not the only form of compensation. It is only one of those many progammes that affirmative action stands for. A member of the non-minority is sharing a part of the obligation for the benefits he inherited unknowingly from past discrimination. Every generation inherits the privileges and the burdens of the society that previous generation leaves behind. Preferential treatment is to be understood as the legacy of the new generation.

13

Social Justice
Perspectives and Presuppositions

Aditya Kumar Mohanty

VALUE-AWARENESS is the *sine-qua-non* of human consciousness. Human consciousness is self-reflective. It is the prerogative of the humans that they can make their actions and thoughts the object of valuation. 'To act' and 'to reckon the action as just or unjust', are patently different. In valuing an action as just one transcends the state of doing an action. Similarly, valuing an action to be just is different from analysing the notion of justness or justice. This testifies to the different layers of self-transcendence which is characteristically human. In understanding the concept of justice one addresses oneself to the questions pertaining to the nature, presuppositions and perspectives of *justice*. Judging an action to be just or unjust is one of the modes in which the moral sense expresses itself.

It is worth noting that the concept of *justice* is by and large invariable, whereas the content of justice is variable, depending on the contingencies of time, place and person. In other words, 'what is justice', hardly leaves room for inter-subjective disagreement, whereas 'what is just' varies depending on the contextual considerations. Needless to say that the very concept and legislation of justice presupposes a corporate living. The action of the individual is said to be just or unjust in relation to one's fellowmen. Similarly, the laws of the state or practices in the society are considered as just or unjust in relation to people's rights and duites. Administration of justice is meaningful with regard to rights and duties. A case where one is deprived of one's legitimate right is an instance of injustice. Similarly, when one does what ought not be done, it is an instance of unjust action. It is not only the actions of an individual, but also the enactments and enforcements of the state or collective body that come within the ambit of justice. Dispensation of justice consists in rational allocation of benefits and inconveniences among the people without preference and prejudice so that, given the contingencies and conflicts of interests, the optimum good of one and all is ensured.

Everyone is equal before the eyes of justice. Dispensation of justice knows no distinction whatsover. Equality therefore, is the very rock-bottom of the concept of justice. No one is too high to be above justice and no one is too low to get the benefits of justice. In a given context, the contingent factors having been given, if an action *X* in respect of *Y* is deemed to be just, the same action *X* performed by *B*,*C*,*D* or anyone for that matter would be just. Besides, that it is just shall be reckoned to be so by anyone or everyone. This shows that the notion of *universalisability* is not inconsistent with the fact that the same action may be just and unjust under different circumstances. For example, '*feeding a hungry beggar*' may be considered just. But it may not be considered just if it is done as a part of the religious rituals of feeding beggars on appointed days. The reason why the former action is just may be that in the interest of social harmony, it is imperative to share the suffering of a fellowmen and the latter action is unjust because the very idea of helping the begging community to survive on charity is to encourage beggary. If there are reasons to call an action just, that holds good for everyone under similar circumstances. It is the reasons which prompt everyone to call the former action just and the latter unjust. It explains why the principles and practices of justice enjoy universal consent.

Behind every pronouncement of justice there are compelling reasons. It is *rationality* that lends the coercive force and accounts for the inter-subjective consensus. This of course, does not preclude the possibility of disagreement or conflicts of opinion with regard to the nature of an action so that a particular action may be reckoned as just and unjust simultaneously, by the parties at conflict. It is commonplace to observe that a favourable verdict acquitting a person is quashed by the higher court making him liable. This does not underscore the contention that *rationality, universalisability* and *equality* constitue the very protasis of *justice*. It simply means that if there are reasons to call an action just there could also be overriding reasons to call the same action, unjust. But it is always the *reason* that is the court of appeal and it is the *reason* which invariably sits in judgement.

Reflection on the notion of *rationality* would bring home the fact that all rationalisations are end-specific or teleolgical. An action *X* is just if it is conducive to end *A* which is construed to be *good* or desirable and an action *Y* is unjust if it leads an end which is not *good* or not worth obtaining. *Rationality* as a faculty is the ability which enables to ascertain whether a given action on the part of the individual or collective body has possible or predictable consequences that are assumed to be good. Justness or unjustness are the two sides of the same coin. An action is good if it leads to a just end or results in just consequences. Thus, one finds that a concept of good is implicit in the notion of *justice*. In other words, *justice* presupposes the righteous use of *reason*. This has also the suggestion that reason could be misused to lend justification to evil. A devil can quote scriptures. But in an instance when reason seeks to justify an end which is not good, it is said to be an instance of bad reason. Hence *rationalisation per se*, is necessarily value-centric.

Needless to say that the ends constitute the heirarchy. Given a particular end one can persist to ask the reasons as to why it deserves to be deemed as an *end* at all. The lower ends find their justification in terms of the higher ends in relation to which they turn out to be the means. Thus one is led to come to grips with the concept of the *ultimate good*, which everyone, by and large, subscribes to. It is this shared notion of *good* that appears to be axiomatic in a given framework or discourse of justice. The principles of justice draw their rationale from the notion of the *good*.

Rawls elucidates the axiomatic nature of *good* by the notion of the *'original position'*. There is the initial agreement, as it were, so that there is the universal consensus as to what is just and what is unjust. It is the shared notion of good that defines the basic principles of justice which, in turn, determine the subsequent pronouncements and practices under the umbrella of justice. There is an unmistakable Kantian strain in Rawls' observations that individuals acquiesce to the principles of justice as free and equal beings and the consent is given behind the veil of ignorance. He acknowledges that such an initial agreement did neither obtain as historical situation nor is it the primitive conditions of culture but an expository device without which the phenomenon of justice with the labyrinth of connections would not be made intelligible. The supposed ignorance or the mutual disinterestedness is significative of the fact that the individuals consent to the principles of justice as autonomous, rational and moral beings. In other words, no contigencies, i.e., no consideration of personal end determines or figures in the act of conceiving what is *good* and what is *evil*. The supposed ignorance is connotative of the absence of prudence or expediency. If *universality* and *objectivity* be the defining characteristics of *justice* then it has to be salvaged from relativity of conditions and subjectivity of considerations. Hypothetically, if the principles of justice are allowed to be formulated keeping in view the empirical contingencies, then the universality and objectivity will be sure casualty.

The supposed equality is nothing other than the contention that despite the contingencies which prevent one from taking any two individuals as equal, there are certian underlying invariables or constants in respect of which all are equal. Divested of the space-time-person contigencies individuals are left with their elemental awareness, i.e., the sense of good or bad along with the capacity to reason, the native knack by which one ascertains an action to be just or unjust. Thus, *moral sense* and *rationality* constitute the universals in respect of which all are equal. It is *reason* which secures *autonomy* or *freedom* to the individual. Therefore, all rational agents are free and autonomous. The principles of justice are autonomous insofar as they are dictated by the *moral sense* and *reason* alone. They are of the nature of the unqualified dictums or categorical imperatives. They are valid regardless of individuals and circumstances.

Autonomy and *objectivity* go hand in hand. *Rationality* implies *freedom*. But *freedom* does not mean unbridled latitude on the part of the individual. If it were so, the autonomy would result in conflict of interests and subjectivity would reign supreme. Exercise of *freedom*, therefore, consists in choosing to act for a righteous end. The shared notion of *good* and ability for *rational choice* explain why the principles of justice are objective. The *objectivity* in respect of the principles of justice is corroborative of the contention that every individual is essentially a rational-moral agent. Moral sense is given but not acquired, as it is embedded in the individual and *collective unconscious*. Hence, for the dispenser of justice all are equal and every individual is an end in himself. *We are all members in the kingdom of ends*.

Equality begets the notion of *right*. The concept of *right* has two-fold connotation. On the one hand, it means the *right* to enjoy what is one's due and *justice* means restoration of the right to the individual. Negatively, it connotes the absence of discrimination. Legislation of justice does not mean equal distribution of mundane resources, which is neither desirable nor possible but equality of right to enjoy what is one's due. Since the contingencies differ from individual to individual and situation to situation *justice* consists in allocation of benefits and inconveniences, due appropriation of rights and duties. The principles of justice, thus, serve as cementing tie in the corporate living. They constitute the basis of mutuality and agreement amidst the disparities. The principles of justice are both constitutive and regulative. They are constitutive of the social fabric and are regulative insofar as they provide direction to one's rational choice. In the absence of benevolent impulse a rational being may act autonomously but shall act unrighteously. In such case, the autonomy would degenerate into capricious living.

If the principles of justice presuppose the notion of an ultimate good, one may persist to ask as to why is it that certain ends are assumed to be unconditionally good. Are they self-justificatory? Do they owe their justification to something extraneous? Needless to say that the concept of ultimate good owes its rationale to a world-view. As a result the alternative world-views generate alternative notions of ultimate end or highest good. Hence, the so-called value-paradigms are in fact relative to their respective world-views. For example, the Upaniṣads espouse the thesis of pan-consciousness, i.e., *Brahman* is taken to be ubiquitous. Hence, the realisation of unity is construed as the *Highest Knowledge* and the state of *Highest Good*. In the social domain, renunciation and sacrifice become the covetable virtues. On the other hand, the Cārvāk world-view, advocating the primordiality of the material components, takes *consciousness* as emergent and derivative. The denial of a transcendent reality or an immanent substance, repudiation of the concept of *before* and *hereafter*, lands one in crass materialism. An individual subscribing to such world-view would obviously treat *maximisation of gross enjoyment* as the covetable goal and in such a framework *sacrifice* or *renuciation* would be discounted as a downright foolishness. It is, thus, amply clear that the concept of good cannot be *ontology-neutral*. As all rationalisations are *value-specific*, they eventually, turn out to be *ontology-specific*. That explains why alternative ontologies generate the alternative notions of good accompanied by alternative modes of rationalisation, resulting in the alternative notions of *justice*. With a change of the metaphysical perspective one begins to discover new patterns in the same reality and new meanings in the same actions.

Man is social, by nature and necessity. The society is collection of individuals with diversities of caste, colour, creed, sex, aptitudes and abilities. Diversity is the law of nature. To opt for social living is to agree to have a shared mode of living. Greater the unity, greater becomes the cohesion in the collective living and more stable is the social order. Social justice is essentially concerned with helping the individual to live the life of mutuality leading to progressive integration and unity. In the search for unitary living the mutual differences are to be resolved in the discovery of the common good. Hence, *unity* is the very pivot of social justice. The constraints on the way of social justice are the factors which promote difference of disunity. In a sense, the perceived differences are either natural of man-made and such differences surface in various facets of social living. The differences may pertian to sex, colour, caste, economic status, social life and so on. The prolonged subjugation of women, male chauvinism have been responsible for the exploitation of women and absence of opportunity for them to manifest their potentiality and grow into completeness. The protracted struggle of the blacks to get liberated from the dominion of the whites is essentially a demand for social justice. The concept of racial superiority is a myth. Human society is one and indivisible. Human beings, irrespective of time and clime, have the identical physiology and they are identical in respect of the primal psychic motivations such as love, hatred, jealousy and have the same inner urge for realising truth, bliss and beatitude which goes in the name of spirituality. Hence, exploitation of one race by another is a fall out from fundamentals of social justice. To promote division by creating artificial barriers in the name of language, political banner, point to the ulterior dimensions of social injustice. Justice, in the economic sphere, means guaranteeing the fundamentals of living to one and all. The right to live and grow is one of the most fundamental rights of an individual. By virtue of being born into the planet one is entitled to have as much as one needs to live and grow. Everyone has equal right to enjoy the endowments of nature. Hence, the man-made disparities perpetuated by the cunning and the vested interests are glaring testimony of social injustice. The thesis of co-ownership of the mundane resources stems from the vision of *Cosmic patrimony (harir pitā, gaurī mātā; svadeśa tribhuvana trayam)*.

Justice presupposes the unhindered role of reason. Hence, the individuals have to overcome the influence of sentiments of sentimental legacies. It is the sentiment which holds *reason* at ransom. A *sentiment* refers to the psychic movement where one runs after the pleasurable without considering the pros and cons, the propriety and impropriety of the action. The sentimental-way is devoid of *rationality*. Shree P.R. Sarkar in his *magnum opus*, *Liberation of Intellect and Neo-Humanism*, undertakes the classification of the sentiments as *geo-sentiment*, *socio-sentiment* and *humano-sentiments*. The sentiment which grows out of the love for the indigenous soil is termed as *geo-sentiment*. It may take the form of *geo-religion*, *geo-politics*, *geo-economics*, etc. An individual under the sway of geo-religious sentiment treats a particular palce as sacred, a particular river as holy. The geo-economic sentiment may prompt the people to say "Although there is dearth of raw materials we must have steel plant in our area." Such sentiments divide humanity on geographical lines, thereby forestalling guarantee of social justice. The *socio-sentiment* grows out of a blind love and unconditional allegiance to a particular social group. We hear the call of the fundamentalists *'The Hindus of the world unite. The Muslims of the world unite.'* History is witness to the dreadful aftermath of the socio-economic sentiments in the form of colonial exploitation and *socio-religion* in the form of religious dissensions and communal upheavals. Still broader is the humano-sentiment wherein the whole humanity is taken as one and indivisible. The orchestrated slogans of the humanists about the nobility, excellence and superiority of man over the non-humans is evidently a commendable attempt to discover a vantage point from which the unity of mankind can be worked out. But this has often proved to be self-defeating an exercise. It has led man to take the human beings as the *ends* and the non-human existents as the means to be sacrificed at the altar of human interest. This has been responsible for indiscriminate destruction of the flora and fauna resulting in disequilibrium in deep ecology. In the attempt to safeguard the interset of the humans the very existence of humanity is in jeopardy. Very much in consonance with the Upaniṣadic vision Shree Sarkar offers a world-view wherein every existent, animate, or inanimate, is seen as the expression of Divine. Hence, it is the vision of cosmic unity that can only serve as the protasis of a holistic of notion of good which, in turn, would pave the way for a social order where social justice draws its strength and sustenance from the pristine values of *Cosmic Brotherhood* and the principles of *live and let live*.

14

Concept of Justice

Dhaneswar Sahoo

I

In view of the literature that has developed on the concept of justice right from the ancient Greeks to the present age, it is difficult to define the term justice. The *Encyclopaedia of Social Sciences*[1] brings out two meanings of the term: (i) it is the faithful realisation of existing law as against any arbitrary infraction of it; (ii) the ideal element in all law — the idea which the law tends to subserve. In both the definitions the idea of law is referred to; but the concept of law equally embraces a vast mass of regulatory matter. The *Oxford Dictionary* gives the meaning of law as: "it is body of enacted or customary rules recognised by a community as binding". Though the purpose of law is the attempt to realise justice in a given social milieu laws change with changing times and are variable from place to place.

The second meaning is too broad as justice is merged with the entire content of morality and it is sometimes difficult to distinguish between the two. Still morality can have a wider scope than justice. Sometimes, strict duties are included in justice, but there are many other things which we admire when others do though they are not under any legal obligation to do

1. Ed. by E.A., Seligman, Macmillan, NY, Vols. VII and VIII, p. 509.

them. Kant's distinction[2] between duties of perfect and imperfect obligations also makes justice to be different from morality. In duties of perfect obligation definite demand is made upon us as, Thou Shalt not kill or steal, etc., but in case of imperfect obligation no such demand can be made as, Thou Shalt serve the destitute or Thou Shalt not refuse a beggar.

There can be some criteriological basis for the application of the term justice in particular contexts and that makes the concept objective. Though the criteria may not be the same in all contexts, the assumption of a criterion in a given situation will be there. At the same time justice is very often used as a subjective ideal in context of utopian models of social transformation. For imagination of an ideal social republic is based on certain preoccupations of justice. Gandhi thought of an ideal social republic based on justice which is a synthesis of some kind of ultimate values like non-violence, equality, etc. In Plato's conception of an ideal state justice is taken as a cardinal virtue along with three others like wisdom, courage and temperance as a result of the division of labour and as the external adjustment of social functions. Justice, Plato considers, is the perfect consummation or harmonious cooperation of the social functions of the three classes; the philosopher-rulers, warriors and the working masses. Even the Marxian political system which accepts value-relativism, for values are the class contradictions at each stage of history, also accepts the synthetic ultimate value of justice composed of some ultimate values as equality, freedom, etc., represented by a classless society. Whether these notions of justice as found in the political systems of Gandhi, Plato and Marx are consistent or compatible with each other is not the issue to be taken up here. But my purpose is a very limited one to point out that any conjecture of an ideal socio-political order cannot do away with the notion of justice.

---

2. See *A Mannual of Ethics*, J.S. Mackenzie, New York, 1945, p. 321.

Not only the utopian models but even social transformations or political revolutions are backed by some notion of justice. Any social reformation or political revolution is definitely goal-oriented and the driving motive behind this goal objective is some notion of justice. So justice presupposes conflict and social antinomies. The gap between the ideal of justice and the disharmony of social reality creates new awareness for social change.

Justice is taken as an evolution-ideal which has sprung from some instinct prevalent in human nature. The instinct of sociability which is dominant in human nature is the cause of, some biological evolutionists maintain, the emergence of social justice in the long process of social stabilisation. Even the animals exhibit social instincts like mother-love, sharing of food, mutual cooperation, etc., and therefore have some sub-human justice which govern their life. Any living species for its survival tries to preserve the helpless offsprings before their maturity and that during immaturity the benefits received are inversely proportional to its potent capacities. Human justice is just a development of the sub-human justice and has been more pronounced or assumes large proportions in varying degrees depending upon conditions of existence and social circumstances.

In a similar vein it is maintained that the impulsive basis of justice is expressed in the feeling of revenge which is an animal instinct. The modern concept of retributive justice is a socialisation of this instinct or in other words a development upon the criminal justice of the prmitive type.

Application of the concept to social sciences, as we speak of economic justice, political justice, social justice, etc., can definitely have some moral bearing and as such they are not independent of moral justice. Any social science for that matter cannot do away with values altogether and therefore sets before it some normative goals lest it will be mechanical. Thus the whole area of discourse on justice can broadly be classed under two heads such as legal justice and moral justice which has also been outlined in the definitions given above.

II

Justice is very often used as a synonym for law. Every state has civil statutes which aim at restoring fairness of justice. Though the end of the legal system may be the restoration of moral values, there may be conceptual difference between the two. For any violation of some legal principle is not necessarily a case of moral turpitude. That makes the moral realm, as already hinted at previously, wider than that of justice. Further a legel system does not have universality of immutability. It has no universality as its precepts are not always the same in all times and ages. It has no immutability as it is not independent of human authority. But the legal system to be a just one must exhibit some characteristic features like equality before law, impartiality, assurance of some fundamental rights, etc. But all these presuppositions of legal justice may not explain all the moral issues associated with a comprehensive theory of justice. The legalistic ideal even if just may have a formal basis without being effective to solve practical issues of social concern. In other words, the scope of legal justice may be limited and may not achieve normative goal to some considerable extent. Though in a country, for example, civil rights are protected by law and violation of them can have legal remedy, that do not make the laws practically operative. Right to life is a fundamental right, but it has little significance if there is no means to live and the state and society at large have no accountability for it. Similarly the cultural atmosphere of a society may not be conducive to give sanction to certain unorthodox views. In a caste-ridden of communally charged social atmosphere liberties or even legal rights remain practically inoperative bacause of social orthodoxy. Society, by and large, may remain authoritarian and may not accept any unorthodox opinion even if it is rational and not violative of legal justice.

The distinction between legal justice and moral justice reveals that while the former is taken as "respect for normal expectations of men as embodied in law" the latter as "to respect for right as embodied in the ideal of social manhood".[3]

Any ethical theory of justice should account for a satisfactory doctrine of distributive justice. It was Aristotle who introduced the concept of distributive justice in contrast to corrective justice. Corrective justice, a branch of legal justice, deals with the infringement of the law and the compensation that one has to pay for it in proportion to the nature of his offence. But distributive justice means what a man has to receive for his contribution and what he has to contribute to the public exchequer in proportion to his possession. This notion of distributive justice or giving a man his due has attracted wide attention in history of moral philosophy to account for a systematic theory of desert.

Considering the complexity and the larger impersonal relations of social life it is difficult to have a theory of desert. Since each man's contribution to society is governed by very many factors a just determination of the reward, both theoretically and practically will be immensely difficult.

Utilitarianism has attempted at a theory of distributive justice. Bentham, Mill and Sidgwick are the chief exponents of this theory. According to this doctrine all people have an equal right to a share of the pleasures that are available. Accordingly the greatest happiness of the greatest number is the ultimate moral standard. The pleasures of others are to be treated as of equal merit as that of our own.

Utilitarian thinkers as well as some others support an individualistic or *laissez-faire* economic theory to account for a just distribution. This theory maintains a natural economic order without government interference to favour maximum

---

3. W.M., Urban, *Fundamentals of Ethics*, Henry Holt & Co, N.Y., 1953, p. 215.

good of individual and community as a whole. Another approach in contrast to this theory to account for distributive justice is the socialistic theory. The socialistic theory takes the ideal of the realisation of social manhood by its maxim "to everyone according to his needs but not according to his abilities".

Each of these views in connection with an ethical theory of desert has some merit and inherent difficulty. The socialistic ideal has an overtone of machanical equalisation and ignores the importance of individual desert or incentive. The individualistic ideal belittles entirely the social and collective effort. B.B. Urban rightly observes that it can justify itself ethically only by an appeal to the fiction of inherited desert or that it rewards no motive except the economic virtue makes it ultimately to be an inhuman distribution. The utilitarian theory of ethical desert has been criticised from various standpoints. Particularily from the standpoint of naturalism and intuitionism the moral desert of utilitarianism seems untenable.

Any satisfactory theory of ethical desert must accept the idea of equality as an essential aspect of justice. It is not only a theoretical presupposition, but in practical operation equality determines, though in a relative way, the extent of legal and moral justice prevalent in a society.

Some hold that men are factually unequal in their talent, capacity, temperament, etc., and from this springs inequality in human society. And ironically, though the present democratic culture owes a lot to the philosphy of Plato and Aristotle, the two great intellectual leaders of humanity, they did not consider it to be ideal that men should be treated as equal. Plato maintained that men are unequal and do deserve unequal opportunities. In a similar tone Aristotle also held that justice is treating equals equally and unequals unequally in proportion to their relevant differences. Similarly, though the spirit of Indian philosophy admits the equality of all human beings on the basis of an imperishable soul dwelling in each of us, the Indian social system has, for centuries, accepted a hierarchical caste-system rooted in gross inequality.

Some differences will exist with regard to biological inheritance and impact of social environment but they are definitely modifiable. That is, the very constituion of human nature admits mutual differences, but that does not mean that this variation cannot be modified by social arrangement or deliberate effort. And even if this is practically impossible, that cannot provide any rational basis for social inequality or unequal treatment to citizens. Rather any civilised society aims at lessening the inequality by providing equal opportunities to all its citizens by legislative and other suitable measures. Social inequality and practical justice are, therefore, inversely related.

III

No society or social system can achieve absolute justice or perfection for all times to come. The reflection of moral ideals in the varied field of social relationships or organisations can characteristically mark a society just or unjust. More it is reflected in social organisations society becomes morally progressive and more they are away from it society becomes morally decadent. Comparison between two social orders makes one relatively more just or unjust. And again what is the best society in one age may not be considered so in another age.

On the basis of this analysis there can be many ways to determine whether social justice is intact or at stake. But two of the conditions can formulate at least some working criteria to detemine the conditions of social justice.

A just society should reflect higher degree of moral symmetry, because moral asymmetry is something counter and detrimental to our moral sense. If people working hard and honestly are deprived of the requirements of life to live on whereas loafers and dishonest persons live exuberantly and good things of life pour upon them it cannot be taken as a healthy sign of a just society. That is, in a society where moral sense of the people is violently affected by the asymmetrical crude realities of social facts and the legal and admininstrative measures have no concern for that, society turns decadent. The second condition is that if people, by and large, from all walks of life become increasingly insensitive to injustice, it cannot be taken as a just society. That is if the moral worth of the means is never given importance in achieving any social end and people from all walks ungrudgingly accept injustice as the call of the time, no doubt it becomes a sign of decadence. There may be very many ways to determine the intensity of moral turpitude in social life but these two conditions, i.e., moral asymmetry and moral insensitiveness provide some criteria in this direction.

15

Social Justice
A Historical Perspective

Himansu Shekhar Patnaik

HISTORY has canonised one consistent impression of human nature, i.e., that man has a multiple nature. While a Walt Whitman might say, 'I contradict myself. I contain multitudes', most often it has been expressed as a dichotomy, as a conflict between good and evil. While in the realm of thought, absolute certainty about good and evil is denied to him as man, he has taken the more modest path of finding "dependable ways of discerning different degrees of probability".[1] Goodness was justice to Moses, wisdom to Plato, love to Jesus, virtue to the Vedas and perfection to Indian Philosophy as a whole. As a religious man, he has tried to achieve goodness through religious morality by trying to substitute "for the liberating experience of Grace, the obsessive fear of committing a mistake". [2]As a social animal, he has tried to establish an objective moral order — "that reality in reference to which a person is wrong when he makes a false moral choice, either in his own conduct or in the judgement of another".[3]

---

1. Elton Trueblood, *General Philosophy*, New York, 1963, p. 61.
2. P. Tournier, *The Seasons of Life*, Richmond, 1961, p. 221.
3. Elton Trueblood, *op. cit.*, p. 212.

Time and education beget experience, experience begets memory, "memory gets judgement and fancy, judgment begets the strength and structure and fancy begets the ornaments of a poem".[4] A process of structural adjustments under stresses generated by cultural innovations from internal and external sources constitutes the development of a social system. Cultural complexes compete within a social system as respective interests of groups or associations. Finally it is resolved either through integration by compatibility or by outright rejection. It also applies to goals and values that normally serve as functional criteria of structural compatibility.

Nature and society are living organisms developing their immanent life as a process of individuation or differentiation. It is combined with coordination of the differentiated elements. A teleological standard of value is reached by varying degrees of individuation that determine the higher or lower rank of things. This applies very much to the pathology of social justice, as a conception of association based upon intelligent reason that also takes into consideration a sub-rational area of instinct.

'Social Justice' is too comprehensive in its connotations to be capable of definition in any simple formula. Justice, derived from Latin word *justitia* meaning idea of joining, is described as the conformity of our actions and our will to law.[5] Whatever is right is according to law or justice (the latin word *rectus* meaning 'according to rule'). But social justice is a philosophy super-imposed on the legal system. An Indian scholar describes it as a "balance between an individual's rights and social control ensuring the fulfilment of the legitimate expectations of the individual . . . consistent with the unity of nation and needs of the soceity".[6] As

---

4. R.L. Brett, *Fancy and Imagination*, Methuen, London, 1966, p.11.
5. *Corpus Juris Secundum*, Vol. 51, p. 31.
6. Bakhshish Singh, *The Supreme Court as an Instrument of Social Justice*, New Delhi, 1976, p. 73.

such, it is an essential part of the great complex of social change for which something may have to be sacrificed for greater good.[7] It is pervasive, the gamut of expanse ranging from minorities protection to eradication of pauperism, from liquidation of vested interests to being the foundation of industrial jurisprudence. Dean Roscoe Paund gives us a division of social justice into six conceptual issues of social interest and eight empirical jural postulates. As such social justice is hypothecated to law and 'lawyers must regard themselves as social scientists' Liberty and equality apart, social justice enjoins to "bring about a social order in which justice — social, economic and political — shall inform the institutions of national life".[8] Allen aptly says, "no obstacle should be offered but rather help afforded to practicable opportunities of self-improvement".[9]

As such, the concept of social justice is a philosophy superimposed on the legal system. In the last Zakir Hussain memorial lecture, Chief Justice Ahmadi defended judicial activism against apprehensions about the lengthening nose of the Supreme Court. Only last December, he had admonished for caution on general matters regarding social justice. In retrospect, judicial activism has appeared as a moral vindication of social justice, though polluting factories have not, as yet, been replaced by purifying plants. So because the concept of social justice varies from person to person and with age and clime. Even the time-machine of H.G. Wells can never bring a consensus on the issue among Manu, Solon, Hammurabi and Confucius.

In Greek physics, harmony and proportion constituted justice, regarded as an ultimate principle. Heraclitus warned, "the

---

7. Kenneth Boulding, "Social Justice in Social Dynamics" in Brandt (ed.), *Social Justice*, Prentice Hall, N.J., 1962, p. 92.
8. Cheif Justice K. Subba Rao in *Golknath* v. *State of Punjab*, 1967, SC 643.
9. C.K. Allen, *Aspects of Justice*, London, 1955, p. 3.

handmaids of justice will find him (the offender) out" and Euripides made the phoenecian Maidens sing, "Measures for men equality ordained". The sophist Antiphon looked upon it as merely conventional and so, contrary to nature. In *Thrasymachus*, it is the interest of the stronger. Plato would define social justice as

> the principle of a society, consisting of different types of men . . . who have combined under the impulse of their need for one another, and their concentration on their combination in one society, and their concentration on their separate functions, have made a whole which is perfect because it is the product and image of the whole of the human mind. (*Republic*, 368 d.)

Plato's social justice would thus be for giving to every man his due. It is not a juristic definition as it omits a lot and includes a lot. The epicureans put a premium on the expedient in needs out of mutuality as socially just. The Romans, while conforming to Plato ("To give to everyman his own", *Digest*, 1.1.10, and "realization of justice in life", *The Theory of Justice*, Eng. trans. 1925, p.127), provided for legal safeguards to protect the slaves and guarantee women's equality. Seneca and Cicero followed Plato in concepts of right and justice. St. Augustine and St. Thomas Aquinas too shared with Plato the absolute and permanent nature of the concept of justice. Marsiglio and Dante were Erastian and Reformationists like Zwingli and Calvin reiterated the equation between the natural (inalienable) rights and natural duties. Bodin waxed eulogy by describing society as a partnership in every virtue and all perfection. Milton, Hooker, Harriongton and Green were Lockean, while Bentham, J.S. Mill and the Utilitarians, like Aristotle, believed that the relative concept that was justice would change with values, conditions and changing times, Bentham was concerned with the primacy of the individual's right to security. While Austin equated social justice with social restraint, J.S. Mill made 'self-regarding' proportional with 'other-regarding'.

As regards the contractualists, Voltaire's cryptic statement, 'we may not have contracted into, but we cannot contract out' tells a lot. The arrogation of the arbitrary authority of Hobbes' *Leviathan* and the dual contract of Locke to keep men in enjoyment of their rights are paradoxes 'reconciled in Rousseau' as Bosanquest observes. The French Revolution and Paine emphasised on the equal rights, the inalienable rights of liberty, property, security and resistance to oppression and legal equality (for the French it meant equality in law and for the British, absence of governmental interference). To Halbach, social justice was the suprement virtue. Burke put a premium on humanity, justice and reason. Kant believed in a system of rights of compulsion and punishment while Bradley stressed state and society as moral organisms. Bosanquet saw in social justice the imperative need for "maintenance of conditions favourable to the best of life". It was, to McDougall, "purely mental or psychological". McIver regards it as a form of service, without any mystical power, Laski said, "the rights of the individual must correspond to his contribution to sociey". The Treaty of Versailles (1919) emphasised that "universal peace can succeed only if based on social justice. The Indian constitution is first and foremost, a social document."[10]

As William Hazlitt said,

> Man is an intellectual animal, and therefore an everlasting contradiction to himself. To pretend that the country or society today is not the survivor of innumerable tragedies is sheer perversity or an ignorance that is more depressing than history itself.

All said and done, it is certain that social justice seeks to adjust the various institutions concerned in the social and constitutional structure of society and state for promotion of harmony on ethical and economic basis. A social order of equality and equity

---

10. Granville Austin, *The Indian Constitution*, p. 50.

is apotheosised by social justice. Social justice is synonymous with moral justice and equality for establishing a just society. It is an essential variable in determining the evolution of society. Its instrumentality alone can make distribution of wealth as equally as possible for sharing of the fruits of labour and capital with reasonable equity.

Social justice differs from legal justice in that it does justice between the classes of society. In more ways than one, social justice is identifiable with natural justice in that each represents "justice in itself-indeed and in truth and is not to be identified with the rules of positive morality."[11]

Harking back to judicial activism in the contcxt of social justice in India, justice is connoted by the term *dharma* (*Vedic Index*, I, p. 390). *Manusmṛti* gives us eighteen titles of law, and the Constitution of India, Fundamental rights and directive principles of State policy. Equality and non-discriminations as per Articles-15 to 17, welfare needs of Acts. 23, 38, 42 and 47 have social justice a more vivid sense of proportion.

If battling against the vicissitudes of life is the ultimate purpose of human existence, we are just as much responsible for the evil we allow as for the evil we commit. Social justice purportedly stands for an objective moral order, or, that reality *vis-a-vis* which a person is wrong when he makes a false moral choice, either in his own conduct or in the judgement of another. To Milton, social justice signified worship of individual freedom. To Hooker, law was essential to social life. Harrington admonished that history and observation must compromise democracy with order and progress. And Green suggested that the State must guarantee ideal rights through law.

Interesting indeed is Pound's concept of social justice, The social interest veers around factors, namely (i) General Security involving peace, public health, etc., (ii) Security and Social

11. Sir John Salmond, *Jurisprudence*, 9th edn., p. 62.

Institutions like marriage, religions, etc., (iii) General Morals standing to nullify those that harm the moral order, like gambling and drinking, etc., (iv) conservation, particularly of food and minerals, etc., (v) general progress manifest in research, trade, etc., and (vi) individual rights involving wages, service conditions, etc. Pound then goes on to catalogue eight jural postulates. There are (i) no aggression, (ii) good faith of parties (iii) no hindrances in enjoyment of one's acquisitions, etc., (iv) due care and caution, (v) cautious storing of dangerous things (vi) right of employment, (vii) social sharing of individual misfortunes, and (viii) compensation to works for human wear and tear in industries.

Article 15 stands for non-discrimination on grounds of religion, caste, race, sex or place of birth; Article 16, for equal opportunity in employment, and Article 17, for abolition of untouchability. The welfare needs are adequately catered to by Article 23 (abolition of forced labour), Article 38 with its premium on welfare promotion, Article 42 thundering for just conditions of work and maternity relief, and Article 47 with its healthful impetus to health and hygiene.

The judicial system is the third chamber. A nation is ranked in political civilisation in as far as its justice, as defined by law, is actually realised in its judicial administration. This was how Sidgwick devised the formula to determine a nation's politico-social civilisation and status. But social justice has invariably been crucified on the cross of undue delay. Delay in looking after social justice has been the taboo, the obnoxious routine of our system. Perhaps we are living under the law of rules rather than rule of law. Far from having the capacity to grasp quickly the issue involved or developing for that matter, a sharp enough sense of relevancy, the commissions and committees do often serve the cause of an eye-wash or intricate wrangles, from public sector undertakings and offices to banks and post offices, the public is at times taken to task for upsetting the employees siesta. The arrogant affluence constitutes the dazzling apex of the State edifice, howsoever internally rickety it might be. In the name of emancipation of women, their tormentors are shielded under the umbrella of power. In a country of millions of people of backward classes and communities, for whom literacy is still a far cry, insecurity continues to plague and feudal vestiges of bonded labour and social ostracism. While seminars wax profusely and eloquently on the urgency of social justice, no practical stock is taken of the legions of instances and practices that continue to impugn personal freedom within the cramped quarters of social justice. In rural India in particular, social justice is utopian enough to render it the perspective of a mirage. It seems, social justice is closed to all demands of futurity in India, and appears relegated to the typology of the pseudological, which understands J.S. Mill on 'self-regarding' and grossly misinterprets him about his 'other-regarding' contentions.

Since 1978 Maneka Gandhi case, the judiciary in general and the Supreme Court in particular has come to assume a more populist tone and tenor. Particular emphasis has come to be laid on what is termed as judicial activism. In a way, it denotes that the function of the judiciary is not only to interpret the law but to make it by approximating to the constitution's passion for social justice as manifest in Justice P.N. Bhagawati's 'goal-oriented', Justice Krishna Iyer's 'humanist-reformist' or Justice Ranganath Mishra's 'community-oriented' approaches. The cumulative results have been the emergence of new dimensions like bonded labour, human rights, slum-dwellers, women protection, and many other jurisprudences. The lesson has been that participative justice is the clarion-call for social justice to bring about socio-economic change. To quote justice Pathak, in the 'Bandhua Mukti Morcha' case, "creation of a system which promises legal relief without cumbersome formality and heavy expenditure" is the goal. Public Law Litigation (PLL) in this regard has gone a long way to increase the people's power. All these speak for themselves on the issue that Social justice is

Justice which is not confined to a fortunate few but which takes within its sweep large masses of people in the country, justice which penetrates and destroys all inequalities of race, sex, power, position or wealth, justice which seeks to bring about equitable distribution of social, material and political resources of the community.

The conception of social justice is hewn out of hard experience, not figured fancifully on paper. If society is on its own, there are no gods to ape. If reason and expediency are human and social property, none can be affronted by their use, through the medium of social justice. Its limits are limits of its use, not a frontier forbidden to penetration. Society must act to its lights. Ideals are guides and goals but they are not worshipful. Otherwise, social justice would continue to be an incongruous mixture of natural rights and physiological metaphor, and as such, a prolonged agony of futility.

The Contributors

Dr. Rajendra Prasad is former Professor and Head of the Department of Humanities and Social Sciences at the Indian Institute of Technology, Kanpur and subsequently National Fellow of the Indian Council of Philosophical Research.

Dr. Debi Prasad Chattopadhyaya, formely Professor and Head of the Department of Philosophy, Jadavpur University is Professor Emeritus in the University. He was the founder chairman of the Indian Council of Philosophical Research.

Dr. Chhatrapati Singh* was Professor in the Indian Law Institute, New Delhi.

Dr. Ramesh Chandra Pradhan is Professor of Philosophy at the Central University of Hyderabad.

Dr. Bijoy H. Baruah is Professor of Philosophy in the Department of Humanities and Social Sciences at the Indian Institute of Technology, Kanpur.

Dr. Sarat Chandra Panigrahi is Reader in Philosophy at Utkal University.

Dr. (Mrs) Mahasweta Chaudhury is Reader in Philosophy at Calcutta University.

Dr. (Miss) Sefali Moitra is Reader in Philosophy at Jadavpur University, Calcutta.

Dr. Kamala Kanta Panda is Reader in Political Science in Delhi University of which he currently is the Registrar.

Dr. Debi Prasanna Patnaik, an eminent linguist is the former Director of the Central Institute for Indian Languages at Mysore.

Dr. Rama Chandra Majhi is senior Lecturer in Philosophy at Ispat College, Rourkela.

Dr. Aditya Kumar Mohanty is Reader in Philosophy at Utkal University.

Sri Dhaneswar Sahoo is Reader in Philosophy in the Govt. College, Dhenkanal.

Dr. Himansu Shekhar Patnaik is Reader in History at Utkal University.

* The General Editor and his colleagues deeply mourn the sad and sudden demise of Professor Chhatrapati Singh who passed away a few months back. Dr. Singh was an excellent scholar in philosophy of law. We mourn with many in Philosophy and Social Sciences the loss of a genius.